PRESUMPTION OF GUILT

PRESUMPTION OF GUILT

HERB BROWN

DONALD I. FINE, INC.
NEW YORK

Library of Congress Cataloging-in-Publication Data
Brown, Herb, 1931–
Presumption of guilt / Herb Brown.
p.   cm.
ISBN 1-55611-259-9
I. Title.
PS3552.R68558P74   1991
813'.54—dc20   90-56083
CIP

Manufactured in the United States of America

10 9 8 7 6 5 4 3 2 1

Designed by Irving Perkins Associates

For
Beverly, David and Andy

For their help and encouragement as I have struggled to improve my writing, I am more than grateful to Tim O'Brien, Bob Canzoneri, Nick Delbanco and Jerome Charyn. Lisa Healy has been marvelously helpful as my editor and Susan Lee Cohen has had a part in this book which goes well beyond what anyone should expect from an agent. Finally, I could not have done without the patience and skills of my secretary, Virginia Tsipas.

They have built also the high places of Bā'-ăl, to burn their sons with fire *for* burnt offerings unto Bā'-ăl, which I commanded not, nor spake *it,* neither came *it* into my mind:

Therefore, behold, the days come, saith the LORD, that this place shall no more be called Tō'-phĕt, nor The valley of the son of Hĭn'-nom, but The valley of slaughter.

And I will make this city desolate, and an hissing; every one that passeth thereby shall be astonished and hiss because of all the plagues thereof.

And I will cause them to eat the flesh of their sons and the flesh of their daughters, and they shall eat every one the flesh of his friend in the siege and straitness, wherewith their enemies, and they that seek their lives, shall straiten them.

BOOK I

1

THE SECRET ELEVATOR, the one in back, the one for judges and special people, transported me, Sergeant Lutz and Mr. Gorman from the garage in the basement up to the ninth floor of the Hall of Justice. I would be testifying in the main courtroom. None of us talked. I heard them breathing. Mr. Gorman was looking at me the way I did at insects for my collection when I made identifications. The elevator doors opened and I stepped out, Sergeant Lutz on my left and Mr. Gorman on my right. I was scared. Mr. Gorman was a prosecutor. He prosecuted people to put them in jail or maybe fry in the electric chair.

3

Coming off the elevator we faced a window which looked out over downtown Columbus. I saw Lazarus, the store where I whispered my presents to Santa Claus when I was little. I used to sit on his lap and pretend so they could take a picture for mother and father. But he had never fooled me into thinking he was the real Santa Claus. Outside the Hall of Justice, a drizzle made it so you couldn't see much farther than Lazarus. I wouldn't testify right away. They wanted me here early.

We turned the corner and walked down a narrow corridor, me still in the middle. My eyes came to the same height as the shiny wood on the handle of the .45–caliber Smith and Wesson strapped to the wide belt Sergeant Lutz was wearing. His handcuffs, clipped to the belt next to the gun, jingled as he walked. I was glad neither of them took hold of my hand. I didn't want them to see how scared I was.

Sergeant Lutz was my friend. He had showed me his gun. He had let me play with his handcuffs when we had to wait around. His gun was an automatic and I knew the difference between a revolver and an automatic. Some officers carried Colt .38 revolvers. I had added the words *revolver* and *automatic* to the vocabulary notebook I had kept since mother helped me start it in kindergarten. I had also added *prosecutor*, a lawyer but not a lawyer like my father. Like mother suggested, I had tried to use my new words in order to master them.

We were in the back corridor, between the courtrooms and the judge chambers. I had been there before. Yesterday Sergeant Lutz drove me to the Hall of Justice in a police car with red, white and blue flasher lights on top. We came up the main elevator because it was Sunday and the Hall of Justice was vacant, no newspaper guys or lawyers or judges or crowd or anything.

They showed where the judge would sit, way high behind

4

a long, tall desk. From up there he could look down and boss the courtroom. When I climbed into the judge's seat, I couldn't see over the bench. My head only went halfway up the leather back and my legs stuck out in front because the chair was too deep for them to bend. The judge would sit up there like a king, with the high desk in front of him and flags on both sides, Ohio's and America's.

After I sat in the judge chair, they showed me the jury box which had fourteen chairs. There would be twelve jury people and two substitutes in case one got sick. We went into the room behind the jury box where the jury people would be locked up at the end of the trial, until they made up their minds if Howard had caused the sore places in my rear end. In the jury room, they had a big table with chairs around it. There was no windows or phone and it was soundproofed. They had their own toilet.

The last thing I did yesterday was sit on the witness chair. It rested on a platform, in the middle of a box with an opening on one side to get in. That was where I would sit when I testified. It faced the jury chairs and the two tables where the lawyers would sit. My legs couldn't reach the floor and I wasn't able to see over the front of the box. "We'll have a booster for you tomorrow," said Mr. Gorman.

"Where will Howard be?" I asked.

"He'll be between his lawyers at this table," said Mr. Gorman, putting his hand on a long, curved table.

It had been quiet in there. Our voices sounded hollow. You could hear the clock on the wall make its thock every time the long hand bounced, which it did once for every minute. It was dark back where the watchers would sit because Mr. Gorman didn't turn on all the lights. I felt like I was in church when no one was there. During school vacations I'd gone with mother to our church in the middle of the week and we'd walked through the sanctuary. Mother was on important committees at the church. The smell of the pews in church when it was empty was like the smell in the courtroom.

"Is Howard allowed to stare?" I asked. Before today they hadn't allowed Howard around when they asked questions about him.

"He can watch," said Mr. Gorman. "But he won't be permitted to say anything. He can't hurt you."

I didn't know. Howard had a fat face. He looked mean when he squinted. He called me his little brother before he got mad at me. I wondered if Howard came early too.

We got halfway down the long corridor in back. On the thick carpet you couldn't hear our footsteps. Mr. Gorman was in a hurry but he slowed himself so I didn't have to walk faster. I wondered where mother was. She had met us for breakfast and rode with us to the garage in the basement of the Hall of Justice. Mr. Gorman told her to use the main elevator and he'd find her in the lobby later. She was probably out there, in front of the main doors to the courtroom. Mr. Gorman said he wanted this last chance to review my testimony just by ourselves.

Mother had kissed me. "You'll do fine," she said. She told me again how proud of me she was. She knew how scared I was. Mother thought awful things would happen if something wasn't done about Howard. Nobody would tell me what they were going to do to Howard if the jury people said he was guilty. They told me I was helping Howard. I was pretty sure they were lying. Howard was going to win. Even if I did have Mr. Gorman and Sergeant Lutz and Dr. Merwin and Dr. Hartenfells and mother and lots more on my side.

We got almost to the end of the long corridor when a door opposite to some bookshelves opened and a man in a black robe came out. The black robe went clear to the carpet and the man was taller than Sergeant Lutz even. The door opened so fast it surprised me. For a second I thought

6

it was Vorlock, a powerful dragon I had once taken a whole week to kill in one of my Nintendo adventures. That was ridiculous to think because I knew the man was a judge. He had glasses and a red face. I wished I hadn't reached for Sergeant Lutz's hand and looked silly.

"Good morning, Judge Van Horn," said Mr. Gorman. Standing between the judge in his black robe and Sergeant Lutz, Mr. Gorman looked short. But Mr. Gorman's shoes shined like a mirror. Mr. Gorman's hair was as black as mine and he smelled good.

Mr. Gorman put his hand on my shoulder. "This is Charles King," said Mr. Gorman. "He's going to be our star witness."

From inside the folds of his black robe the judge brought his hand out to shake mine. "How do you do, young feller," he said. He talked like he had a bad cold. "As long as you stick to the truth," he said, "you will be safe in my courtroom." He didn't smile until after he said "my courtroom."

"Just relax," said the judge. "Nobody is going to hurt you." He said that because he felt how cold my hand was. The judge's hand was enormous and he brought his other one out from under his robe to hold mine between his. Sergeant Lutz and Mr. Gorman had told me the judge would protect me, but I couldn't relax just because the judge said to. I didn't see how the judge or Mr. Gorman or mother or Sergeant Lutz or anyone could help when I climbed into that witness box. I'd be by myself in front of jurors and lawyers, people and newspapers and Dr. and Mrs. Landis who were our neighbors besides being Howard's parents. It was me that had to say what Howard did. I had to look at Howard when I told. Mr. Gorman said that was important. I had to point at Howard when Mr. Gorman asked if I saw him in the courtroom.

"Clay," said the judge to Mr. Gorman. "We hit a bit of a

7

snag. I've got to take two guilty pleas and a sentencing hearing before we start."

"How long do you think?" Mr. Gorman glanced at me before looking back at the judge. Those glasses the judge was wearing didn't have rims.

"Let's shoot for ten," said the judge. "My bailiff has alerted the jury commissioner. We'll keep them downstairs and bring them up at ten."

I looked at my watch, one of the presents I received on my birthday, a month ago. I was eight. I was in the third grade and in the gifted section at the Canterbury School. Mother had been extra nice to me since she started forcing me to tell about Howard. My watch had indicators for the day and month. It added, subtracted, multiplied, divided and played songs. It wasn't quite eight-thirty. That meant almost two hours for me to wait.

The same door the judge came from opened again and a man in a blue suit stepped out. I hadn't seen him before but I knew who he was. He was Mr. Mansfield, the main lawyer for Howard Landis. When we practiced, Mr. Gorman had showed me pictures of Mr. Mansfield and his picture looked exactly like him. He was the one who would try to trick me in front of the jury.

Mr. Gorman told me Mr. Mansfield might try to get the blame off Howard by making it look like father did things to me. Mr. Gorman had made me practice answers and questions for hours and hours. I had to protect father from Mr. Mansfield.

Mr. Mansfield was staring at me. What had he and the judge been doing in the judge chambers? Mr. Mansfield was my enemy. He saw how scared I was. He looked cross at me before he shook hands and said good morning to Mr. Gorman. Mr. Mansfield was carrying a black bag, about twice the size of my father's briefcase. There would be room for thousands of papers and it had probably cost a hundred dollars. The initials "B.D.M." were in gold grooves on its top.

I bet Mr. Mansfield and the judge were talking about the case. Maybe they were planning to gang up on me. Maybe Mr. Mansfield told the judge I wasn't telling the truth and that was why the judge had said about me being safe if I stuck to the truth. The judge was smiling at Mr. Mansfield. The judge was only pretending to like me.

"I'll get these other matters disposed of as quickly as possible," said the judge. "You boys be in my chambers at ten." The judge opened a door on the other side of the corridor, a door between bookcase walls. The judge disappeared through the door. It was his secret passage and went into the courtroom with steps that came out right behind his enormous high-up desk. They showed me the secret passage yesterday.

A policeman pushed past us. In front of him was a man in handcuffs wearing a blue shirt with a number on its back. I bet he was a robber or a burglar. His hair was messy. He smelled. That policeman was not as neat as Sergeant Lutz who had perfect folds in his pants and shirt and everything shiny.

I wondered how many people were in the courtroom, waiting to watch me testify. Other than Dr. and Mrs. Landis I wondered if I'd know anyone. "It will be just like when you went before the grand jury," Mr. Gorman told me. "Only now you've had practice and it will be easier." He had lied about that too because there hadn't been watchers in the grand jury room and Howard hadn't been there and I didn't have to answer Mr. Mansfield's questions. Besides, the grand jury was the scariest thing I'd done in my life. All those people stared at me from behind their tables, trying to decide if I was lying. That was what they were doing even if a lot of them smiled. I was in the middle of an enormous room with blue drapes on the windows and a high ceiling. Mr. Gorman had to help me with my answers. I threw up just before I went in. Outside the door there was a policeman with a gun to keep anyone from sneaking in or out. Or getting close enough to listen through the door, Mr. Gorman said.

In the grand jury room, I sat under a tray of lights that made me hot and feel like I would have to throw up again. When they made me raise my hand to swear to tell the truth, I had to look away from a black man who was frowning at me. Sometimes I would forget what Mr. Gorman asked and he had to do his question again. A lady with a machine sat on a stool, making the buttons on her machine jump every time I started to talk. I guessed she was putting down what I said and later Mr. Gorman told me I was right.

After Mr. Gorman asked his questions in the grand jury room, he told them they could ask questions. I wished he'd warned me. I wondered who would ask about father—or about all my visits to Dr. Hartenfells and me trying to stop her from blaming Howard. I couldn't help looking to see what that black man would ask. But he didn't ask anything and neither did anyone else. They just stared at me. That was when the most of them smiled. They kept smiling as Mr. Gorman took my hand and led me to the door which the policeman had to unlock to let us out. Mr. Gorman said the people on the jury wouldn't get to ask questions this time. Maybe he told me the truth about that.

There had been so many questions and I'd talked to so many people since mother discovered my bloody undies, I couldn't remember all I'd said to all of them. Besides that machine in the grand jury room, I'd been on tape recorders and twice, at least, even VCRs. I knew I'd say something wrong when I had to testify to the jury. Mr. Gorman might not stay friendly if I said wrong things. I could get people in trouble. Mother wouldn't be proud of me anymore.

10

This wouldn't be better than the grand jury, not with the judge and Mr. Mansfield and Howard and all the watchers. But I couldn't have got out of it. Even if I got sick, they would just have the trial later, Mr. Gorman told me. "This is something you must do," mother stressed. We'd told so many people, called in the court and the police and the judge. We'd got Howard in trouble. Back in first grade I had learned how bad it was to turn in false alarms for fires. You could be put in jail. And all that was was getting some firemen and their trucks to race out on the streets and blow their sirens. This was the court and a judge and doctors and police and lawyers and it could take two whole weeks. Like mother said, it was very important. It had gone too far to quit.

"Charles, this will be your room while we wait," said Mr. Gorman. We entered a small room with yellow walls, a soft chair in the corner and four wood chairs around a table. The paint on the chairs and table was cracked. The only thing on the table besides some paper cups of old coffee and an ashtray that spilled over and needed to be dumped was a telephone. There was a bookcase on one wall and a window on the other side. The window let me see out into the back corridor where we came after we got off the elevator. You could pull a curtain to keep people in the corridor from looking. At one end of the room they'd hung a picture of fruit and at the other end a picture of a vase of flowers. The flower picture was crooked.

Mr. Gorman had things to do. Sergeant Lutz would stay with me. "Do you want me to close the curtain?" Sergeant Lutz asked. I shook my head.

Sergeant Lutz picked up the telephone and called someone. He told them to bring up my *Yes and No* quiz books, my book *When the Dinosaurs Ruled the Earth* and my vocabulary notebook. Since it wasn't to be a long wait, there would be no need to bother with my school books.

11

Since yesterday, I'd been in protective custody, living in a room at the Rosewood Center. Mother and Sergeant Lutz had promised me I could go home the minute the trial ended. I was in Rosewood because they didn't want the Landises, their lawyer or the news people or others—even the children in my class—asking me things. Father might be part of the cause too. They didn't say that but mother and Sergeant Lutz decided on protective custody for me after mother caught me talking to father in church on Sunday.

Father had promised to come to the Hall of Justice before the start of my trial. I wondered if he might be out front or if he knew to come to the back. He should. Father was a lawyer. He was with the law firm of King and Braxton but it was not his firm as I foolishly imagined when I was five. I kept looking out the window and into the corridor for father.

Father didn't do criminal cases. He could be talking to mother out in the lobby. Maybe that was the problem. Father and mother didn't see me at the same time. They were separated and still angry. Father had to move out of our house because he was sick. It wasn't the kind of sick that kept you from being a lawyer or going to work. I thought father was getting better but I wouldn't ask mother till after the trial. I hoped they weren't arguing again.

In the beginning, father had tried to talk mother out of blaming Howard Landis. That was before they separated. It was before father smashed up the garden room where we used to eat supper; me, Vivian, father and mother. But it was after he broke furniture in the bedroom and punched holes in the wall. If father got over being sick I thought he might come back to our house with me and Vivian and mother. This trial was messing everything up.

Because of protective custody and the trial I would be absent from school. Ms. Trawick, my teacher, was assisting

12

me to meet this challenge. I had assignments and books. She would provide special attention when everything was over. Ms. Trawick and mother had worked this out in their conferences.

Mother had said they wouldn't let the trial disrupt my school. Mother promised to do her weekly reviews. Every day I was to add new words to my vocabulary notebook. "This will be a difficult experience," mother told me, "but we profit from difficult experiences." She said the notebook and doing her weekly assignments would give me "continuity during this challenging time." When my notebook got brought up, I would need to add *plea, media, sentencing, bailiff* and *voir dire examination.* Meeting challenges was very important.

Voire dire examination was an interesting part of trials. It meant the jury people had to tell the truth when the lawyers asked questions. It was to make sure the jury people could be fair and weren't against one side or the other. Telling the truth was the most important characteristic of trials. Mr. Gorman had said the voire dire examination in my trial would take all morning and so I wouldn't testify until after lunch. With the judge putting off the start, it might be later. I knew a lot about trials. Much more than when I followed father on shadow day in the first grade. Back then, father brought me to the courthouse, even though he wasn't that kind of lawyer.

During the last year, though, the more I had learned, the more scared I had got. Mother and Mr. Gorman thought it should work the other way. I wished father would get here. What I remembered most from shadow day was how murderers had been tried in the same courtroom I would be in. Murderers had sat in the same witness chair. When the jury decided they did it the judge made the murderer stand up. Then he told them they had to die in the electric chair. "Fry in the electric chair" was what Sergeant Lutz told me when I asked questions. He told me that next year Mr. Gorman will be assigned to murder cases and have people put in the electric chair.

"Nothing like that will happen to Howard," Mr. Gorman told me. He had been annoyed with Sergeant Lutz for discussing murder cases and frying in the electric chair with me. "We are doing this to help Howard," said Mr. Gorman. "Not to hurt him."

Mr. Gorman planned me to be the first witness. "After you finish, the trial will be easier for you," he said. How did he know? I still had to stay in protective custody. That was because either he or Howard's lawyer could bring me back to answer more questions. They could do that right up to the very end. I didn't think Mr. Gorman deliberately told lies, but he kept things from me and he made things sound too easy.

Since I might have to go back in the courtroom for more questions, I would not be allowed to listen to the trial. Neither could mother. Witnesses couldn't stay in the courtroom to hear each other because they might hear something that changed their mind. It might help them lie. I was supposed to say only what I knew and not what other people said. I wondered why they'd been practicing me for almost a year with doctors and people helping me say what happened to me.

It wasn't fair. My sister Vivian didn't have to be in protective custody. She was twelve, four years older. Her testimony would be much easier. She could keep going to school, practicing her violin every day and eating supper with mother like nothing had happened.

Why wasn't father there? He should have got there. He had promised. Maybe they had called him and said to wait because the judge was doing things that would keep the trial from starting on time. It was nine-fifteen. Father

14

should of come by this time even if he waited. Maybe they weren't going to let him see me.

I caught myself sucking my thumb. I knew better. "Stop thumb sucking" was always on mother's weekly list along with work hard to keep from biting my fingernails. Sergeant Lutz had been watching me and that remembered me I had my thumb in my mouth. It got there without me knowing. Sergeant Lutz was looking at my hands. I had made a mess out of the paper cups they brought hot chocolate for me in, and coffee for Sergeant Lutz.

Howard Landis walked by in the corridor. He saw me. He was with his lawyer. He looked in and slowed his walking a little. Then he looked away. Neither Sergeant Lutz or Mr. Gorman had told me exactly what would happen to Howard. "The judge decides that," said Mr. Gorman. Everybody, even the doctors, had told me how much what I was doing would help Howard. The way Howard looked at me wasn't like someone who thought he was being helped. Howard was pretty fat. He had on a suit and tie so you couldn't see all his blubber. His hair was slicked down. He lived next door and because of that I didn't see how I could keep away from him after the trial. Howard was part of what I was getting protected from in protective custody. If I won Howard would go to jail.

Sergeant Lutz watched me watch Howard. Then Sergeant Lutz got up to pull the tan curtain across the window. He lit a cigarette. I didn't tell him the danger of cancer or how mother didn't tolerate smoking by people who came to our house.

My books and things got brought in, and another cup of hot chocolate. I spilled a little on the table because of the cup being too hot. Some dripped on my brown pants. Sergeant Lutz dabbed at it with his handkerchief.

Mr. Gorman had told me to wear the oxford shoes, brown pants and plaid shirt. He and mother looked at the things she brought to the Rosewood Center. Mother wanted me to wear my jacket and tie but Mr. Gorman said what I had on would be better. Mr. Gorman was the expert on trials. Mother said it would be all right for him to decide. I hadn't understood how wearing a tie and jacket would make any difference. I asked Mr. Gorman. He smiled and said "We want you to be comfortable." Leaving my jacket at home hadn't made me comfortable. I had known it wouldn't. Not even if I was an adult. But I hadn't told Mr. Gorman.

I hadn't told anyone how I felt living in the room at Rosewood Center, with its concrete-block walls and eyes that stared at me when I was alone at night. Last night was the worst. I laid in my bed thinking about the trial, looking at the two windows high up on the concrete-block wall. They were covered by thick wire. One didn't completely close. The block walls were painted bright blue and they had pictures on them of baseball, football and basketball players, good examples for other boys who had stayed in my room. Over the desk was a picture of Abraham Lincoln. Rosewood was like a jail to give boys who cause trouble a chance to do better. There were also girls, but they stayed on the third floor.

I was wondering if they put me in a room with wires on the windows to keep someone from doing something to me. When I layed there in bed, thinking about the start of the trial, I got scared. I didn't remember when I fell asleep but I remembered waking up screaming, with a man standing in the doorway asking if I was all right. I also remembered the dream.

The spider was in the long cedar closet in the master bedroom. I heard the spider swishing in and out between the clothing and garment bags. I reached for mother, but she was gone. I was in her enormous bed all alone.

It was dark and the closet doors were closed, but I saw

16

the spider in there, growing. I heard the closet door being rolled open on its rollers. The spider was coming out. Its eyes were the size of golf balls. They were red and they glowed. They were looking at me. It was an enormous spider with long, skinny legs. It had blood on its face. Two of its long legs grabbed the bedspread. It pulled the spread off. Then the sheet.

It stared at me in my jammies. With its legs spread it filled the whole room. Its eyes were up high on the ceiling, looking down at me. Blood seeped out of its eyes. That spider could grow or shrink if it wanted. It made a scraping sound as it felt with its legs, one on either side of me, along the sheet. "Please," I begged. Me and the bed were trapped under the spider. Around us was a web so thick I couldn't see through it. I couldn't of got away if I tried. The spider was bending its legs, lowering itself on top of me. It was going to bite me and eat me. It had sharp teeth.

My scream couldn't get through the thick web. The spider wasn't moving. It knew no one could hear and I couldn't escape. I screamed and kicked. Its mouth opened and black ink came out, smothering me.

Then I saw the man standing in the doorway. I told him I was all right and he left. He didn't turn on the lights. He didn't question me. He didn't see that under the covers of my bed, I was shivering.

It was important to keep my dream a secret. There had been others but none that scary. I didn't dare tell them. Especially to Dr. Hartenfells or mother. They would ask questions, try to get things out of me.

I wished this was over. I wished they'd just tell the jury what I already said a thousand times. I had said it to the grand jury and to Dr. Hartenfells and Mr. Gorman and Sergeant Lutz and Dr. Dean. They had taken notes and made that machine recording in the grand jury. That

17

should have been plenty. They could easily have just showed stuff to the jury.

Sergeant Lutz gave me a cookie. He always had a cookie or candy hidden somewhere, or he would get me orange pop or something. I didn't feel like a cookie.

Mr. Gorman came back in. "How are we doing?" he asked.

"Just fine, thank you," I said.

"It may be tomorrow before we finish getting a jury in the box," he said, looking at Sergeant Lutz. "Mansfield's got this psychiatrist to advise him during voir dire. With that bullshit, it's going to take forever."

Mr. Gorman said mother would have lunch with us. We'd meet her down on the fourth floor in the prosecutor's office. They'd bring in sandwiches and Cokes. Mr. Gorman didn't say anything about father. I almost asked but decided not to.

"Why don't you do one of your *Yes and No* puzzles?" Sergeant Lutz asked when Mr. Gorman left.

I started one where you connect dots to see what picture you've made. I pushed it aside. I didn't feel like connecting dots. I wished they'd open the curtain. I wanted to watch for father even if Howard went by again.

"Want to look at my automatic?" asked Sergeant Lutz.

I shook my head.

"You're going to do great," said Sergeant Lutz. "You don't have to worry because Mr. Gorman will do everything and the judge will be there to protect you. All you have to do is give answers like you did before." He grinned. "Only there won't be as many questions," he said. His grin changed to a smile and he pushed me on the shoulder like he was being playful.

I wouldn't be great. So long as I told the truth, the judge said. I had an awful problem and it got more awful the longer we waited. It was worse than that dream.

18

There was things I'd never tell. No matter what. Even if they caught me in my lies. It wasn't my fault. I hadn't meant to lie. But they had kept after me and after me. It had turned into an awful problem. I was lying about Howard Landis.

2

MY TROUBLE STARTED a year ago, the day my parents were expecting Mr. and Mrs. Gerlach as company for dinner. It was Friday. I usually liked it when company came, but this time I had been praying all week that mother would never find out what happened to me.

Mr. and Mrs. Gerlach were my friend Mitzy's mother and father. At least Mr. and Mrs. Gerlach were not bringing Mitzy along like they sometimes did. Mother told me Mitzy wasn't coming but I wouldn't be absolute sure till they got there.

Mitzy and I played together, sometimes at our house, sometimes at hers. Mitzy was always asking questions, making me talk about things I didn't want to. She didn't care if she got me in trouble.

I was not an ordinary seven-year-old, not a boy who got called Chuck or Charlie. I had just finished the third week in second grade. I was the youngest in my class at the Canterbury School and I was in the gifted section. Mitzy was also gifted. Our teacher's name was Mr. Shirley. Mr. Shirley knew all our names on the first day and he was friendly. He said we would have more work to do at home than we did last year. I expected second grade to be more challenging. Mother had told me the reason I went to Canterbury School was so I could be challenged.

"What is challenged?" I asked. Mother appreciated questions. Even when she was busy, like she was then, downstairs preparing for Mr. and Mrs. Gerlach, mother took time to understand what I was asking. Then she answered and kept on answering if, as I usually did, I had additional questions. If she was too busy, she reminded me of my question later.

Mother had explained challenged to me and, together, we wrote *challenge* in the notebook she and I kept of the new words I added to my vocabulary. We were careful about spelling and checked words in the dictionary before writing them in the notebook.

Mother and I played a game where Mother came into my room and asked me words from the notebook. I almost always got them. When you wrote a word down at the time you learned it, it stayed with you. That gave me a large advantage in school. Even in the gifted section, none of the other children knew as many words as myself. They spelled atrocious. If I won at mother's game, she rewarded me with extra time to play Nintendo. If I used a new word

21

correctly mother would mention that when we did our weekly review. Using new words was important.

One of the best days in first grade was when Ms. Graham praised me for knowing the word *vocabulary*. "You used the word correctly, Charles. And you pronounced it properly," said Ms. Graham.

On the very same day, Ms. Graham complimented me on my word selection when I responded that oceans were larger than lakes. "We want to avoid overworking the word *big* when we have a better alternative," said Ms. Graham. Mother was pleased when I told her these compliments. At supper mother would ask Vivian and me to report on what we accomplished in school.

"You see, Charles," said mother on that day. "Our attention to vocabulary is paying dividends." That led to an interesting discussion about dividends and produced two new words for my notebook.

I was to stay in my bedroom until I got invited to join the Gerlachs for dessert. My bedroom was large. It was above the three-car garage on the end of our home. I had crank-out windows facing the golf course. The windows over my built-in desk looked into the leafy maple trees between our home and the residence of Dr. Landis. Howard Landis was our baby sitter. I liked Howard. He had told me I was like a little brother. I didn't like the way Mitzy made fun of Howard because he was fat and played with me like he was another kid. I thought she might of made up stories about Howard which she told to her older brother.

My room was nice and neat, my collections and books and everything in their place on the shelves, the bed made with the map-of-the-world bedspread lined up. All my clothes were in drawers or hanging in the closet. If Mr. and Mrs. Gerlach came upstairs it wouldn't embarrass me if they observed my room. But I didn't want the challenge of Mitzy.

22

My Sony television sat in the middle of the long book-case wall. I decided to try again on my Nintendo fantasy-adventure. It would take my mind off of things. For three weeks I had been keeping charts, slaying monsters, ac-cumulating powers, trying to stay alive and defeat the evil forces. I was facing Vorlock, a powerful and clever dragon. I had been killed by Vorlock five times but because I saved my position, I could start again without going back to the beginning. I kept trying new tactics but Vorlock was awe-some.

He got me again. I yelled and threw my charts on the floor. It took a few minutes to sort them out and get every-thing in place. I almost ripped them up. I shouldn't have tried to kill Vorlock while I was thinking about what hap-pened to me. I'd been scared and sweaty and not feeling good. I was afraid it might happen again. In a way I wished it would if I could be sure no one found out.

I was doing better at controlling my anger. I didn't have temper tantrums like I did when I was younger. Luckily mother didn't hear me yell. Mother did not tolerate temper tantrums. She would have imposed consequences.

My sister Vivian and I had eaten. Later we would be in-vited to join mother and father and Mr. and Mrs. Gerlach for dessert. Luckily it was nice and warm so mother and father could entertain the Gerlachs on the terrace.

Father was home. I had heard the garage door go up when I was fighting Vorlock. A few seconds later my fa-ther's gray BMW with silver trim came into the driveway. Father always activated the garage door with his electric opener when he rounded the corner onto Country Club Way, which was the street where our home resided. When I rode in the car, father let me use the electronic opener. I also got to call mother on the cellular telephone to tell when we would be arriving. When father left his law office he called mother on the cellular phone so she could prepare his martini. Before we ate, mother and father did martinis on the terrace or in the leisure room, dependent upon the weather.

Father was a partner in the law firm of King and Braxton. My father was Stewart King III and his father, my grandfather, was Stewart King, Jr. and his father had been Stewart King who founded the firm.

I was not named Stewart because of my mother. "You are special," mother explained to me. "Not just another Stewart King. We don't want you to carry the burden of wearing someone else's name." I wasn't sure what mother meant or what burden father carried by being Stewart III, but I remembered how mother looked when I asked. She had given me my tubby bath in our large bathroom with colorful tiles from Mexico. She was rubbing me with a large towel. We were going to have company that night too. Mother dropped the towel and put both hands on the sides of my head. She put her face in front of my nose, so close I could smell her perfume and her hair. She smelled like the roses where I found the scarab beetle for my insect collection, only not that sweet. Mother's hair was dark like mine, only cleaner and beautiful.

"You are special," she said and her eyes looked into mine the way Moose, Mitzy's golden retriever dog, looked at Mitzy when Mitzy was holding a treat in front of Moose. I would have liked a dog. I would have liked a tracking dog.

If Mitzy's dog, Moose, belonged to me I could teach him to track. I had been interested in tracking since last winter when I found deer tracks in our backyard. Father didn't believe me but mother took me to Tremont Library and Ms. Perkins located a book for us and it proved I was right. My chance for getting a tracking dog would depend on when I quit sucking my thumb. A dog was out of the question until I stopped my thumb-sucking. Too much danger of germs and contracting disease.

24

Kevin and Scott and Mitzy all had dogs and mother let me play at their houses. So mother may have had other reasons. I realized dog paw marks wouldn't look good on the peach-color carpet in the master bedroom. Dogs did provide good protection and if it was a large barking dog, they scared people away. But we had many security protections, lights that turned off and on at different hours, an electronic and laser alarm system that connected to the police station, light beams that watched for burglars when we went out, private guards who drove by the house when we took vacations. I'd practiced dialing 911 and could do emergency calls in the dark. Unfortunately, we did not require a dog for protection.

I cranked open a window on the golf course side. I pushed a chair to the window. I liked to spy on mother and father. Listening to grownups—or adults as I should of called them—was the most interesting thing I did. I had my own telephone and could pick up the receiver so quiet no one could tell.

I saw father checking the outdoor grill, making sure he had his charcoal shaker, starter fluid, briquettes, cooking apron, fork and his Lawry's Seasoned Salt. Mother was pinching wilted geranium blossoms and pulling tiny weeds that had sprouted in the four large urns which stood at the border of the upper level of our patio-terrace. Mother was wearing a green blouse and pants with bright colors in large flowery swirls. I had gone with mother when she bought those pants in the Canterbury Mall Boutique during one of her shopping sprees. *Shopping spree* was what father sometimes called mother's trips to the Canterbury Mall. I hadn't put *shopping spree* into my notebook of words, but when adults used a phrase like *shopping spree* in the way father did, I remembered.

Outside my window, the sun had just dropped into the trees on the other side of the sixth fairway. Behind and

25

above the trees the sky was red and orange and purple. The breeze was barely making the leaves on the trees flap against each other. It seemed unlikely that it would rain. It was hot but might get cooler in the evening.

Occasionally a golfer would play a shot from just beyond the edge of our yard. We adjoined the sixth hole. My father said "you have to be long and slice" to reach our yard, but a few did. Most golfers at Canterbury, even the whackers as my father called them, would have never come into someone's yard to retrieve their ball. I kept the balls I found in the bottom drawer of one of my built-ins.

Father disappeared. There was a wall of doors opening from the dining room onto the terrace, another door from the center hall and finally double doors opening from the kitchen to the deck. The deck and the steps from the deck down to the lower level of the patio-terrace were constructed of large, hand-hew timbers. Father had gone through one of the dining room doors.

The roar of crowd noise startled me. "Ladies and gentlemen, the pride of the Buckeyes, the Ohio State Marching Band." The announcer blared the words loud enough to be heard above the cheering. The drums rolled. Our stereophonic system had an instrument panel that transmitted sound to the kitchen, living room, dining room, leisure room, master bedroom, game room which was in the basement, or to the terrace. Two in the golfing foursome who were playing the sixth hole heard the drums. They waved. Father was playing my favorite Ohio State marching band tape. When I was little I used to march, like I was in the band marching onto the field in Ohio State stadium. The band started to play "Buckeye Battle Cry" and suddenly the music stopped. Mother had quit tending to the flower boxes. She stood with her hand on her hip, glaring at the doors where father disappeared. Mother did not like marching band music. She preferred Prokofiev.

26

"Stewart, you aren't going to make an ass out of yourself again," said mother when father came out.

"Lighten up, Babs," said father. "I'm just making sure everything is set to go. Gerlach is a nut about his Michigan Wolverines."

"You play that tape every time they come over," said mother.

"You got it," said father.

"Doesn't it get through to you? They laugh at you. Super Fan, they call you."

"Look, Babs. Gerlach didn't even graduate from Michigan. He only went to law school up there. You think I'm not going to remind the bastard who kicked whose ass in Ann Arbor last November?"

"I don't know why we see so much of the Gerlachs anyhow," said mother. "They are shallow. So materialistic."

"I'll tell them you said so," said father.

"You are disgusting." Mother went to the steps. Without looking at father, she climbed to the deck. "And vulgar," she said as she went into the kitchen.

Father looked sheepish. He glanced at the golfers. Three of them were watching the other one take his stance to hit. The golfers acted like they heard nothing.

I hoped mother and father wouldn't get into one of their fights, not with Mr. and Mrs. Gerlach about to arrive. Not with everything else on my mind. I put my hand on my forehead and it was cold, clammy. I pushed the chair back to its regular place and closed the window. I thought mother was coming upstairs.

Mother came in my room and headed to the closet to pick clothes for me to put on when I came down for dessert.

"Something smells funny," said mother. "Charles, do you know what it is?"

"No," I said, coming to the closet door. But I knew. I felt

sick. She bent down, looking at the box of Lincoln Logs. She started moving boxes. She found my undies.

"Charles, did you put these here?" she asked.

"No," I said. "Are they mine?"

"Charles," she said, stepping out of the closet. "How did these get here?"

"Maybe I lost them," I said.

"Not under boxes in the corner." She had the waistband of the undies in her fingers and walked to the window holding them to the light. She held the undies away from herself. Her fingernails were long and peach-color.

"Charles, is this blood?"

"I don't think so."

"Have you been bleeding during your eliminations?" she asked.

I shook my head.

"Why did you hide these, Charles?" She was staring at my blood-spotted undies.

"I didn't."

She looked at me, not exactly cross but like she had hundreds more questions. She knew I was lying.

I heard the crunch of a car on the gravel.

"The Gerlachs are here," said mother. She sat the undies on my desktop and laid out my shirt, corduroys, socks and loafers.

"We will talk about this later," she said, taking the undies with her. At the door she turned. "Charles," she said, "mother is very disappointed that you are hiding something from her."

Mother walked back in the room, to where I was. She put the undies on the dresser and her hands on the sides of my face. She was only inches from me and I could see the lines and marks where she put stuff on her face and eyes. "Do you understand?" she asked. Her hands pressed on my head. "Do you understand that mother is very, very disappointed?"

"Yes," I said.

"Mother will expect a full explanation," she said, taking the undies with her.

I wanted to lie down but I had to know what they were going to do.

I cranked the window open again. I pulled over a chair but stayed back, behind the curtain on the side, so they wouldn't see me.

Mr. Gerlach was wearing yellow slacks and a polo shirt that was the color of lime sherbet. He had thick wavy hair and his glasses were on top of his head, the stems pushed into his hair. He was wearing boat shoes and no socks. He had his arm around mother's waist as they followed Mrs. Gerlach, who had stepped out on the terrace first. He had a Rolex watch, like father's. Mother must have done something with my undies. She was smiling at Mr. Gerlach, as if she'd forgot about me. Or else she was pretending not to be worried about blood on my undies.

Mrs. Gerlach was wearing fancy sneakers with baby blue liners. She had on a tennis dress. She was carrying a sweater because on September days it could get cool on the terrace when the sun went down. Mr. and Mrs. Gerlach had wonderful tans, just like Mitzy.

Father grinned at Mrs. Gerlach. "Bambi, you look good enough to eat," he said. "Are you ready for a silver bullet?"

"Stewart, you make the best martini in Columbus," said Mrs. Gerlach. "And I'm ready. God, am I ready. What a week." She looked at mother as if a longer explanation would be necessary after she received her drink and became comfortable in one of the wrought-iron chairs.

Father went into the kitchen. He frosted glasses in the freezer compartment and kept his martini pitcher in the refrigerator. While he was gone, mother talked to Mr. and

Mrs. Gerlach, complimenting Mrs. Gerlach for winning the B-flight singles championship in tennis. Maybe she wouldn't bring my undies up with Mrs. Gerlach. I was afraid that would be the first thing mother would say. Then I'd of been in large trouble. When father came out with drinks, mother went inside. I wondered if mother had told father about the undies. I didn't think so or he wouldn't be laughing.

Mother came back with a tray of shrimp and oysters spread over lettuce and ice. There was red sauce in a cup in the center of the tray. Mother handed out small plates and let everyone pick from the tray, serving herself last.

"What do you think of Mr. Shirley?" asked Mrs. Gerlach.

"I'll tell you what I think," said Mr. Gerlach. "I think he's a silly fag."

"Fritz," said Mrs. Gerlach, looking cross at Mr. Gerlach, the way she sometimes looked at Mitzy. Mrs. Gerlach was mean. She whipped Mitzy. One time Mitzy showed me her welts. I leaned closer to the window. I had to hear what they said. Mrs. Gerlach turned to mother. "I do wonder though," said Mrs. Gerlach, "whether he is neglecting the fundamentals."

"In what respect?" Mother crossed her legs and sipped from her drink. I relaxed, but only a little.

"I realize he has them learning things we didn't touch until high school, but what about spelling, for example? Some of Mitzy's work is deplorable."

"I'm pleased with what Mr. Shirley is doing for my Charles," said mother.

"Does Charles like school?" asked Mrs. Gerlach. Suddenly I was breathing so hard they might hear. Now mother would tell, and then what?

"My Charles loves school," said mother. Usually I like to hear conversations about me and Vivian and Canterbury School. But I wish they'd talk about something else.

"I can tell you this," said Mr. Gerlach. "Children need structuring. They require discipline."

"You can have success with different methods of parenting," said mother. "The important thing is for the child to know it is loved."

Mother or father never spanked me or Vivian. I wondered if mother was thinking about that. To make me tell about my undies. It wouldn't work if she tried.

Mother listened as father and Mr. Gerlach teased each other. Then the Gerlachs invited us to their cabin. "We'd love that," said mother.

I had to go to the bathroom. I felt sick in my stomach. But I had to hear everything they said.

But Mrs. Gerlach only told about her awful week. They were having their house painted. The painters had been messy and were not reliable about when they came and went.

The Gerlachs, mother and father were laughing. Each had taken a second martini. I had been thinking how to get out of going to the cabin with the Gerlachs and missed what they talked about after house painters. Father was telling about "this asshole" who lives down the street on the side away from the golf course. I knew the house. They didn't spray for weeds and dandelions. They didn't use a fertilizer service. They let their grass grow, sometimes to seed, and they didn't trim when they mowed.

Mrs. Gerlach laughed so hard she took a handkerchief out of a green canvas bag with a daisy patched onto it. She wiped her eyes while father told how the neighbors got madder and madder, held meetings to decide what to do about the trashy lawn. Finally Mrs. Landis, Dr. Landis's wife and Howard's mother, drove her tractor-mower across the street to cut a criss-cross swath through the tall grass when the assholes weren't home. That made the ass-

31

hole angry and he had been threatening to sue. Only the simple shit didn't know who did it.

It was a great relief to hear about assholes and simple shits. Mother disapproved of those words and never used them. But she didn't seem mad when she said "Please, Stewart" to my father every now and then. Maybe mother was not so upset over my undies as I thought.

Mrs. Gerlach went inside. She wanted to check on their babysitter. "We're using a new sitter tonight. She's only twelve," said Mrs. Gerlach.

"Everything is hunky-dory," Mrs. Gerlach said when she came back.

"We're fortunate to have a very responsible boy next door," said mother. "He's a high school senior."

"I suppose having a boy as babysitter is fine," said Mrs. Gerlach.

"Howard is wonderful with my Charles," said mother.

"I know," said Mrs. Gerlach. "I guess it's my prejudice. But you do hear stories about boys who like to babysit. There was that incident in Worthington."

"What do you mean?" asked mother. Mother was leaning forward.

"Nothing," said Mrs. Gerlach. "I shouldn't have opened my mouth."

Mother didn't say anything more but she stayed quiet while father, Mr. and Mrs. Gerlach talked about Dirk, Mitzy's brother and the star of the Tremont High School football team. Ohio State's coach, Pepper Jordan, had come to see Dirk play and had even been to Mitzy's house. Sometimes Dirk was there when I played with Mitzy. I didn't like Dirk. I was afraid of him, partly because of what Mitzy told me even if I didn't believe all of Mitzy's lies.

Father took the cellophane off the thick steaks and put them on the grill. They sizzled. Flames jumped from where

the juice dropped onto the hot coals. The smell coming off
the grill floated up to my window.

"Time for din-din," said father.

The four sat at the large round table with a large um-
brella sticking up through the middle. It was nearly dark
and the colorful Chinese lanterns looked lovely, strung
along the outside edges of the upper terrace.

"Stewart," said Mrs. Gerlach. She put her fingers on father's arm. "What do you think of the president's Supreme
Court appointment?"

Father finished chewing his bite of steak. He wiped his
mouth with his napkin. He stared at the lanterns for a second, picked up his martini glass and moved it closer to the
center of the table. "I'm terribly worried," he said. He
glanced at mother and Mr. Gerlach before looking back at
Mrs. Gerlach. Father was frowning. "It is difficult to predict
how any justice will turn out," said father. "But a number
of his decisions disturb me."

Mrs. Gerlach nodded as father spoke.

Mr. Gerlach and mother joined the conversation. Pretty
soon they were talking about education in Japan, China
and Russia. "We are not keeping pace," said Mr. Gerlach.
"Thank God for Canterbury School," said mother. "Our
children are being challenged there." Mother didn't think
the Chinese and Russian children were beating me and Vivian. But I didn't know how I could keep mother from being
disappointed when she asked her questions about my undies. Because I wouldn't ever tell.

"My goodness," said mother, looking at her watch. "Did
anybody realize it was nine o'clock?" Mother, hurrying, disappeared into the house. Carefully I cranked the window
shut. I pushed the chair back to where it belonged and
opened up the dinosaur book I got at the library.

"Charles," said mother when she came into my room.
"You haven't changed clothes yet."

"Is it time for dessert already?" I asked.

Mother helped me. She brushed my hair. She stepped back and looked at me, starting with my loafers. She moved my belt to make the buckle line up with the buttons on my shirt. "We look just fine," she said, smiling. She didn't say a word about my undies. I followed her. Vivian was already in the kitchen. Mother held each of our hands and we went out, onto the terrace.

"Hello, Mr. Gerlach. Hello, Mrs. Gerlach," I said.

Mr. Gerlach clapped me on the shoulder. "How's it going, old sport?" he asked. He held out his hand with the palm up and asked me to give him "some skin."

"Just fine, thank you, Mr. Gerlach," I said as I slapped his hand.

Mother brought out a key lime pie. Since our trip to the NASA Space Center, Disney World and Epcot Center where we rented a treehouse at Lake Buena Vista, key lime pie, which we ate lots of, had been my favorite.

Father put two extra chairs at the table. They scooted closer to make room for me between Mrs. Gerlach and my father, for Vivian between Mr. Gerlach and mother.

Mr. Gerlach did a trick. He pulled a quarter out of Vivian's ear and then one out of mine. He gave the quarters to us. "You are gold mines," he said. "Anytime I need money, I know where to go."

Father and mother laughed so I grinned but I wondered if Mr. Gerlach thought I was dumb enough to believe he got those quarters out of our ears.

Mrs. Gerlach told Vivian that her dress, which was blue with ruffles at the end of short sleeves, was darling. Vivian stood and turned so they could see the bow in the back.

The pie was delicious. I ate, watching bugs get zapped on the bug zapper which was mounted on a pole at the side of the patio, just beyond the Chinese lanterns. Not as many bugs were getting zapped as a month ago. Spring and early summer was the time when I found the most specimens for my collection.

"Charles, Mitzy tells me you have been studying dinosaurs," said Mrs. Gerlach. "Is that something we're interested in?"

"We saw some at the Museum of Natural History in Washington on spring vacation," I said. I wondered if they saw how I jumped when Mrs. Gerlach said "Mitzy tells me."

Mrs. Gerlach twisted in her chair, leaned toward me and put her elbows on the table. She rested her chin in her hands and looked right into my eyes. Her hair fell to her shoulder on either side of her face and she was smiling. "That must have been fascinating," she said.

"I want to go to Dinosaur State Park in Connecticut," I said. "You can see tracks right where the dinosaurs made them."

"I wonder if any of those dinosaurs made it out to Ohio," said Mr. Gerlach and he winked at father.

"My favorite is Tyrannosaurus Rex," I said. "He was fifty feet long and as tall as this house. He weighed eight tons. He had long sharp teeth like those steak knives." I pointed to the ones on the redwood table where mother had stacked dishes before serving dessert.

"It makes you wonder, doesn't it," said Mrs. Gerlach, who was still looking right at me. "What became of such a creature? Did they just get so big they ran out of food?"

"We don't know," I said. "Maybe a star exploded too close to the earth and radiation poisoned them. Scientists have many theories."

"Radiation," said Mr. Gerlach, shaking his head and stroking his chin. "Something to think about, isn't it?" he asked, looking from father to Mrs. Gerlach to mother.

"Guess what George Washington's favorite dinosaur was?" I asked.

Nobody knew the answer.

"George Washington didn't have a favorite dinosaur," I told them. "Because no one knew about dinosaurs when George Washington was alive. The word wasn't even used till forty years after he died."

Everybody laughed at my joke. I felt a little better. Mrs. Gerlach asked Vivian a question about her violin lessons. Mother told me to go inside and get the last two boxes of my insect collection because Mr. and Mrs. Gerlach might like to see them.

When I came back Mr. and Mrs. Gerlach looked at my specimens and asked questions. I got a chance to tell them that an ant has no bones. "Just a crunchy shell and that's why they go crunch when you step on one." Mr. and Mrs. Gerlach laughed again.

"We've been looking forward to hearing you play," Mrs. Gerlach said to Vivian.

We all went into the leisure room. "The sound isn't true out of doors," mother said.

Vivian played a sonata. I didn't like sonatas—or etudes either. I didn't like the screechy sound of Vivian playing her violin every day. Screech, screech, screech coming from her room like it wouldn't ever stop. But I knew how hard Vivian practiced and was proud of the difficult thing she had been able to accomplish.

Everyone, me too, clapped when Vivian finished and did her curtsy. We kept clapping until my hands got tired. The Gerlachs went back out on the patio with father.

Mother walked me and Vivian upstairs to our rooms. Mother didn't ask questions. She was in a hurry to rejoin the Gerlachs on the patio.

I laid in my bed in my jammies, thinking what could I do, what story could I tell mother that she would believe? I couldn't fall asleep.

3

I WOKE UP to shouting and crashing. Something slammed into the wall. It sounded like the house was falling apart and I could feel my bunkbed shake. "Let go of me." That was mother's voice.

I heard a thud. "You're fucking hysterical," yelled father.

"I am not hysterical," mother shouted. "And I am not making a federal case. But I am going to have Charles examined by Dr. Merwin."

"That's crazy," shouted father.

"This is not my imagination," yelled mother. "And I am not going to pretend that what I found doesn't exist."

37

I put my head under my pillow and pressed the ends of the pillow against my ears but I still heard them.

"You can't face a problem," screamed mother. "The blood on these underpants won't go away just because you'd like it to."

"Fuck you, you bitch," yelled father.

"You're drunk," shouted mother.

The door slammed. I heard mother crying. Maybe she got hurt.

The garage door went up and a car engine started. I got out of bed and went to the window. You could hear gravel shoot away from the tires as the BMW turned from our drive onto Country Club Way. I was shaking and my jammies were wet. I stood at the window. There was a full moon. I sat in the chair beside my bed, still trembling. I wished those undies would disappear. I should have put them in a trash can at the shopping mall.

After a little bit, I went to the door and stepped into the hall. The doors to the master bedroom, the two guest rooms and to mother's utility room were closed. I kept walking, being careful in my bare feet to make no sound. At the end of the hall, I went down the steps to the landing. Vivian's room was above the leisure room, in the ell of our house. The door to Vivian's room opened onto the landing. I turned the knob and went in.

Vivian was sitting up in her bed with pillows wedged between her back and the headboard. No lights were on but I saw her face by the light of the moon which came through the windows and her lace curtains. She wasn't crying. Shadows flickered on the wall opposite to the windows.

"Can I get in bed with you?" I asked.

Vivian nodded.

She was shaking. She put her arm across my shoulders

38

and pulled me close. She moved over so we could share her pillows.

"Did anyone get hurt?" I asked. "I heard loud crashes. I heard screams."

"I don't know," said Vivian. "Mother hates him." Vivian couldn't be right. They didn't hate each other. Not after the fun we had at Disney World and Epcot Center. Not after I saw them laughing when they were talking with the Gerlachs down on the patio. It was my fault but I didn't tell Vivian.

I was remembering the sounds from their bedroom. "Mother might of got hurt," I said. "We better go see."

"No," said Vivian, louder. She pulled away from me a little. "I don't want to," she said.

"But what if . . ."

"I don't have to," she said.

I didn't want to go back there by myself. Maybe father left so fast in the car to get a doctor. I felt my key lime pie coming up. I made it to Vivian's toilet. I felt better when I came back.

"It's not daddy's fault," said Vivian.

I heard mother calling my name. I heard her in the hall. She opened the door.

"Oh God. There you are," she said. She was wearing her silky blue robe with the sash pulled and tied at her waist. Her hair was tangled. When she came closer, I could see she'd been crying and rubbing her eyes. Makeup was smeared on her cheek and face. I ran into her robe. She held me, then walked me to the bed where Vivian was still sitting, propped against the pillows. Mother sat on the edge of the bed, between me and Vivian.

"Your father and I have a problem," said mother.

"Did father beat you up?" I asked.

"Not this time," she said. "But your father is a sick man. He needs help."

I was remembering those crashes and the thumps against the wall. "Will he come back tonight?" I asked.

"I don't think so," said mother. Mother seemed more tired than angry or scared. Mother took hold of my hands. I was waiting for her to ask about the undies.

"Are you going to get a divorce?" asked Vivian.

"I don't know," said mother. "Your father needs help, but we want to do what is best for you."

With everything mother said, it seemed worse. I kept thinking of mother and father and Mr. and Mrs. Gerlach laughing on the patio; then them arguing about me. "It's because of me, isn't it?" I asked.

"No," she said. She hugged me. She held me tight.

"Do you hate father?" I asked.

"I don't hate anyone," she said. "I feel very sorry for your father."

"Because he's sick?" I remembered her saying that but I didn't know what she meant. I didn't remember father ever being sick.

Mother nodded. She still had her arm around me. She pulled my head against her shoulder.

"If he's sick," I asked, "when will he get better?"

"I know you have questions, Charles," said mother. "And I'm sure Vivian does. We'll talk tomorrow, when we're rested."

"Where did father go?" I asked.

"Your father will be all right tonight," she said. "You don't need to worry."

"Can I sleep in your bed with you?" I asked.

Mother hesitated, then said yes. She offered to let Vivian come too. "I'll be all right here," said Vivian.

The master bedroom was a mess. I saw my blood-spotted undies on their dresser. Glass from the mirror on the back of the closet door was all over the peach-color carpet. A lamp laid on the floor with the pedestal broke. The lampshade was ripped and lying at the end of the king-size bed. The cactus was turned over and so were two rubber trees. Dirt was spilled all over the carpet. There was a jagged hole in the wall, next to the bed. I'd never come into their room, with its peach-color carpet so thick my toes sank in, when it didn't look as perfect as the pictures in *Architectural Digest*, the magazine mother kept on the table in the formal room downstairs.

"Did father do this?" I asked.

"Yes," said mother.

Mother saw me looking at my undies. I kept glancing at the dresser, where they were. "We'll talk about that tomorrow too," she said.

Mother smoothed the sheets and straightened the blanket. We always slept under a blanket because our climate control was set to keep the bedrooms cool. Mother held a corner of the sheet and blanket in her hand, so I could get in first. Then she slid in next to me. She was still wearing her blue robe.

"Charles," she said. "Mother loves you very much."

She wouldn't if she knew how my undies got blood on them. But I didn't say anything.

"Did you hear me?" she asked.

"Yes," I said.

She kissed me on the ear and rolled on her back. She adjusted her pillow under her head.

"Are you afraid of father?" I asked. "Is that what you mean by being sick?"

"We'll talk in the morning," she said.

"When will father get well from being sick?" I asked.

"It is very hard for me to think right now," she said.

WHEN I woke up, the bed was empty.

"I let you sleep late," said mother when I came downstairs. "Would you like a waffle for breakfast?"

41

I nodded. "Where's Vivian?" I asked.

"Vivian went to Holly's home. She will be spending the day with the Schofields."

Mother told me that after she cleaned the bedroom, she would take me to Mamsy and Paw-paw's. They were her mother and father, my grandparents.

"Your father and I are meeting for lunch," said mother. "We have things to negotiate."

Mother said our talk would have to wait until after she and father met.

"We won't be going to the football game?" I asked.

"Not today," she said.

Before we left I entered two new words in my notebook. They were *approximately* and *negotiate*. Mother helped me look the words up in the dictionary. I was specially interested in *negotiate*.

IT was late afternoon when mother came for me at Mamsy's. Mamsy hadn't asked questions like usual because mother must of told her not to. I got in the Volvo with mother. She looked fresh and clean in her blue slacks and white blouse.

"I wanted to talk with you before we go home," said mother. "I know you are worried about last night."

"Where's Vivian?" I asked.

"I have already talked with Vivian," said mother. She looked both ways before backing into the street.

"I think you know," said mother, "how children sometimes say things they don't mean."

I nodded.

"Adults do that too," said mother. She explained that she and father were angry last night but that today they have been able to talk. She told us that she and father have some problems but they are going to face them. She was sure everything would work out. She said most people have

42

problems. It was healthy to face them. She and father would be doing that.

"I thought father was sick," I said.

Mother slowly nodded. "Your father will be getting some help," she said.

"You mean a doctor?"

"Something like that," said mother.

Mother slowed the car and looked at me. "I don't know how much of our argument you heard." She kept looking at me.

I was worried about my undies but afraid to say.

"Are you thinking about what I found in your closet?" mother asked.

I nodded. Lots of times mother knew what I was thinking.

Mother pulled the car into a restaurant parking lot.

"I am not going to ask you about your underwear. Your father and I have agreed that you should see Dr. Merwin. We both want to be sure you haven't been hurt."

"I haven't," I said.

"We want Dr. Merwin to make sure."

"When do I have to be examined?" I asked.

"I'll be taking you out of school a little early on Monday," said mother.

I was glad she wasn't asking questions. I was still sore, like I had been all week, but not bleeding. I could be better by Monday.

"Charles," she said. She put her arm around me. "Is there anything you want to tell mother?" she asked.

I shook my head.

"Is there any question you want to ask mother? Mother wants to know what is worrying you."

"Nothing," I said.

43

She looked at me. Real hard. She smoothed my hair and straightened the tip of my polo shirt collar. She didn't believe me. Finally she started the car. Mother was disappointed in me even if she didn't say so.

4

MOTHER WENT TO the window, one of two with holes to talk through. Nurses in white dresses sat at desks behind the glass. Mother told the nurse we were there. At Dr. Merwin's office you always had to wait. A kid on the floor was going *erm-erm-erm* with one of Dr. Merwin's play cars while his mother patted the back of a baby who had his face in her shoulder.

The nurse didn't make us wait this time. Me and mother were led through the door, into the back. We got put in a small room. Mother took the chair and I climbed up to sit

45

on a black leather table that had sections that go up and down at either end. Pictures of pandas and deer and other friendly animals hung on the walls.

Another nurse came to tell me to take off everything but my undies. As I took something off, I gave it to mother who folded and placed my clothes on top of some shelves at the end of the table.

The leather table was cold on my legs. A strip of white paper down the middle wrinkled when I moved. Mother told me not to be ashamed no matter what Dr. Merwin asked. I was pretty sure mother had called Dr. Merwin on the phone. She wanted him to ask her questions for her.

"Sorry to keep you waiting," said Dr. Merwin who came in chuckling. He patted my back. "Had a wee bit of an emergency," Dr. Merwin said to mother. Dr. Merwin's nurse was standing behind him.

"Okay, big guy," said Dr. Merwin as he lifted me off the table. He tore off the paper and his nurse put on a new one. She clamped it in place while Dr. Merwin got a flashlight out of his pocket. It was the size of a pencil.

"Flop down here on your tummy," said Dr. Merwin, making the paper splat as he smacked the table. He gave me a boost.

He pulled my undies down. He put on rubber gloves. He spread my rear with his fingers and leaned down with his flashlight.

"Ouch." I couldn't help it when he touched sore spots. I twisted away.

"Sorry, big guy," he said. "We'll try to be more careful." I felt more hands. The nurse was spreading me so the doctor could push around with his fingers. He was fucking me. I didn't know what that word meant until ten days ago and I hated it—it would never go in my vocabulary notebook. But that's what Dr. Merwin was doing; fucking me with his fingers. He smeared some medicine in there. It stung.

46

"Okay, let's flip over on your back." Dr. Merwin helped me so I didn't fall off. He talked fast to the nurse. I couldn't understand all his words but the nurse was making notes on a clipboard.

Dr. Merwin played with my weenie; holding it up, looking underneath with his flashlight.

"Okay, big guy. Let's put on our clothes," he said. He looked at mother. "We've got ourselves a problem," he said. Mother's face was white as paper.

"Let's go to my office," said Dr. Merwin. "Have you seen my office?" he asked me.

I shook my head. I didn't want to either, even when he promised to show me his skeleton.

Dr. Merwin held my hand. Mother was right behind and the nurse behind her. I heard a kid bawling in one of the rooms with a closed door. Dr. Merwin didn't pay attention to the bawling kid.

He had a lot of skeletons, one full-size hanging from a pole. He had skulls and parts of skeletons on his shelves. His office was enormous with a bathroom and shower, a TV and a mini-refrigerator. He offered me a Coca-Cola and opened one for himself. Me and mother said "No, thank you."

He had me sit behind his desk in his chair which could turn completely around and rock back. The doctor sat on the corner of his desk facing me with his leg swinging. Under his white coat he wore blue pants and plaid socks. Mother sat on his sofa and the nurse stood between me and mother, holding her clipboard. All three were staring at me.

"Charlie, do you study science in school?" the doctor asked.

I nodded. I wasn't fooled by his pretend interest in my school but I kept nodding when he asked more school questions.

"A doctor is a scientist," he said. "A doctor looks at people and he sees things. What he sees tells him what happened." He leaned forward, clasped his fingers across his knee. "Charlie," he said, "I know what someone has done to you. I know you feel very, very bad about it." He kept looking at me. "Do you understand what I'm telling you?" he asked.

I did but I didn't move, except to shift my eyes to see the nurse. Dr. Merwin noticed and told the nurse to go outside.

"Perhaps it would be better if I left as well," said mother.

"Charlie," said Dr. Merwin. "What do you say? Do we want mommy with us or should mommy go outside and read a magazine?"

I knew mother wouldn't be reading magazines if she went outside. I couldn't answer his question, though. I couldn't think, except about Dr. Merwin looking up my rear, using his flashlight, studying to detect what happened to me. I looked at mother but she didn't tell me what to say. Dr. Merwin saw me look at mother. He was watching everything.

"Let's try it just between me and Charlie," he said.

Mother left. The door clicked shut.

"I know you don't want to talk about this." Dr. Merwin looked at me, expecting me to agree. I nodded. "It probably seems to you like you've done something wrong. Maybe you are afraid you'll be punished."

I nodded.

"Maybe the hardest thing is to tell me who hurt you. You may feel it is a secret and this person would be angry, that this person will hurt you if you tell." His eyes were trying to see what I was thinking. I didn't dare move.

"Sometimes," said Dr. Merwin, "it is hard to tell because the person who has hurt us is a friend, even someone we love."

I wondered if someone might of fucked Dr. Merwin. He

48

talked like it had happened to him. But I didn't ask. I didn't dare say anything or move.

"Charlie, you can help the person who hurt you. Even if it is your daddy or your sister. Even if it is your mommy." He studied me as he mentioned each of those.

"Your mommy tells me how much you like the boy next door. Howard, I believe his name is, the boy who stays with you when mommy and daddy are away."

I didn't move. Except I couldn't stop from blinking.

"Do you and Howard have secrets?" asked Dr. Merwin. "Has Howard ever told you that something you've done together should be a secret just between you and Howard?"

Dr. Merwin saw me move. He saw my eyes. He knew. But I couldn't tell the secrets between me and Howard.

"Charlie, you are a smart little boy," said Dr. Merwin. "I think you know that you must tell me what happened. You know it is wrong to hide what happened."

"No." I shouted at him. I didn't dare move, but I couldn't help myself. He slid off the desk to hold me. I hit him with my fists. I kicked him. "Let me go," I yelled. "You can't make me tell."

Dr. Merwin reached behind himself and pushed one of the buttons on his telephone. The nurse came in. Dr. Merwin told the nurse to take me to the waiting room. Dr. Merwin wanted to talk to mother.

The nurse gave me Kleenexes. I couldn't stop crying. But I was glad to be out of his office. I didn't think they'd torture me. They couldn't make me say what happened. I never would. I wasn't dumb. The more they found out, the worse it would get, even if they pretended the opposite. What we did was worse than I thought. I saw that from mother and Dr. Merwin and the nurse and how hard they tried to make me tell. If they knew everything it would be . . . I never would have wanted to see mother or anyone ever again.

There were kids and mothers all over the purple-color carpet and in every chair in the waiting room. They watched me wipe my eyes as the nurse pulled me in by the hand. I stood there being stared at while the nurse got another chair and put me in it. The nurse behind one of the windows looked out every few minutes to see what I was doing.

Each time the door into the back opened, I looked. It was always some kid coming out with a mother who was smiling, or it was a nurse coming to tell a mother that Dr. Kubek or Dr. Stamford would like them to step in back. There were many doctors and nurses back there.

My nurse came in. She looked at me, then went to a mother whose kid had yucky white stuff on his face and arms. "An emergency has come up for Dr. Merwin," said the nurse. "He thinks Dr. Kubek should look at Shawn this afternoon." Shawn and his mother followed the nurse into the back.

Emergency. Mother had been back there for hours. Besides, I knew she and Dr. Merwin had talked before we came. He knew about Howard's and my secret games. Maybe Vivian spied on us. I had to take a pee. What did the nurse mean by emergency?

The nurse spying out the reception hole saw me wiggling in my chair. She came out. She took me back to pee. I saw other nurses and two mothers with their kids but I didn't see mine. The reception nurse waited outside the toilet which was in a closet. After I peed she returned me to my chair.

What was I going to say to mother? Would they make me go back in there for more of Dr. Merwin's questions? Maybe I should of told how me and Howard played horsey-ride and monster. They knew anyway. Maybe Howard noticed my rear when he babysat last week and I took my tubby. He might of told about my being sore back there.

50

Dr. Merwin came out with mother. He had his arm across her shoulders. There were still people in the waiting room and they were watching. They'd been watching me all the time. I bet someone told these mothers it was me that caused the emergency by refusing to tell the terrible thing I did.

"I will call Dr. Hartenfells and fill her in," Dr. Merwin said to mother. "Hartenfells is first-rate."

I was surprised to see Dr. Merwin smiling. He came to me with his hand out. He wanted to shake hands. Everyone in the waiting room was surprised because doctors were supposed to stay in back. Only nurses came out.

Dr. Merwin walked with me and mother to the corridor that led to the elevator. In the corridor he squatted down so that his pens and the tools in his white coat were almost touching my shoulder.

"Charlie, your mommy and I have had a nice visit," he said. "Mommy tells me what a fine young man you are. I can see that myself." He moved his feet. I heard his bones creak under his white coat. "Mommy and I have a plan," he said. "You know what a plan is, don't you, Charlie?"

I nodded.

"Good," he said. "I know you trust mommy and I think you realize that mommy knows what is best for Charlie."

He stopped talking. I had to blink but I looked back without dropping my eyes.

"We trust mommy, don't we?" he asked.

I nodded.

"Good," he said, standing up. He reached inside his white coat. He pulled out a green sucker on a stick. He shook my hand again, then put the stick in my fingers.

"We're going to make this problem go away," he said, still smiling. "Charlie, you haven't done anything wrong, and this will turn out fine."

Mother took my hand. We didn't talk on the way to the

garage. We had parked on the middle of the ramp going up to the third level. We got in mother's Volvo, but mother didn't start the motor. It was pretty dark sitting inside the car.

"You and Howard have done some things that mother doesn't know about," she said.

I couldn't be sure whether she was telling me or asking a question. She sat there looking at me. She wouldn't start the car unless I answered.

"Maybe," I said.

"I imagine Howard makes it seem like a game," she said.

"Maybe."

Cars left and came on both sides of us. People looked in. One lady asked if we had car trouble.

Mother remembered Howard taking pictures of me at the pool with his camera. "How many pictures has he taken?"

"Howard took lots of pictures," I said. If I answered the Howard questions that might satisfy them. Mother wasn't asking about my sore rear. She wasn't questioning my answers. She knew the answers before I said them anyhow. She was excited, fogging the windshield with her breathing.

"You and Howard played some games," she said, looking at me with her face close to mine.

I nodded. Someone must of told.

"Tell me about those games," she said.

I had to tell mother something. If I didn't they'd never stop. I decided that the easiest time to tell her about would be the time Howard came to babysit with me and Vivian after an argument between mother and father two weeks ago. Not the terrible argument where father broke glass and messed up the master bedroom. The time I would tell about was when mother and father had been getting ready for a party. Howard was standing right in our front hallway when father yelled up the stairs, "All right, bitch, take all night. We're already an hour late." Father slammed the door and went out to wait for mother in his BMW. A few minutes later she went by without saying goodbye to me. She slammed the door too.

Vivian wasn't downstairs when that happened. I could hear the screech of her violin from her room. I ran up to my room and locked the door. By closing the door I could almost shut out the violin.

There was a knock, not loud like mother or father's. "What?" I asked.

"It's me," said Howard. "Come downstairs and we'll play a game."

"I don't want to," I said.

"Well, let me in," said Howard. "We can play Nintendo."

"No," I said. "Leave me alone."

"I know how to come in if I want," said Howard. "Your mom showed me."

"I don't want you to."

"Okay," he said. "I'll just sit here and talk through the door."

"No," I said.

"Okay, I'll talk and you listen."

I didn't answer. I couldn't force him to go away.

Talking through the door, Howard told me his parents got in arguments, just like mine. He used to think they would never speak to each other, that his mother might leave and never come back. "Only it never happened," he said.

I tiptoed to the door to hear better.

"Grownups are like kids," he said. "They get mad and make up."

He made me feel better. But I'd seen Dr. and Mrs. Landis in their yard working on their flower garden. I'd seen them in church. They wouldn't argue or yell at each other, throw tantrums and drive away mad.

"I'll play horsey-ride with you," said Howard. "Or monster."

Howard thought up good games and they were fun. "I don't feel like playing horsey-ride or monster," I said.

"Then let's play Nintendo," he said. "Just fifteen minutes. Then I'll go downstairs to do my homework until your bath and bedtime."

I opened my door. Howard had green sweatpants on. His fat bulged out. He was so fat and large that I asked him—about last year—why he didn't get on the football team. He told me he liked being the manager. He was at all the practices and games. Lots of times he told me about the team and exciting plays and who got clobbered. The Canterbury School didn't have a good team like Tremont High where Mitzy's brother played.

Howard took a comb out of the waist of his sweatpants. He combed his hair, looking at himself in my mirror to get the part perfect. He smiled at me. He rubbed his arm across his mouth. "You are my friend," he said. "My best friend."

I didn't believe that, but Howard was nice and I was lucky he lived next door and liked to babysit. He wasn't bossy like Nancy Watts who was Mitzy's babysitter.

"Do you like me better than Vivian?" I asked.

He nodded.

I liked hearing that because mother had emphasized how she didn't like me or Vivian better than the other.

I told Howard how much challenge the spider-monster was giving me in my video adventure. That was the monster I fought before Vorlock. Howard asked if he could try. Howard was outstanding at video adventures. Howard was going to be a doctor. He would be a pediatrician like Dr. Merwin. When he was younger, Howard was in the gifted section at the Canterbury School, just like me. He had a scholarship for Oberlin College after high school. Mother and father talked about that in the garden room after supper one night when we were having family discuss time. They said Oberlin was outstanding, better even than Ohio State. Mother said Howard was brilliant.

I didn't know if I wanted Howard to kill the spider-monster. That would be like me cheating. But I thought I could watch Howard and after he went home I could go back and try by myself. That wouldn't be cheating. But it wouldn't count as much either.

Vivian came by my room. She was finished with violin practice and had her homework done. She said she was going to watch television in the leisure room. When Howard came we got to watch more television, but I didn't think mother knew.

The spider-monster killed Howard faster than me. Howard backed his chair away from the screen. "Here," he said, patting the tops of his legs. "Sit on my lap and let me watch you try."

I wanted to kill the monster with Howard watching. I squirmed to get comfortable and Howard scooted the chair closer to the screen. He steadied me with his hands and put his head on top of my shoulder.

I danced away from the monster, trying my powers. It took the monster a long time to kill me. But I was extremely disappointed. For a minute I thought I could kill the monster with Howard watching.

"That was a great try," said Howard. He wrapped his arms around me and gave me a hug.

"I've got an idea," said Howard. "Do you know the story of Achilles?"

I nodded. That story was in a picture book that mother read to me. It was about a Greek warrior whose mother dipped him in magic coating so no one could kill him. Only

55

she forgot the place she held him when she dipped him. "Do we have to hit the monster in his heel?" I asked, wondering which one because the monster had so many arms and legs.

"I don't think it's the heel," said Howard. "But I notice he protected himself when you got close to hitting under his bottom arm on the left."

"He did?" Howard was brilliant to see that.

"Let me try again," said Howard.

I slid off his lap but he pulled me back. "No, you sit right here and watch," he said. "You aren't in the way at all."

Howard was right. The spider-monster was protecting himself where Howard said. But the monster won again. I wanted the next turn but it wouldn't have been fair after Howard figured the monster out.

"Right in the armpit, you ornery sucker," Howard yelled as he started the next fight. Howard got him. Then Howard put the adventure back to before, for me to try. It took three tries. But I did it. I felt outstanding. I wanted to tell mother and father. But that made me think of their argument. I stopped feeling good, even when Howard hugged me and said, "That was super."

"Let's play monster," Howard said. He meant the game he made up; not spider-monster on video.

The way you played monster was you hid. Howard was the monster. The monster was blind, so Howard wore a handkerchief over his eyes. The monster tried to find you. You had to be quiet. You could hide anywhere downstairs except the formal room and the dining room where no one was allowed to play. When the monster found you he had to decide if you were poison or safe to eat. He did that by smelling and feeling you. Howard made me giggle when he smelled and felt me. After that he always said, "Yuck, you are poison," and let me go.

Monster and horsey-ride were secret between Howard

56

and me. Not even Vivian knew. Howard said mother might not let him sit with me if she thought we were wasting time on silly make-believe. Howard said these games would be ruined if other people knew. Howard was especially right about Vivian. Besides, I liked secrets. I hated having to tell mother about our games.

The monster got close to me. I was in the kitchen where I pulled out the homemade-ice-cream maker and some pans so I could wedge into the cupboard under the utility island. The monster found the pans. I should not of moved them because that's how he knew where I was.

He got my foot. His hands came up my leg, reaching in. He tickled me and I giggled. I closed my eyes. He pulled me out, keeping hold of my ankle so I couldn't run away. It was against the rules to move except when the monster got you. Then you were allowed to.

I was wearing shorts and the monster bit my bare leg. Not hard. Just pretend.

"Mmm," he growled in a deep voice. "This might be something good to eat."

He bit me again and I giggled. He tasted where he bit with his tongue. He spit out, spraying me a little.

"Yuck," he said. "This tastes like poison."

I giggled and twisted to get away. My sneakers came off and I almost did.

Sometimes Howard and me played horsey-ride, my favorite of all Howard's games. Howard got on all fours. I climbed on him. My sneakers were spurs and I dug them into him to make him go faster. I held the ends of a belt which went through his teeth. I pulled back to make him slow or stop. I could make him turn by digging him on the side. Sometimes I dug him hard cause he said I could. He was so huge it didn't hurt.

After we played monster that night, Howard helped me with my tubby bath. I was pretty dirty. Howard sat on the toilet while I washed myself. I played in the water until he said I had to get out and get dried. He helped dry me.

BY the time I finished telling mother about horsey-ride and monster, it had gotten pretty dark. We were still sitting in the Volvo inside the medical center garage. Lights from cars going past flashed across the inside of our car. Those cars had their windshield wipers going. I heard rumbles. It had to be storming and raining outside. I wasn't sure how long we'd been there. I looked at my watch. It was only five but it seemed a lot later.

"Did Howard always help you take your bath before bedtime?" asked mother.

"Lots of times."

"Did he touch you?"

"Sometimes." I had to look away from mother because she was making it seem terrible.

"Oh God." Mother was breathing like she had run a long way. "Why didn't you tell mother?" She took her hands off the steering wheel and whammed them back down.

Suddenly she started the car.

It was pouring rain when we came out of the garage. Mother had to concentrate on her driving and we didn't talk. "I know I sound upset," mother told me when we got home. "Mother is not upset with you," she said. She told me I would be seeing another doctor, a different kind of doctor than Dr. Merwin, "a doctor who specializes in this type of case."

"What kind of case do I have?" I asked.

She shushed me off to my room to do homework, saying it would be better if Dr. Hartenfells explained. "Dr. Merwin said we should involve a third party." Mother was talking to herself more than me.

When the telephone rang, I eased up my receiver to listen. It was probably someone about me. With everyone telling things, I didn't have much chance.

The phone call was father, telling mother to have his martini ready because he was about to leave the office.

"You may need a double," said mother.

"Honey, what happened?" asked father.

"I'll tell you when you get here," said mother. "Maybe by then I can get myself collected."

"Jesus Christ, Babs. What is it?"

"It's the situation we've been talking about," said mother. "Stewart, I have not been exaggerating."

"Oh, Jesus Christ," said father.

Father's car raced into the drive. After his call, I hadn't been able to do anything except lie on my bed and think.

They were taking forever with martinis, but I didn't feel like eating anyway. I wished I could put on my jammies and go to bed.

Vivian busted into my room to say it was time for supper. "They're fighting again," said Vivian.

"What about?" I asked.

"You," she said and she ran out before I could ask anything. I had to force myself to go downstairs for supper.

5

ALL WEEK I waited to see what would happen. Mother had been friendly. She studied me when I was eating and at times when she thought I didn't know, but there were no more questions. I wasn't sure if mother and father had argued about me the night we came home from Dr. Merwin's office. When I got downstairs to eat, they were being nice to each other. Vivian could of lied.

On Sunday morning we went to church. Father was an usher. His place was the center aisle. He wore a red flower on his coat and assisted people to seats, handing them programs. Sometimes mother attended worship service and sometimes she joined an alternate study group. This Sunday she was in the large sanctuary, worshiping where father ushered.

Vivian and I knew our Sunday school locations and didn't need assistance. After church we would meet mother and father in Fellowship Hall where they had coffee and discussion with members of the congregation.

I didn't like Sunday school. It was not school. You didn't learn anything. We spent the whole hour cutting out pictures of David, Goliath, Saul, David's sling and Goliath's spear. I pasted pictures on a sheet of purple art paper. Other children cut out the same pictures but had different color paper, some pink, green, orange, blue and yellow.

I had better ways to spend my time. Only two children in my Sunday school class were in Canterbury School and neither of them was gifted. Sunday school was where I thought about things, dinosaurs, my insect collection, my video-game adventures, how to train a tracking dog—stuff like that.

But this time I was thinking about how my undies got bloody. I was praying that what I told mother when we sat in her Volvo in the medical center garage would be enough explanation; that mother was satisfied.

"Don't our posters look lovely?" asked Mrs. Phillips, the Sunday school teacher. Our posters were taped to the walls.

Most of the children said yes. Some clapped their hands and one squealed.

"Before we leave this morning," said Mrs. Phillips, "I want you to look at these lovely posters while I read you something from the Bible which was written by the David you see in your posters."

Mrs. Phillips was sitting on a baby chair in the middle of the room. We were all in baby chairs, in a circle around her.

61

"Yea, though I walk through the valley of the shadow of death, I will fear no evil; for thou art with me." That is what Mrs. Phillips read. "Think about those words and think about David this week," she said, turning her head to glance at the posters on the wall. "Think about David going out to face Goliath." She told us to put our posters up in our rooms as reminders.

"Was that before or after he killed Goliath?" asked a fat girl. Mrs. Phillips didn't understand and smiled at the fat girl. "Those words you read," said the fat girl. "Did David write them before or after Goliath?"

"Now that is an interesting question," said Mrs. Phillips. "Let's see what we think."

There was noise out in the hallway. Church was over. Kids rushed to grab their posters. Some tore out. Some would wait until their parents came for them. Probably Mrs. Phillips would answer the fat girl's question next Sunday.

I found mother and father in Fellowship Hall. They had their coffees in their hands and were in a conversation with Reverend Ethridge, the senior minister. Fellowship Hall was full of people and they all looked happy. I heard people talking about Ohio State's great win and the debate for the presidential election, which would be on television on Tuesday. The people were surrounded by watercolors of skiing, snow scenes, frozen streams and falling-down barns. The art in Fellowship Hall got changed to a different artist every three months. You could buy pictures if you wanted.

Father was telling Reverend Ethridge of his and mother's enthusiasm for a special drive to raise money for Reverend Ethridge's television ministry.

"We want to make our home available for the small group-feedback buffets," said father.

Mother nodded and smiled. "It is time for the mainstream church to have a voice on television," said mother. "We certainly get enough of the other kind."

Dr. Ethridge smiled. "If Jesus Christ were alive today," said Dr. Ethridge, "I'm quite certain that television would be vital to his ministry."

Vivian hurried toward us, carrying a painted can. It was to collect money for a walkathon. The money would go to Central Community House to help the less fortunate children.

Reverend Ethridge put a quarter in Vivian's can. Then Reverend Ethridge squatted to shake hands with Vivian and he squatted even lower to shake mine. His preaching robe picked up dust from the floor.

Mamsy and Paw-paw joined our group and accepted mother's invitation to come home with us and eat Sunday lunch in our garden room. We called father's parents Grampaw and Gramaw to distinguish them from mother's.

The sunlight beamed through the glass roof of the garden room into Paw-paw's eyes, making him squint and making his bald head shine. "Son, what subjects do you like in school?" Paw-paw asked. Paw-paw owned an insurance agency. He went to the office every day but he said other people did most of the work.

"We don't have formal subjects at Canterbury School," I told Paw-paw. We finished our pasta salads and mother went through the double doors to the kitchen to get the strawberry shortcakes she promised.

"Don't they teach arithmetic? Reading? Composition? History? Geography?" Paw-paw's eyes darted from Vivian to me to father and back as he pronounced each subject. Vivian was scuffing her black church-shoes on one of the Mexican tiles, tracing the design with her toe.

"We cover all those," I said. "But Mr. Shirley doesn't go subject by subject. He starts with an interesting question every morning. Then our study follows the different topics that come up, according to what interests the children show."

"At the end of last year, Charles was reading at a fourth-grade level," said mother as she put a strawberry shortcake in front of me, on the glass-top table. "His mathematics is up to junior high level. Vivian's scores on algebra place her in the upper thirtieth percentile for high school freshman. The students at Canterbury are, on the average, performing at two grades above level." Mother, who had finished serving dessert, pinched a dead leaf off one of the plants. There were plants all along the glass walls and hanging from the beams, under the glass roof. There was always a green leafy smell in the garden room. Mother took great pains with the plants, often sticking a gauge in the soil to see if they needed water.

Mamsy kept shaking her head in wonder as mother described what Vivian and I had accomplished in school. Paw-paw looked at me. He seemed to have a question, but wasn't asking it.

"It's up to Mr. Shirley to make sure all the subjects get covered by the end of the year," I said.

"Well, I don't understand," said Paw-paw. "But if it's working, that's the bottom line." Paw-paw reared back in his chair and used a toothpick to get food out of his teeth.

"THIS week," said Mr. Shirley, "we want to understand the checks and balances in our government." Mr. Shirley had on his gray slacks, plaid tie and blue blazer with the Canterbury School emblem. Pretty soon he'd take his blazer off, hang it on his chair, and loosen his tie.

Last night I read the assignment: "Understanding our Government." It wasn't too long and there were interesting diagrams along with pictures. But this was more challenging than anything we did in first grade. If mother hadn't discussed the assignment with me, I wouldn't have understood. We added seven words to my notebook. I thought I understand checks and balances. It was the same idea as a game Mitzy made me play where paper covers rock, rock breaks scissors and scissors cuts paper. In the game you made either a rock or scissors or paper with your hand and then, like if I had scissors and Mitzy had paper, I got to slap her wrist with two fingers as hard as I could. If we played very long, we could make each other's wrists red and puffy.

Mitzy had pestered me on the playground this morning. I told her to mind her own business. She wanted me to promise to come to her house on Saturday. I told her I couldn't. "You better start being nicer to me," she said, "or I'm going to get you in trouble."

She saw how scared I was when she said that and she giggled. I wondered if Mitzy knew about all mother's done. Maybe mother told stuff to Mrs. Gerlach. It was impossible to keep away from Mitzy at lunch, recesses and before school on the playground. Besides, I was afraid people were watching us. I noticed Mr. Shirley looking at us when we talked this morning.

"Now Congress is made up of how many . . ." Mr. Shirley paused and looked around ". . . two branches." Often Mr. Shirley answered his own questions. "They are? . . . anybody . . . yes, Mitzy."

"The Senate and the House of Representatives."

"Very good, Mitzy. Does anyone know the name we use to describe a Congress that has two branches? Yes, Charles."

My hand was the only one raised. "Bicameral," I said. It was one of the words mother and I looked up last night.

"Very good, Charles. Let's write the word *bicameral* on the blackboard and then we'll talk about why we have a bicameral legislature."

Mr. Shirley wrote fast in large clear letters. His rear end bounced under his blazer as he wrote.

Mr. Shirley spent several minutes talking about Congress. He put more words on the blackboard. We learned that Ohio had two senators and that our mothers and fathers would be voting to elect one this November. Ohio had twenty-one representatives who were often called congressmen. "Really I should say congresspersons," said Mr. Shirley, smiling at Mitzy who was one of his pets.

Mother had explained to me how Mr. Shirley explored the limits of our potential. He did that by asking questions no one could answer, along with the easy ones. He watched to see that the material did not get away from us. Mother discovered this on the first partnership night. At Canterbury School, they held parent-teacher partnership nights every other Monday. Mother almost never missed and father usually went too. Tonight would be a partnership night.

"Who can tell me why we have so many representatives in Ohio when Nevada has only one?" asked Mr. Shirley.

"Ohio is bigger," said Mitzy. "The big states get more. All states have the same number of senators."

"That's right," Mr. Shirley beamed at Mitzy. "But can we find a better word than *big?* Yes, Charles?"

"Ohio is larger," I said.

"Charles," said Mr. Shirley. "We may start calling you Large Charles. You surely do like that word."

The other kids laughed. I felt my face turn red but I couldn't figure out what I said wrong.

"If you watched the football game on Saturday, you remember the run by Steve Jeffords," said Mr. Shirley.

I remembered. It was the play that made father jump up and shake his fist at the television.

"We wouldn't call that a large play, Charles. We would call that a big play. So *large* is not always a better word than *big.*"

The kids were laughing hard now.

"Let's look at some words," said Mr. Shirley. He wrote *large, heavy, important* and *numerous* on the blackboard. "Now, *big* can be used to replace any of those," he said and he offered examples.

Mr. Shirley was looking at me. I hated him and his fat rear, writing words on the blackboard and underlining them, whirling around in his blue blazer and smiling as he explained.

"Charles, you were right to see that *big* is overused. When we can use a more specific word, we want to do so."

He was trying to be nice. He saw how I felt. Most of these kids had been in my room last year when Ms. Graham praised me for saying *large*.

He explained how Nevada was a larger state than Ohio. I knew that. I just wasn't thinking. He kept rubbing it in, saying that *big* in this instance was a better word than *large* though still not good. "When we use a word we want to do two things," he said. "We want to be clear and we want to be precise." He wrote *clear* and *precise* on the board and underlined each.

Finally he got to *populous*. Populous was the word he was looking for. Mr. Shirley used it several times in sentences.

"Charles, what is the most populous state?" he asked.

I shook my head like I didn't know. Heather Knowles gave the answer. California. I knew that. I hoped he was through asking me things. I couldn't answer anything. Heather grinned at me. Heather was another one I was avoiding. Only she wasn't pestering me like Mitzy.

At recess every kid had a question for me and they all called me Large Charles. I tried not to cry but when it was time to go back to class, I couldn't help myself. Mr. Shirley saw me rubbing my eyes.

"Charles, you are my outstanding learner," said Mr. Shirley. "I'm amazed how quickly you grasp ideas. It's unusual for someone your age."

I didn't feel better. He was making it harder to stop crying. He had his arm across my shoulder and the kids were looking at me. Mitzy was making the words *Large Charles* at me with her lips but she was behind Mr. Shirley and Mr. Shirley couldn't see. I wished somebody would kill Mitzy.

"Sometimes we learn from mistakes," said Mr. Shirley. "Sometimes we learn more when the mistake is painful." He led me to my desk and kept his hand on my shoulder as I sat. "We've all benefited because of Charles," he said to the class. "All of us will be more careful as we chose the word that will give more clarity; when we select *great, heavy, major, important* or *numerous* instead of *big.*"

He walked to the front of the room and announced a game. The game would be to make a list of the words one could use where somebody with a limited vocabulary might say *big.* Heather Knowles wrote twenty words on her paper. As a class, we thought of fifty-seven words. Mr. Shirley was delighted. He joined in the laughing when words like *humongous* got said out loud. I was afraid I might have to be excused to throw up. I hoped not. The nurse would call mother. Mother would find out how I'd been feeling all week and would start in again on her questions.

Mrs. Stedman, who drove our car pool on Mondays, picked us up after school. At home, I went straight to my room to do the mathematics exercises for tomorrow. It took until supper to finish because I kept thinking about the stupid way I said large all the time. Also, what could I do about Mitzy? Mother brought me a glass of milk and graham crackers at five-thirty but she was busy and didn't linger.

"What was the most interesting thing that happened in school today?" mother asked. We were eating in the garden room, all four of us, and a hard rain was pounding the glass roof and one side. Ordinarily I liked sitting out here in the rain even when there was lightning and thunder. Mitzy and her dog Moose and Mrs. Gerlach were afraid of thunder. Once at their house, Mrs. Gerlach took us to the rumpus room in the basement until the thunder quit. It was not logical to be afraid of thunder when you were inside a modern house. That was one time I got the best of Mitzy.

"Charles, did you hear me?" asked mother. Because I was youngest I told about my day in school before Vivian. "We are already going to be late to the parent-partnership meeting," said mother.

"Charles made a fool of himself," said Vivian. "That's why he isn't answering."

"Charles," said mother. "You didn't say anything when you came home."

"Everyone at school is calling him Large Charles," said Vivian.

I knocked over my chair, getting up. Running through the kitchen to the stairs, I heard father. "Charles, you have not been excused." I ran to my room and locked the door. I saw some girl I didn't know sitting in the leisure room. Probably she was the new babysitter, in place of Howard.

Mother was knocking on my door. I didn't answer. They put a nail through the hole in the center of the doorknob. My room did not have a real lock. The door opened. Father was standing behind mother.

"We do not tolerate temper tantrums," said mother. "You are grounded for one week from playing Nintendo."

"I don't care," I said. Father was unplugging my television. It would go to one of the guest bedrooms.

"Come downstairs immediately or there will be further consequences," said mother.

"No," I said.

Father came back. He picked me up. He carried me

downstairs, into the garden room and placed me on my chair. He was out of breath.

"Now," said mother. "Either you tell us what is going on or I'm going to take you with me to the parent-partnership meeting where you and I and Mr. Shirley will get to the bottom of this."

"You tell," I said to Vivian. "Since you know everything."

Vivian had finished her lamb chop and tossed salad. She was staring into her dish of raspberries and cream.

"Did Mr. Shirley punish you?" asked mother.

"No," I said.

It took a long time, but mother's questions forced me to tell. The whole time father stood beside my chair with his hands folded, twisting his tie in his fingers. Vivian finished her raspberries and they let her go to her room to practice her violin. It was after eight.

"Stewart," mother said to father. "I am absolutely furious with Donald Shirley. I intend to confront him tonight."

"The meeting has already started," said father.

"So," said mother. "The other parents need to hear what I have to say."

"Babs, you're overreacting," said father. "Let's stay home from the meeting."

"I didn't expect you to go," said mother, glaring at father.

"You are making this worse for Charles," said father.

"Whenever there is a crisis—"

"Babs, honey," father interrupted. "This is no crisis."

"You are the invisible father," said mother. "You are the father who isn't there. You disappear at the first sign of trouble."

Father looked at me. I couldn't think what I could do. Father looked helpless.

I heard Vivian's violin screeching from upstairs. I wished I was in my room too.

70

"Stewart," said mother, "you might have the decency to act like an adult."

"Bitch, bitch, bitch," said father.

"Obviously you don't care what happens to your children," said mother. "Or how you carry on in front of them."

"You mean *your* Charles and *your* Vivian," said father, imitating the way mother said *"My* Charles did this" when she told other mothers about my accomplishments.

Mother stared at him, her arms shaking.

"I've had it with you trying to run everybody's life," said father.

"That's too bad," said mother. "Because that's the way it has to be in this family."

"I can't stand the sight of you," father said through his teeth. Spit sprayed onto his raspberries and cream. He knocked over his chair, getting up.

"Then why don't you leave?" Mother's voice wasn't loud but her face was shaking.

"Then you and your doctors and shrinks can go right ahead and destroy the boy," said father.

"I can hardly believe you are doing this." Mother's voice was so low I could barely hear her.

"You started it, bitch," said father.

"Get out," yelled mother. "You get out or I'm calling the police."

I ducked when father picked up his chair. He swung it, crashing dishes to the tile floor. He threw the chair at the glass. It crashed through, onto the terrace.

"Keep on," said mother. "Break everything. The partners at King and Braxton will be impressed."

I was on the floor. Father ran into the kitchen. I screamed. He had a knife.

"No," I shouted. "No."

He didn't hear.

Mother screamed.

He threw the knife. It broke more glass in a garden room window. "Fuck you," he yelled.

I heard the car engine in the garage. Mother was sitting in her chair with her arms folded. The tabletop had been smashed. It looked like a glass spider web. Rain was pouring in, on to the flowers and Mexican tile floor. Mother was trembling.

She helped me off the floor. She put her arm around me and took me to my room. "Get into your jammies," she said. "You can play Nintendo until I come back. Then we'll talk. After that mother will read you a story and put you to bed.

"Stay here," I said.

Mother hugged me. "Mother will be right back," she said.

"What do you have to do?" I asked.

"I need to look in on Vivian," she said. "I will send the sitter home. Then I need to take pictures of the garden room."

"To make people see about father's temper tantrum?" I asked.

Mother wrapped her arms around me again. "Charles, this has been a terrifying day for you, hasn't it?"

"Are you scared of father?" I asked.

"This is hard for us," said mother, "but we will be all right." She told me how each of us had to do our best, me, Vivian and her; how the challenges I'd have in the next few months would be the greatest ones in my life. She needed help from me and Vivian. "Can I count on that?" she asked, holding me at the ends of her arms.

I nodded.

"I know I can," she said. "Mother will be back and we'll talk some more in a few minutes."

When mother finally came back she told me that Dr.

72

Hartenfells would be seeing me on Thursday and that Dr. Hartenfells would make me feel better.

"What kind of doctor is Dr. Hartenfells?" I asked.

"She helps children who feel bad and are afraid," said mother.

6

It HAD BEEN two weeks since father smashed the garden room and left our house. We had to work harder, me, Vivian and mother. We had to do more than our part, like on a football team. If we did, everything would turn out fine.

School was not too difficult—except for Mitzy. Mr. Shirley was especially nice to me. He often invited me to sit next to him in the lunchroom. Children still called me Large Charles, but I got invitations to two birthday parties from children who didn't invite me last year. In a way I didn't mind being called Large Charles. I was not fat and was shorter than everyone except Chad and Kevin. When children called me Large Charles they said it different than they did at first.

I had been to see Dr. Hartenfells two times. Dr. Hartenfells was friendly but tricky. "I'm the kind of doctor that children like to tell things to," she told me. Her office looked like a kindergarten playroom.

I didn't want to tell her anything, even about my insects. If you told her things she used that to get you to tell more.

Dr. Hartenfells was a real doctor because it said "F. J. Hartenfells, M.D." on her door. She was smart. She knew more about dinosaurs than anyone I'd met, even Mr. Shirley. She listened to every word I said and sometimes I didn't know I said something until she asked her next question. It surprised me that a person so smart and tricky would think I might tell secrets just because she gave me a glass of chocolate milk and two pecan sandies. I didn't know how long I had to keep going to her. "That depends," is what mother said. They wanted me to give up awful bad.

It was another Sunday morning and I was dressed in my wool pants, long sleeve shirt, tie and cardigan sweater. Mother, Vivian and me were going to church. "We'll feel better if we keep doing those things that are important to us," mother said.

We had not seen father, but mother said I would in due time. Mother was extremely mad at him. She had taken pictures of the busted-up garden room and the mess on the terrace. She used our VCR camera. She put that knife in a plastic baggie, being careful to put on a rubber glove and use only her thumb and one finger. She was preserving fingerprints. Kevin Engle had a fingerprint set and that was something I planned to put on my Christmas list.

Mother was letting me sleep in her bed with her. That was how I found out she felt awful even though she had been cheerful to me and Vivian. In the middle of the night I heard her crying.

In Sunday school, Mrs. Phillips told the story about Abraham taking his son Isaac to the top of a mountain and building a fire to burn Isaac as an offering to please God. Mrs. Phillips looked at us and smiled as she spread her book. She held up a picture, moving it slowly so we could all see. The picture showed Isaac loaded with wood for the fire. Abraham was carrying a knife and a little bowl of fire that looked like the eternal flame we saw at the memorial to President Kennedy in Washington, D.C. Only the one Abraham had in his hand was enclosed by a grill and was much tinier.

I didn't understand why Mrs. Phillips kept smiling while she showed the picture and told about Abraham making his son carry wood to build the fire. But after she finished I realized she knew all along how God would interrupt after Abraham tied Isaac on top of the bonfire and raised up the knife to kill him.

Mrs. Phillips said the reason God liked Abraham so much was because Abraham loved God enough to kill his son. She said that was why God said he didn't have to kill his son. I hated the story. Mrs. Phillips smiled too much and talked in a silly voice, stopping every few words to look at all of us.

I wondered how old you had to be for God to talk to you like he did to Abraham. What would God sound like? I would have liked God to say something to me. I wished God would answer my questions. I wished God would make Dr. Hartenfells and Dr. Merwin and my bloody undies go away. I knew God was the smartest person in the world because he knew hundreds of languages. Maybe you were ready for God to talk to you when you started worshiping in the sanctuary.

I wondered if God talked to mother or father. I hoped he

didn't because mother would ask him about my sore rear, and God might tell. Mother or father had never said anything about talking to God. Maybe you weren't supposed to tell when God talked to you. But Abraham must have told. How else would anyone know the story Mrs. Phillips told us?

After Sunday school I went down to Fellowship Hall. Mother was looking for me and came as soon as she saw me in the doorway. Vivian was with her. Mother was nervous and her coffee spilled from the cup into the saucer as she looked around to see who she wanted to talk to. Mother walked toward two ladies.

"Wasn't Reverend Ethridge superb," said one of the ladies.

"Yes," said mother. "But this is hard for me. Stewart and I are getting a divorce."

The lady touched mother's arm. The other lady saw that mother's coffee cup and saucer were jiggling. The first lady was looking at mother like Mr. Shirley looked when he explained what a promising student I was. There were people behind us and more to the side of Vivian. Those people stopped talking and two of them made glances at mother but now they were talking again.

"It came to a head two weeks ago," said mother.

"Oh, Babs," said the first lady. "Do you think coming here so soon is a good idea? Why put yourself through this?" The ladies looked worried.

Mother handed her cup and saucer to the lady. Mother reached for my hand and, at the same time, Vivian's. Mother's hand was cold. "We feel it's important to go on with our lives," said mother. Mother squeezed my hand so hard it hurt.

"You are a brave woman," said the first lady. "I admire your strength." The other lady nodded.

"The sermon spoke directly to me this morning," said mother. "I'm glad we came."

Mother was looking across the room, between the ladies' shoulders. I saw too. It was father. He was wearing the dark blue suit he wore when he ushered the center aisle in the sanctuary. He had on his red usher tie and a red flower in his lapel. He saw mother and me and Vivian.

Somebody moved and I lost him. I thought he might of waved. I kept looking, trying to see him through the people with their coffee cups and saucers. I moved my head and stood on my toes. I felt mother looking down at me. She was. So were the two ladies.

The first lady wanted to have lunch with mother. "I've been through a painful divorce with my sister," she said. "But now, five years later, sis looks at it as a growth experience."

Mother nodded. I could see she wanted to talk longer but not then.

When we finally got in the Volvo to go home, Vivian asked, "Why did we have to come to church?"

Mother had put the key in the ignition. She took her hands off the steering wheel and turned to look at Vivian who was in the back seat. I was in front, sitting next to mother.

"Sweetheart," said mother to Vivian. Mother made sure I was listening too. "There is nothing of which we should be ashamed. I should have made this decision sooner."

"But we didn't have to come to church," said Vivian. "I saw daddy there. It wasn't fair not to talk to him."

"You'll have a chance to do that, sweetheart."

"When?" asked Vivian.

"As soon as it can be worked out," said mother.

"Where is daddy living?" asked Vivian.

"He's taken a room at the athletic club for the time being," said mother.

"Won't he have to get his clothes and things?" I asked. Almost all his clothes were still in the closet. I had checked every day.

"Yes," said mother. She put her hand on my shoulder and kept looking at Vivian. "I can see that you are both thinking about your father," said mother.

Vivian had her arms crossed, her bony fingers wrapped around her arms. She was wearing a short sleeve blue and white polka dot dress with a white collar and white around the ends of the sleeves. She was looking out the window, away from mother.

"Vivian," said mother, "a long time ago your father and I loved each other and we wanted to get married in order to make a home, to have you and Charles live with us as a family."

Vivian, still looking out the window, turned her head farther away from mother. The side of her face was hidden behind her hair.

"That has changed," said mother. "It will be better for you and Charles as well as for your father and me if he finds someplace else to live."

"Because he might hurt us?" I asked. "Is that what you mean when you say he's sick?"

"I'm afraid," said mother, "that what happened a week ago could happen again. It might get worse."

"But you haven't even talked to him," said Vivian, who had her nose pushed against the window.

Mother was thinking father might kill her. Or us. Even though she didn't say so. Vivian wasn't there when that happened.

"You were mean to him," said Vivian.

"I know," said mother. Vivian turned away from the window to look at mother. "We haven't been nice to each other," said mother. "That's why it is better if we don't live together."

79

After lunch mother reminded me and Vivian to complete our weekly planners. What we did was to list five goals to be achieved in the next week. Mother would list five of hers for us. These charts would go up on bulletin boards in our bedrooms. When we finished a task, mother stuck a blue star next to the thing we did. If I missed one task it got added to next week's list. If I missed more than one, they got added and I lost television and Nintendo privileges. But I had got my list done by Friday.

When mother came to my room she had changed into slacks and a blouse. She had taken a shower and smelled wonderful. Mother and I pulled up chairs to my desk and sat close.

Mother was disappointed with my list. "I hoped we'd see something about making progress with Dr. Hartenfells," said mother. What I had decided to do was a science project for extra credit in school. The project would be to hatch brine shrimp and observe their behavior with my magnifying glass. My other tasks were to clean my closet, set the table for one meal, clear the table, and vacuum the floor and seats of mother's Volvo. Mother said those were fine but I should not neglect the most important part of my life.

Mother's list had two chores like the ones I listed. I was to write a thank you note to Ms. Perkins for giving me extra help at the Tremont Library. There were two hard ones on mother's list. The first was to cooperate with Dr. Hartenfells. The second was to write two pages about something nice that happened to me this week.

"What if there isn't anything?" I asked.

"There will be," she said, smiling.

Before she left, mother reviewed my good and bad behavior. She listed behavior in a space at the bottom of the chart. "Too much thumb-sucking" was noted like it often was. Also, I did not cooperate as well as I could with Dr. Hartenfells.

The best thing I did was to be brave enough to meet with Dr. Hartenfells without mother. I also got myself ready for Sunday school.

"The next few weeks will involve some restructuring for us," said mother. "Mother is counting on you to do more things for yourself. Dr. Hartenfells can be a great help to you."

We looked up *restructuring* and wrote the word in my notebook. Mother kissed me before she left.

I knew Dr. Hartenfells and mother talked about my visits and I knew Dr. Hartenfells had told mother to make me cooperate when mother gave me my weekly assignments. I hated Dr. Hartenfells.

7

It had only been four weeks but it seemed like father had been gone longer. "Does he ever want to see me?" I asked mother.

"Your father wants to see you," she said.

"Does he have to wait till I finish Dr. Hartenfells?"

"No," said mother. "In fact you and Vivian will spend a weekend with him. He has moved to a condominium so he has a nice place for you to stay. He will take you to the Illinois football game."

I was glad. Only it was scary too. I was thinking about

father all the time. One afternoon, when Mrs. Engle picked us up for car pool, I thought I saw father's BMW parked on a street near Canterbury School. It probably wasn't. If it had been father why wouldn't he park closer and get out of his car? I wasn't positive it was even a BMW. I didn't say anything to Vivian or mother.

Thursday, two days ago, I told Dr. Hartenfells about horsey-ride and monster. She knew anyway. I told her my rear got sore because of Howard giving me a tubby bath. It was the worst afternoon of my life. She had naked dolls and she kept me there forever. She was very pleased and said how brave I was and how much better I would start to feel. She didn't get mad when I kicked her doll and said I hated her.

I had to tell her something. If I didn't I would go to her office two times a week for the rest of my life. Every night when I went to bed I thought. I couldn't think of anything except to let them blame Howard. But I never said Howard stuck anything in my rear.

Dr. Hartenfells didn't force me to say much and she never suspected me of lying. That was because of her talks with mother and Dr. Merwin. Dr. Hartenfells knew my lie before I lied it to her. She thought it was the truth.

When I was about to leave she told me I had made more progress than any other child she had ever seen. She saw millions. It surprised me that so many children had terrible secrets. I didn't think any would be as awful as mine, though.

Dr. Hartenfells was right. I did feel better after Thursday.

I was in my room on Saturday afternoon. Mother had just finished weekly review. We had weekly review a day early because Vivian and I would be visiting Paw-paw and Mamsy overnight and all day Sunday. Since we didn't have Howard as a sitter anymore, Vivian and I went to Mamsy and Paw-paw's a lot.

In my weekly review mother told me she had "an excellent report from Dr. Hartenfells."

"What did Dr. Hartenfells tell you?" I asked.

"Only that you and she have reached the point where you trust each other. 'Charles should start feeling better about himself and everything that has transpired,' were Dr. Hartenfells' exact words," said mother. We added *transpired* to my vocabulary notebook.

Mother was so proud of my week, she didn't add extra challenges because of my failure to do the story about a nice thing happening to me. This was the second weekly review where I failed that. All mother said was, "You have been worried that mother—and maybe Dr. Hartenfells—blame you for what happened. You probably have been thinking you did something wrong. This week you will not worry as much so you will notice the nice things that happen to you. It won't be as hard to write the story."

She still wanted me to write the story and was keeping that assignment on my chart. She said we must not let our troubles keep us from carrying on our lives. She praised me for doing that. Mr. Shirley had told mother that my schoolwork was as good as always.

Me and Vivian being able to spend a weekend with father was probably another result of the excellent report from Dr. Hartenfells.

From my window, I saw Howard backing his car out of the driveway. I often watched him come and go. He drove a red Ford Mustang and used to give me rides. I hadn't talked to Howard since I got taken to Dr. Merwin. He never looked up at my window to wave or see if I was in my room. Mother was extremely mad at Howard; and at Dr. and Mrs. Landis. Mother avoided them in Fellowship Hall. They used to always find each other to visit. Mrs. Landis stopped coming into our yard or dropping in for coffee. I didn't know exactly what mother had said to Howard or

Dr. and Mrs. Landis, but Vivian told me that mother tried to talk to Howard. Howard's father wouldn't allow that. Vivian said Howard's father hired a lawyer. I asked mother why they hired a lawyer and if that meant they would sue me. She said that wouldn't happen and that the lawyer was because the Landises knew what Howard did and were trying to protect him.

"Protect him from who?" I asked.

Mother said Howard needed help from doctors and lawyers. She said I shouldn't worry because nothing that Howard or their lawyer did could hurt me.

I didn't understand about helping Howard. It sounded like he was being helped like Dr. Hartenfells was helping me. I also saw from the way mother's face colored when she answered my questions and from the way mother pronounced every word distinct in a low voice like she did when she got the maddest at me, that mother hated Howard and his parents. Mother said I could pursue any other questions I had about Howard with Dr. Hartenfells. Then she told me again to stay away from Howard and to let her know if he tried to see me or talk to me. Then we put *pursue* in my notebook. I wouldn't be pursuing any questions with Dr. Hartenfells.

MAMSY and Paw-paw took Vivian and me to church. We didn't stay for conversation in Fellowship Hall. We didn't see father. Mother was at a retreat for the Junior League Executive Committee. It started last night and would go all day today.

Mamsy and Paw-paw's house was across from Cardiff Park in old Canterbury. We were eating Sunday dinner in the dining room. Mamsy sat at the end of the table nearest the kitchen. I couldn't eat everything on my plate. There was ham loaf, mashed potatoes, lima beans, jello salad and cole slaw. Mamsy baked a peach pie for dessert.

Mamsy had been asking me and Vivian questions while we ate. Were we having trouble in school? What were we getting to eat? Did mother seem tired or cross? Could Mrs. Yoder, our Amish cleaning lady, come an extra day each week?

"Of course," said Mamsy. "I can imagine the extra expense might be a consideration."

"We are comfortably situated," I told Mamsy.

Paw-paw smiled. Mamsy said she didn't mean that, only that with Vivian's piano lessons and Canterbury School and everything, there could be a strain. *And everything* meant father having left and having to pay for another place to live. I wasn't sure if Mamsy knew we paid Dr. Hartenfells for two visits a week. If Mamsy knew, Mamsy would of asked questions.

Mamsy was over sixty. She asked silly questions and said dumb things. Maybe mother didn't want Mamsy to know about Dr. Hartenfells or my sore rear.

Sometimes Paw-paw came to our house to stay with us. Mother must have told something to explain why Howard wasn't sitting. Maybe mother made up a lie.

"You tell your mother I'm free any night this week if she needs me," said Paw-paw. Paw-paw probably didn't have much else to do.

After Sunday dinner, Vivian had to practice her violin. Paw-paw took me across the street to play on the slide and swings in Cardiff Park. It was a sunny day and I was glad to get away from the screeching because Paw-paw's house wasn't as spacious as ours.

"Look, Paw-paw," I said. We stopped walking. Under an apple tree there was a praying mantis in the grass. It was fighting another insect, almost the same size. The praying mantis killed and ate the other insect.

"I wish I could get him for my collection," I said.

86

Paw-paw promised to watch the praying mantis while I ran to ask Mamsy for a shoebox.

We captured the praying mantis, poked air holes in the box, put in grass and leaves and twigs. I didn't have anything this good in my collection. Mr. Shirley and Ms. Perkins at the library would help me find books about him.

I knew then what I could write for my nice thing that happened to me.

IT was dark outside. Through the dead leaves which were in full fall color when there was sunlight, I saw lights from the windows in Howard's house. On my desk, beside my writing tablet, I had the shoebox with twigs, grass, a few rocks and dirt on the bottom. Having my praying mantis beside me would help me write my two pages. I had one hour until bedtime. I wrote the title on the first page of my tablet.

The Nicest Thing That Happened This Week
by Charles Bateman King

"Not often is someone lucky enough to watch a true adventure," I began. "But that happened to me on Sunday when I was with my granmother and granfather. It was exciting. It was the nicest thing that happened to me last week."

Then I wrote out everything that happened, just as it happened; how I almost didn't see the mantis and almost stepped on it, how some of the apples on the ground beside the mantis had turned squishy, how the mantis ate another insect that I thought might also be a mantis, how I captured the mantis and had nourished it in a shoebox, how I took it to school and did research on mantises in books and with Mr. Shirley and Ms. Perkins at the library, how I found out that mother praying mantises ate their babies and after that ate the father, how it was unusual to find a mantis in Ohio, how some mantises could eat frogs but mine ate the flies I gave it, how lucky it was we had a bug zapper to produce a lot of dead flies, how I demonstrated my mantis eating flies with my class at school circled around, how I liked watching the mantis in its box on my desk in my room, especially when it raised its legs like it was praying.

> I will never forget the fight and how my praying mantis ate up the other one. It was a true life adventure. It was the nicest thing that hapened to me in a long time.
> The end.

My hand was tired because I wrote fast. I had almost three pages and I could have written more. The hard part would be to check my spelling. I knew I missed some words. Mother would understand if I didn't catch all the mistakes.

I wondered how long my praying mantis could live in the box eating flies. Mr. Shirley was going to see what he could find out at Ohio State. If I could keep my praying mantis alive and keep a log of my observations, I'd receive extra credit. If my praying mantis died, I'd add it to my insect collection. The book said a praying mantis laid as many as two hundred eggs and they came in a papery container. I didn't think a praying mantis fucked two hundred times to get two hundred babies and I didn't think father fucked mother to get me. I wished I'd never heard that.

THIS had been my best week since mother discovered my undies. Dr. Hartenfells did not schedule me on Tuesday because she was testifying in a court case. On Thursday she stayed in bed with the flu.

It wasn't until Friday that my assignment was ready to

show mother. Mr. Shirley assisted me with my spelling after I corrected many errors by using my dictionary on Thursday night. "Wonderful," said Mr. Shirley. "Charles, you must write stories. Develop the talent this shows." He went on and on. He liked this better than anything I'd done that year. He was going to take me to see a friend of his, a professor at Ohio State who used to live with him in his apartment and who had written a book about helping children write stories. Mr. Shirley made me feel proud except I wondered if he knew how hard it was to write three pages when you have to check spelling. Or if he knew how much time it took.

Because of what Mr. Shirley said, I was eager to show mother. I handed my story to her in the kitchen and followed her into the garden room where she sat to read. I was sitting across the new glass-top table that was delivered two days ago to replace the one father smashed. Watching, I couldn't tell if mother liked it. When she finished she looked at me and smiled.

"I had no idea that such an adventure was attached to your praying mantis," she said.

"I wanted to surprise you," I said. Then I told her the nice things Mr. Shirley said.

Vivian came into the kitchen to get a glass of milk from the refrigerator. "May I share this with Vivian?" Mother asked, still holding my three pages. I nodded, but I knew Vivian wouldn't think it was any good. Mother called for Vivian to come in the garden room. "I want you to read what Charles has written," said mother.

"He made this up," said Vivian. She was looking at my three pages like they smelled. "Charles, I was there," said Vivian. "You shouldn't say things you never saw."

"I did too," I said. "My praying mantis is right up in my room."

"Charles." Vivian looked at me like she was disgusted. "I was at Mamsy's when you found it."

"You weren't in the park," I said. "You were playing your screechy violin."

"If you don't believe me ask Paw-paw," Vivian said to mother.

"Perhaps some of what you read about your praying mantis and some of your conversation with Mr. Shirley has influenced your story," said mother.

"Yes, but everything happened just like I said." I was thinking of running because I didn't want to cry.

"Well, it's a wonderful story," said mother. "I'm just as proud of you as Mr. Shirley."

"But it happened like I said." My three pages were on the glass-top table. I grabbed them and tore them into tiny pieces. I couldn't help crying.

"He's such a baby," said Vivian. "And a liar."

"Vivian!" Mother sounded cross. Mother sent Vivian to her room and told her to stay there. Mother would have more to say to Vivian when mother went upstairs. We didn't get spanked but I hoped Vivian got a terrible punishment. Vivian didn't like to hear when I did good things in school. But I hadn't done anything to her.

After Vivian left, mother took me to the bathroom and cleaned my face with a warm washcloth. The pieces of my three pages were left all over the garden room. Mother held my hand and I went with her into the formal room and sat beside her on the long blue couch. Ordinarily we didn't use the formal room except for company. I wasn't allowed to play in there. Vivian was permitted to play the baby grand piano which was in the end opposite to the fireplace.

"I can appreciate how hard you worked on your story," said mother. She could understand that I was upset. She was pleased and was not criticizing me. "Sometimes it is

90

hard," she said, "to separate what we do from what we imagine we do."

"But it happened just like I said."

Mother pulled me close to her and kept her arm across my shoulder. She smelled cool and clean. She was dressed from her Junior League luncheon. She looked pretty in her white blouse with tiny flowers all over it.

"Sometimes we want to embellish a story and we include things we read in books or that someone has told us."

"I didn't," I said knowing I would have to look up *embellish* for my notebook.

Mother ran her fingers across my back, like she did when she kiddled me before going to bed. She said we'd talk again when I was not so upset. The important thing, she said, was my ability to express myself. Together we returned to the garden room. She watched me pick up the pieces of paper and throw them in the wastebasket.

DURING the next week mother didn't ask about my praying mantis. She did talk to Mr. Shirley. How else could he have known I tore up my papers?

I'd given my praying mantis a name. It was Mantis Rex. Mantis Rex was tinier but he looked like a dinosaur, especially when he raised up and stretched his long front legs to eat flies. If Mantis Rex grew to dinosaur size he would be awesome.

I told Dr. Hartenfells about Mantis Rex and how I found him, how I wrote my story and nobody believed it. Dr. Hartenfells was interested. Most of what we talked about on Thursday was Mantis Rex and how I felt about not being believed.

Dr. Hartenfells did not seem as tricky. I was sorry I tore the story up because I wanted to show it to her. I would try to rewrite it. She said spelling didn't matter to her. She also said she was mad at mother and Vivian for how they acted when I showed them my story. I told Dr. Hartenfells not to be mad at mother because it really was Vivian's fault.

Dr. Hartenfells didn't bring out her dolls or ask questions about Howard. I had been hoping she was satisfied but at the end on Thursday she said something that scared me enormously.

"Next week I've asked two people to join us when we talk," she said.

"Who?"

"One is Dr. Dean. I want her to give you some tests."

"What kind of tests?"

"Tests that will help me to help you."

"Like school tests?"

"Sort of. They will speed our progress. They aren't the kind where you pass or fail. These are like games."

"Games?" I asked. I remembered those dolls.

"One of the games will be to make up stories," she said. "You did so well with your mantis story."

"Who's the other person?" I asked.

"Sergeant Fred Lutz. He's a policeman."

"A policeman?" I was really scared.

"He wants to help you. He's a very nice man."

"How can he help me?" I asked.

"Charles," she said and she got down on her knees right in front of me. "Howard Landis did things to you and he may do them to other children. We have to stop him. We have to help him. You will feel much better when we do. When you grow up, this will be as important to you as going to school."

"Do I have to do both? The tests and see the policeman?"

"Let's wait until next week," she said. "I can see you are imagining things that are much worse than they are. You have already done the hardest part."

"We have to punish Howard because of what I said?"

"Not so much punish. We have to stop him and we have

to help him. We can't pretend that what Howard did never happened."

"I lied about Howard," I said. "Howard didn't hurt me."

She smiled at me. "Our time is up," she said. "We'll talk again on Tuesday. And I hope you'll write out your mantis story and bring it to me."

She didn't believe me about lying. The only way to make her believe would be to tell what really happened. I would rather die. Besides, they might do terrible things to other people; worse than they were going to do to Howard. Because what happened was worse than being touched during a tubby bath.

Also, I realized that mother had been lying to me when I asked why Howard had a lawyer. I used to think only me and bad people told lies. Now I knew that everybody lied. It was bad to lie, but if you had a good reason maybe you didn't become a bad person just because you lied.

They had all been hiding things from me. My trouble was going to get worse.

8

FATHER WAS ON his way to pick me and Vivian up. The next day we would go to the Illinois football game. We would stay in his condominium for two nights. On Sunday he would take us to church where mother could bring us home after Sunday school. I was a little bit afraid. Father might be mad at me. I would like to talk to Vivian but I was still mad at her though not as mad as I was.

Mother made sure I had warm clothes in my suitcase because the weather forecast for the game was snow flurries. Father waited in the car for me and Vivian. Mother was looking for him from the window but she didn't come out.

Vivian got in the front seat and me in the back with our suitcases. Vivian kissed father. I wasn't sure what to do since Mother was watching from the living room window. "Are we ready for a big weekend?" asked father. We said yes. Vivian fastened her seat belt. Father seemed in a hurry to get out of the driveway. The top of father's hat touched the ceiling. I had forgot how tall he was.

"I've missed seeing you two," said father. He reached his hand through the space between the seats where his tape-holder compartment was. He squeezed my leg with his hand. "I want to hear about all you've been doing," he said.

Father's condominium was in Waterford Tower. After we parked in the garage and came in the lobby, we were greeted by a man in gold braid uniform who showed me and Vivian the security system, how he could watch us get out of our car to make sure no one robbed us.

"Daddy, this place is neat," said Vivian when we got to the fourteenth floor and went inside. There was windows on three sides and you could see for miles. I noticed the balcony and father took us out on it. It was after dark. The Scioto River wound around us, through downtown and out, like a snake, to Canterbury. The bridges which crossed the river were lit with white lights like on Ferris wheels. I could identify the Capitol, father's office building, the historic state penitentiary and Ohio State Stadium where we would see the game tomorrow. The cars on the streets below looked toy size.

Father had supper ready to shove in his microwave. I set the table while Vivian assisted in the kitchen. The dining room bulged out with windows so we could eat and keep looking at the downtown buildings.

During supper Vivian and me told father what we'd been

doing except I didn't talk about Dr. Hartenfells and neither of us told things we did with mother.

Along with cake and ice cream, father brought in two packages, one for me and one for Vivian. They were wrapped in white tissue with red ribbons, exactly the same.

"It's nobody's birthday and Christmas isn't for over a month," I said.

"That doesn't matter," said father. "These are because I'm so doggone glad to see you two."

They were radio-tape players. Mine had an Ohio State Marching Band tape in it and Vivian's a Beethoven violin concerto.

Vivian threw her arm around father. "Thank you, daddy," she said. "I miss you so much."

I thanked father but I didn't copy Vivian and kiss him. Father had always liked Vivian better. Father asked me about things at school but he was more interested in Vivian's recital which would be at Ohio State University. It was for Dr. Botti's students. Father promised to go.

After we tried out the tapes in our new players, Vivian and me explored father's condominium. The wood floors were polished and the rugs looked like the kind I'd seen in museums. The furniture was much too good for children.

"This unit isn't mine," said father who was watching Vivian rub the rounded top of the dark wood paneling which came up to my chest on the walls. "I rent from a partner in our firm who is on a temporary assignment in Washington."

"He must be rich," said Vivian.

"He is." Father laughed and explained how the man helped elect the president and was appointed by the president to help the president keep lakes and rivers from being polluted.

"When he comes back, where will you live?" I asked.

"I'm not sure," said father.

96

"You might be back to our house by then," I said.

"I don't think so," said father.

"Stop asking stupid questions," said Vivian. She went into the main bedroom. The picture of dolphins playing in the ocean, which I made in the first grade, was hanging above a chest. I made it from pieces of different-color cloth I cut out by using patterns Ms. Graham gave me. Father had it framed. I gave it to him for Christmas but I didn't realize he liked it this much. There were pictures of me and Vivian on top of a bookcase.

Father refilled his drink glass from a bottle that said Bushmills Irish Whisky. He carried his glass as we looked at things in his condominium.

I saw the green marble pen holder with a clock between the two pens which mother gave father for his birthday. It used to be on the desk in father's study. He also had the fancy clock that was two feet tall and showed its moving parts under a glass tube.

"Why do you have so many bedrooms?" asked Vivian.

"That's how many there were." Father laughed. "When this became available, I took it just like it was."

"I can see why," said Vivian. "But does anybody use the other bedrooms?"

"You and Charles will be the first," said father.

"I thought that was why you wanted three bedrooms," I said.

"There's a place for you two anytime you want to come," said father.

"Does Charles have to come every time?" asked Vivian. "I mean, I know there are rules."

Father said he and mother and the lawyers were working things out.

Father made a crackling fire in the fireplace which was between where me and Vivian were sitting in the living room. Father sat on a short davenport facing the fire. Vivian and I and father sat around talking like grownups.

Father asked what we wanted for Christmas. What I wanted most was a bicycle. I was the only one in my class who didn't have one. Father smiled but didn't promise anything.

Father promised to take us to the Michigan game next week. If Ohio State won, father would like to take us to the Rose Bowl in California.

Vivian and I asked about the airplane, where we would stay and what we would do. "You tell your mother I'm thinking about the Rose Bowl," father said to Vivian. "Tell her how much you want to go."

"I will," said Vivian.

"Me too," I said. I wanted to go just as bad as Vivian. Vivian didn't even jump up when Ohio State scored touchdowns.

If we went to the Rose Bowl and did the things father said, we would be gone on Christmas. Talking about Christmas and presents made me wonder. Who would decorate our house? Last year father planned it even though he paid people to help. We had a sleigh with Santa Claus and reindeer leaping from our yard on a rainbow ending on the chimney. There were millions of lights, all of them white, sparkling from our pine and spruce trees. It was so great that traffic jammed up from people who drove by to look.

We won first prize in the secular division. There was also the comedy division, the artistic division and the sacred division, which was what mother and father said they would enter this year because the winner of the sacred division usually won the John W. Bricker Grand Prize named after John W. Bricker who lived there, was a United States Senator and ran for vice-president of the United States where he carried the state of Ohio against Franklin D. Roosevelt, the only president elected more than twice. I could name all the presidents in order. More people saw our house than the one that won the John W. Bricker prize. It was unfair.

The next morning, father had to go to his office. Vivian wanted to stay in the condominium to practice her violin. Father considered that, called someone on the telephone, and decided she would be safe. I thought so, with all the guards. Father wrote numbers for Vivian on a piece of paper.

"There is security downstairs," he said. "You mustn't open the door for any reason."

I liked going to the office with father. I was glad Vivian didn't come. We'd be back at noon to get Vivian to go to the game where we'd eat hotdogs for lunch.

The morning was cold but bright sunny, perfect for football. White mist came off the river, into the sun. The trees along the banks were almost bare. It wasn't far to the office and we could of walked, but father took the car. Some days he walked he said. He parked in the garage underneath the State Capitol Building which had a tunnel to father's building. Father's name, Stewart D. King III, was in silver letters on a black plaque to reserve his space in the underground garage.

"Good morning, Mr. King, I see we have Charles with us," said the pretty lady in a yellow dress who sat behind a circular table facing the elevators. Her desk was in the middle of an open space with furniture, vases and potted plants.

Father was wearing his L.L. Bean jacket, brown corduroys and hiking boots. He was dressed for the game. He would not be seeing clients this morning. "Susan, it's too nice a day to be inside," said father to the pretty lady.

"I wish," she said and laughed. Her white teeth showed when she smiled.

Father's office had oriental rugs on a floor made of pol-

99

ished blocks. It was called parquet. He had a desk and a table where people could hold conferences. He had four telephones, one next to a soft leather chair that swallowed me when I sat in it. From the windows you could see down on Ohio's state capitol.

Father gave me a yellow tablet and a pencil. He had puzzles for me on his shelves. I got the one where you put golf tees in holes and jumped the tees to try and have only one left. If you did that, you were a genius. I tried to make genius while father looked at messages and opened his mail.

"Nothing here that can't wait," he said. Father came around his desk and sat in a chair close to me. There was only a small table with a lamp, telephone and notepad between us.

"I've been wanting to talk with you," said father. "I'm glad it worked out that we could have this time together."

"Me too," I said.

"One of my partners has done some checking," he said. "Also your mother has told me a little. But I want to know from you. What is going on? How do you feel about it?"

I knew what he was talking about. He was leaning forward, looking at me with a smiling, worried look.

"It's bothering you, isn't it?" asked father.

I lowered my head.

"Charles," said father, "I don't want to fight your mother. Your mother has many fine qualities. But I have as much responsibility for you as she does."

He wanted me to nod and I did. But he was wrong. Mother made my rules and decided about me.

"I have thought from the first," said father. "Too much is being made out of this."

"I don't have any choice," I said.

"Let me ask you something." Father reached across the

small table for my hand. "Do you know what a molester is?"

I nodded. I knew that long ago. We got lectures in school. Last year from Ms. Graham and this year the nurse had come to talk to Mr. Shirley's class during the first week.

"What do you do," asked father, "when someone tries to touch you or asks you to do a bad thing?"

"You report them to your teacher and the nurse."

"Have you done that?"

I shook my head.

Father was watching me close. He probably had more questions. "I'm going to put a stop to some of this," he said.

"Can you, father?"

"I hope so."

What did he mean, *hope?* That wasn't a promise. "Will I have to go to Dr. Hartenfells anymore?" I asked.

"I don't know," he said.

Father wouldn't stop anything. And if I had to keep seeing Dr. Hartenfells, she'd keep after me and after me. She'd bring in more people, like the policeman and the test-giver doctor.

Father saw how disappointed I looked. "Charles," he said. "I'll talk to some people. I can be pretty persuasive." He smiled.

"Will you talk to mother?" I asked.

"I certainly will."

"What if you think one thing and she thinks another?"

"Let me worry about that," he said.

Father needed to make phone calls and then we'd go to the game. I returned to my genius puzzle. Father watched me while he sat behind his desk talking to people on the telephone.

Mr. Jay Gordon came in. He was one of father's partners and was using mother's ticket to go to the game with me, Vivian and father.

I stood up to shake hands with Mr. Gordon.

Mr. Gordon turned me upside down. When he set me on my feet he messed up my hair. "Ready for the big game?" he asked.

"I sure am," I said.

"Who's going to win?" he asked.

"The Buckeyes!" I held up my fist and shook it.

"Atta boy, tiger," he said. He looked at father. "Is this going to be the fourth King at King and Braxton?" he asked father.

Father laughed and shrugged his shoulders.

"What do you want to be when you grow up?" he asked me.

"Paleontologist," I said. That was an easy question. I wanted to look for fossils and bones, study dinosaurs. I'd known that since first grade.

"Wow," said Mr. Gordon.

"When I was seven, I wanted to pitch for the Cleveland Indians," said father. "I wanted to be Bob Feller."

I looked to see if father was teasing. He never told me he wanted to be Bob Feller. When Mr. Gordon left I'd ask who Bob Feller was.

"Let's get Vivian and go to the game," said father. "It's going to be a great afternoon."

The football game was outstanding. Illinois brought its band. An Illinois Indian chief did an Indian dance. His feather headdress went clear to the ground and flew all over the place as he jerked his head up and down and side to side. The Illinois Indian chief faked a fight with Brutus Buckeye. I had often watched Brutus Buckeye during games and once I had the privilege to shake hands with him. He said "Hi, Charles" to me. He was like a chocolate pumpkin, with hands and legs. Buckeye was a nut. It grew on Ohio's state tree. The Indian chief pretended to scalp Brutus Buckeye. That was ridiculous. Ohio State was undefeated and number one in both polls and would clobber Illinois.

Father kept asking me and Vivian if we were cold. He tucked the blanket around our legs. The wind was cold and it gusted in from the open end of the horseshoe stadium.

Steve Jeffords, Ohio State's star, got hurt in the first quarter by some dirty bastard.

Father jumped up all the time. Our blanket came off and got gunked up in hot chocolate that Vivian spilled. "Jesus H. Christ," said father.

Two turkeys plowed in front of us, going out for hotdogs. They tramped on our blankets. "Jesus H. Christ," said father.

"I'm sorry," I said. Mr. Gordon didn't notice any of that because he hardly ever took his binoculars out of his eyes.

At half time the dirty bastards were ahead by seven to six. Father asked if we needed anything. I shook my head no. "You stay put," he said and went out. Mr. Gordon went with him.

By the end of the game Ohio State won by thirty-four points to seven points. Father kept offering a bottle in a leather case to Mr. Gordon. "To ward off the chill," he said each time. After one Ohio State touchdown father picked me up and hugged me and turned clear around. Then he hugged Vivian. Luckily we were far enough ahead that father didn't mind when he had to take me to the bathroom.

We left our seats just before the game ended. We went down to the track which made a circle around the football field. Vivian and I stayed close behind father as he pushed through people. We were trying to get to the Ohio State tunnel. We made it. We got next to the rope the policemen held to let the players through. Number 77, who was giant size, gave me a chin strap. The chin strap was sweaty and had 77 written on it with magic marker. It was a wonderful game.

"Chuck, what's your sport?" asked Mr. Gordon. We were in the car, stuck in traffic, trying to get out of the parking lot. It took me a second to know the question was to me because no one calls me Chuck.

"I like football," I said. "Ohio State football."

"I mean sport to play," said Mr. Gordon. "Are you in one of those peewee football leagues?" He turned to look at me in the back seat.

I shook my head. Besides Nintendo and games like Chinese checkers, I played kick-the-can and tag. Next year I'd take physical education. I'd probably play soccer. I'd had swimming lessons and ski lessons. I didn't think any of that would count.

"Tell you what, Stewart," Mr. Gordon looked at father. "You ought to give your boy boxing lessons."

"How's that?" asked father.

"They've got a great program on Saturday mornings over at the A.C.," said Mr. Gordon. "Our two ate it up. Made scrappers of them."

"How does that sound to you?" father asked me. I thought he was mostly being nice to Mr. Gordon.

"Hell, Stewart, you don't ask the boy," said Mr. Gordon. "You have to expose him. He doesn't know whether he'll like it. Right, pal?" Mr. Gordon swiveled to look at me again.

I nodded my head in agreement.

"Hell," said Mr. Gordon. "He may not like it at first. But it's good for a kid to get biffed on the nose, maybe bloodied a little. Finds out it doesn't kill him. Learns to fight back."

"I boxed as a boy," said father. "It was required in gym class back then."

After we let Mr. Gordon off and got back to father's condominium, father told me he'd set up a private boxing lesson for me at the athletic club.

104

I didn't know. It would of been good to beat up Kevin Engle. If father wanted me to, I'd try.

ON Sunday morning we were late for church because of breakfast and getting all of my and Vivian's things. We were tearing along the river road when a siren came on and I turned to see the red, white and blue flashers of a police car. Father pulled over and pushed the button to lower the window.

"How fast do you think you were going, Stewart?" The policeman asked after father handed over his driver's license.

"That isn't my name," said father.

"Oh," said the policeman. "That's what it says on this license." He bent down and squinted through the window at me and Vivian.

"My name is Mr. King to you," said father, whose fingers were jittering on the steering wheel. Father demanded the policeman's badge number and name. The policeman ordered father to follow him to the police cruiser. Out the back window, I saw the policeman speaking on his walkie-talkie radio.

"Asshole," father muttered to himself as he got into our car. He was holding a slip of paper. "He'll find out who he's fucking with."

All the way to church father mumbled, "Goddam asshole." Father was probably upset because he was late and it was his responsibility to escort worshipers to their seats on the center aisle. The church parking lot was full so father had to park in one of the handicapped spaces. He was so mad he didn't hug me or Vivian. If mother saw where father parked she would be upset. The sticker on mother's Volvo said, "This car does not park in handicapped spaces." People who did made mother as mad as those who smoked cigarettes in restaurants.

WHEN mother came to my room for weekly review, she was angry. She had been with Vivian and knew about father asking us to miss Christmas and go to the Rose Bowl. I could tell mother had asked Vivian lots of questions about father's condominium and what we did. Mother knew everything. She couldn't of known about me and father's conversation at the office though. I wished father wouldn't of asked us to the Rose Bowl. Mother would get even madder when he talked to her about Dr. Hartenfells.

"Father has the pen-holder clock you gave him for his birthday," I told mother to make her feel better. "It's right on his desk."

"Did he talk to you about the Howard Landis situation?" Mother was so mad she didn't hear about the pen-holder clock. "Well, answer my question," said mother. She wasn't giving me time to think.

"Yes," I admitted.

"I thought as much," said mother. "When I learned that he left Vivian in the apartment and took you to his office."

"I felt myself starting to cry. "He wants to help," I said.

"Just how does he propose to help?" asked mother.

"He says I shouldn't have to answer more questions. He doesn't think getting more doctors and the police is a good idea."

"I can see you encouraged him," said mother.

I couldn't help crying and I didn't care. "He says he's got as much right to boss me as you," I said. "He's got lawyers in his firm to help him."

"We will see about that," said mother. "You will not visit your father again until this is straightened out. And you are not going to take boxing lessons, in case you thought you could hide that from me."

"You're mean," I told her.

"Charles, I am more than disappointed," she said. "You

106

will not influence me by crying, throwing a tantrum or acting like a baby. I have turned myself inside out for you and Vivian. I will not see you destroyed by your father."

"But I didn't lie. You didn't ask about boxing," I said. "I didn't tell father to try to stop you."

Her dark eyes rejected my excuse. "Right now I am just about out of sympathy for you," she said.

She told me she had to get ready for a dinner meeting at Central Community House. Paw-paw would be coming to stay with me and Vivian. She would be with children who did not have my health, my intelligence and my advantages. "I do not want to hear that you have talked to Paw-paw about any of these things," she said.

"I won't." I was crying so much it was hard to talk. "I promise."

"Mother puts little trust in your promises after what went on this weekend," she said.

"I hate you," I screamed. "I never want to see you again."

"Well, maybe you won't," she said. She slammed the door as she left.

I sat on my bed. My hands were cold and my face was burning.

When Paw-paw came he wondered if I was sick. "You look peaked," he said. I showed him Mantis Rex. Then I told him I had to do homework. He told me he liked to see a boy who took his schoolwork seriously and let me be in my room by myself.

I didn't feel like doing anything. I wished we hadn't gone to visit father.

When Paw-paw came to put me to bed he took me to the master bedroom. He knew mother let me sleep with her since father left. But I was afraid mother might be mad when she saw me in her bed. After what happened. I couldn't fall asleep. I was still awake when I heard mother's car. She came straight upstairs and opened the door.

"Charles, I'm so sorry," she said when she saw me awake. "I should have left my meeting. I felt awful. It isn't your fault."

"That's all right," I said.

She slid in next to me with her clothes on. She rubbed my back. She said the way she left was worse than me trying to get father to interfere with Dr. Hartenfells.

"You aren't mad at me anymore?" I asked.

"No," she said, hugging me.

"You wouldn't leave me—even if you were mad, would you?"

"Mother will never leave you," she said. "No matter what."

She sounded honest.

"You shouldn't be forced to choose between me and your father," she said. "My problem is with your father. He and I will work it out. Can you forgive mother for blaming you?"

"Yes."

She rubbed tears out of my eyes with her lilac-smell handkerchief.

"You are growing into such a fine boy," she said. "Mother is so very proud of you."

"Do I have to see the other doctor and the policeman?" I asked.

"Yes," she said softly. "But mother will go with you if you wish. Mother didn't know you were worrying this much. I thought you and Dr. Hartenfells were making progress. I haven't been as attentive as I should be." She kept rubbing my back.

I felt better even if I couldn't get out of the policeman. I told mother that if I shouldn't get presents from father when it wasn't my birthday or anything, I'd give the tape player back.

"No," she said. "I would never ask you to do that. Mother knows you love your father."

108

"I love you more," I said. I sniffled and she wiped my nose.

"You are probably wishing your father would come back and live with us," she said.

"Yes." I could barely hear my voice.

"Sometimes mother wishes that too," she said. "When you grow older you will understand that everything does not happen the way we want it to happen."

I knew that. You didn't have to be older to know that. But I didn't tell mother. "I'm awful sorry I said I hate you," I told her.

"Mother knew you didn't mean it," she said.

9

I HADN'T SEEN father since the Illinois game. Mother didn't talk about him. I had to talk to Vivian. Vivian was practicing her violin. I waited outside the door for her to stop but she didn't. It kept screeching away in there. Daily practice was indispensable to one who planned to give concerts. Dr. Botti said a day missed meant a loss of accomplishment.

I was about to go back to my room when the violin stopped. I went in. Vivian was sitting on a folding chair which sat on top of the box father made for her. The box reminded Vivian that violin playing was a performance. The box had room for her music stand.

110

Vivian's violin and bow were on her lap. She was making marks on her music sheets with a soft tip pen. The folded hanky she put between her face and the violin had dropped on her powder-color carpet.

"Get out of here, Charles," she yelled. She put her violin and bow on the chair and came to push me out the door.

"I have to see you," I said.

She stood in front of me with her legs spread. She had on her sweatshirt that said "American Suzuki Institute." Her bony fingers were on her hips the way mother's were when mother discovered I made a mess in the kitchen.

"Why?" she asked.

"Father promised to come to your recital."

"So."

"Did he?"

"Charles, I'm busy. You know you're not to interrupt my practice."

"It's not fair," I said. "Mother won't let me see father anymore. Besides, he likes you better."

"You are too going to see daddy," said Vivian. She wrinkled her nose and pushed her glasses back. "We're staying at his condominium this weekend."

"Why didn't anyone tell me?" I asked.

"Probably because you're trying to get out of telling the truth about Howard Landis." She went to sit on her bed.

I took a few more steps into her room. "I thought you were finished with your practice," I said.

"You ruined it anyway."

"Who said I'm trying to get out of anything?" I asked.

"Charles," she said. "I saw you and Howard when you had the lights out and he was grabbing you and laughing. I know he always followed you into the bathroom when you took your baths. He took pictures of you."

"Who did you tell?" I asked.

111

"It's the truth," said Vivian. "So I told Sergeant Lutz and I told mother and I told father."

"When did you tell father?"

"On the telephone, dummy. I talk to daddy all the time."

"You call him at his office?"

Vivian stared at me.

"Do you?"

"None of your business," she said. She got up to put away her music, fold her stand and put her violin and bow in their case.

"Why did you tell father about Howard?" I asked.

"You ask dumb questions," she said. "And you blab everything."

"I do not," I said. "I can keep secrets."

"You better go back to your room," said Vivian. She saw me rubbing my eyes. I wished I could learn to keep from crying when I didn't want to. "Everybody is mean to me," I said.

"You ruin everything," said Vivian. "It was because of you that they had their fight and because of you we haven't got to visit daddy."

"You said they hated each other."

"I did not."

"You did too. You were right there on that bed. You're a liar." Vivian ran at me. She grabbed me and shook me. I tried to punch her in the face and break her glasses but I missed. She twisted my arm behind my back and pushed me down on the powder-color carpet. She had me on my stomach and she got on my back. She had hold of my arm so she could jerk it and hurt me if I tried to get away.

She held me down and told me that father wanted to know what was going on. Father asked her questions so she told him the truth. She knew father had talked to mother. They had lunch together. They agreed to things and we were going to visit father every week. We would spend part

112

of Christmas with him. We would get to take a three-week fishing vacation with father this summer.

"Unless you ruin it," said Vivian. She let go of my arm and pushed me.

I rolled over onto my back. "I won't ruin it," I said.

"You better not," she said.

10

THE WHOLE WORLD knew about me. After Sergeant Lutz
and Dr. Dean came Mr. Gorman and the grand jury.

Then it was in the newspaper. The children at school
found out and started being extra polite to me. It was like
when we were nice to Kevin Engle because his father died
of a sudden heart attack at Canterbury Mall. They picked
me to carry the flag on recognition day at which I won top
score in mathematics and a prize for my Mantis Rex story.
I had seen Dr. Hartenfells so many times I couldn't possibly keep track of everything I'd told her.

Mamsy and Paw-paw asked questions when I went to their house or they came here. "Is your schoolwork suffering?" Paw-paw wanted to know. "Can't your mother give up some of her meetings so that she isn't away so many nights while this business is going on?" Mamsy asked.

Last Friday, Mitzy sat next to me on the bus when we came back from our field trip to visit the capitol where we met Governor Leonard and saw how state government worked.

"What did you tell them about Howard Landis?" Mitzy asked in a whisper.

"I'm not allowed to talk about that," I said. I looked for an empty seat but couldn't see one.

"Did you say he fucked you or something worse?" she asked. "I know there's worse," she whispered.

I was afraid someone might of heard her use that word. I told her to quit asking questions or she would be in trouble with the police, that they told me to report people who asked me questions.

"It must be bad," she said. Then she asked why I didn't come to her house anymore.

"I'm too busy," I told her.

"You're just a sissy," she said. She asked what they were going to do to Howard and how they found out. I wanted to put my hands over my ears.

Mr. Shirley saw her bothering me. He stared at us.

"I won't ask questions if you promise to come to my birthday party," Mitzy said. Mitzy's birthday was July sixth, two days after the parade and fireworks. I went last year and the year before.

"I might tell people you got me to take my clothes off and did things to me," she whispered.

"That's not true," I said.

She giggled. "Maybe they would believe me and maybe they wouldn't," she said.

"They wouldn't because I made friends with the police," I said.

She giggled again. "Are you going to come to my party or not?" she asked. "If you don't I might tell other things."

I told her I would come to her party. This was the last week of school and her birthday was a long way off.

Mitzy was allowed to invite two people to stay overnight after her birthday party. She was going to ask me and Heather Knowles. "You just wait, Charles," she whispered. "This will be the best birthday party you ever went to."

In Canada, on the fishing vacation with father, we caught some major fish, over a foot long. Vivian, father and I each had a room. Mine looked over the water from a cabin at the top of a rock as high as our house. Steps were carved out of the rock so you could walk down to the water where a pier for our boat was bolted into the stone. Vivian practiced violin every morning. Sometimes father took me fishing early, and we'd come back to get Vivian after she finished her violin. That was good because I was getting to where I couldn't stand the sound of her violin.

One morning father came to my room. "This is a great day for pickerel," he said.

It was drizzling and I planned to stay in my room to write a story about a boy my age discovering dinosaur tracks on an island like the one our cabin was on, then finding a cave in the rocks with a live dinosaur in it.

Instead of weekly planners, mother made out lists for me and Vivian to take on vacation. I was supposed to write a story. Mr. Shirley told mother my creative talents should be stimulated over the summer months.

Father saw mother's list on top of my chest. "What's this?" he asked.

I didn't answer since he could see by reading it.

"This is fucking-A ridiculous," he said. Then he saw my

vocabulary notebook and my dictionary. Mother assigned me to add twenty words by the time we went home.

"Please don't," I said. I was shaking, afraid he might wreck my notebook or tear up the list.

"Get your rain pants and poncho," he said. "We're here to fish and have fun."

Father had trouble starting the engine. Because it was so damp, he said. It was misty with light rain splatting off our ponchos and rain pants. Finally father got the motor going and we putt-putted to our favorite place. We anchored on top of the edge of an underwater shelf which stuck out from the cliff side of an island. The cliff towered above us, into the rain gray sky. We had fished and ate many delicious walleyes from here.

Our boat rocked a little due to a pickerel chop. As we waited for fish, father smoked a cigar. He asked about my story-writing and especially about the interest Mr. Shirley took in me. He had lots of questions on what kind of person Mr. Shirley was and the times Mr. Shirley took me to visit that professor at Ohio State who had lived with Mr. Shirley in an apartment.

We caught one nice walleye fish. I took it off the hook. It was squirmy but I held it on the edge of the boat so father could bash its head with a sawed-off baseball bat. You could still see the fish gills open and close but it didn't wiggle anymore. We knew it would be safe from jumping out of the bilge water on the bottom of our boat.

I doubled up a new minnow, pushed my hook through it twice and dropped it in the water, letting the line out enough to have it just above where father said the shelf would be. We had bobs on the line to tell us how deep.

"We haven't talked about Howard Landis and your trial," said father.

I shook my head. I thought father and mother made a treaty. She would decide anything to do with Howard. Fa-

117

ther wouldn't interrupt or ask questions. We got to visit father.

"How do you feel about Mr. Gorman and what he wants you to do?" father asked.

"Fine," I said. I wished we'd catch another fish or something so he'd quit asking questions.

I explained how I had made friends with Sergeant Lutz, that Dr. Hartenfells was nice and didn't force me to do anything I didn't want, and that mother didn't have much to do with trial preparations because Mr. Gorman and the doctors were in charge. I wanted to keep visiting father and thought that was worth lying for. I told father that nothing interfered with my schoolwork or my activities.

"I'm proud of you," said father. "It seems like you're adjusting nicely to a difficult situation."

"I am," I said.

"A lot of adults do not do as well when they face the courtroom," he said. For the first time since his questions started he smiled.

I smiled back.

"Maybe they are right," said father, looking over the side of the boat. He was talking through the mist, more at the cliff than at me. Then he turned to face me. He slapped his hand on the wet knee of my green rain pants. "This will be over soon," he said.

"I know," I answered.

He flipped his cigar into the water and put his other hand on my other knee. He leaned forward. I could of touched his face. Drips of water off the bill of the hood on father's slicker was all that was between us.

"Son, I want you to remember this," he said.

I nodded. He hardly ever called me son.

"If things go bad," he said. "If this trial starts to worry you, if something comes up where you don't know what to do—you call me."

He stared at me through the drizzle. "Do you understand what I'm saying?" he asked.

I said I did. But I didn't. Not then, not after we caught two more walleye and not since. I couldn't figure what kind of bad things father expected. How could I call him without mother finding out? What help could he give if mother said no?

Father lit another cigar while I put bait on both our hooks.

"This vacation has been good for us," he said, watching me jam the hook through the minnow.

"It's been lots of fun," I said.

"You're becoming a young man," he said. "You're not a little boy any more."

He told me it was time to develop myself physically, that he would make sure I had that opportunity. He didn't want me to be a bookworm. We talked about football, boxing lessons, maybe going to camp next summer. He promised to take time from his office so we could do things together.

"Your mother loves you," he said, "but you need to do more than play Nintendo, collect insects and look up words in the dictionary. Maybe after the trial is over we'll go hunting."

"Shoot animals?" I asked. Mother opposed guns and war and killing. I didn't watch violence on TV. I never played with toy guns. She wouldn't tolerate hunting.

Father pushed my hood back and rumpled my hair with his wet hand. It was raining harder, getting my head wet. "You're too serious," he said. "I want to see you have fun, break a rule now and then, raise a little hell."

"Raise a little hell?" I asked.

"Just teasing," he said putting my hood back and fixing it so the rain wouldn't come down my neck. "You're a great little feller and damn if I haven't enjoyed being with you." Father shook my shoulders, not hard. One of the fish poles went overboard. Father paid no attention to the pole which sunk out of sight. Then he laughed. He sounded loud and crazy out in the middle of the water, surrounded by mist, with the cliff behind him, looking at me and laughing harder because he could see I didn't know what was funny.

Father got the fish pole back by maneuvering the boat to where the bob sat on the water. Then he pulled the line to get the pole up.

"We've caught ourselves three good ones to clean for supper," said father. We've had a hell of a good morning. Let's take 'em in and show Vivian."

He jerked the cord and the engine fired right off.

I didn't tell mother about father's offer to help or his plans for hunting.

I was telling less and less to anyone. If you didn't tell, you didn't get questions.

I was watching Howard through my window again. Howard was mowing their lawn. The front was complete and he was doing the back, going from their deck to our side to the golf course in a square. The square shrunk as he went around. The For Sale sign was still in their yard. I had hoped to see a Sold sign when I came back from fishing. Then I would be able to play in our yard, capture golf balls and insects. I stayed out of the yard to avoid Dr. or Mrs. Landis or Howard.

I wouldn't tell that I'd been watching Howard mow his lawn or how seeing Howard got me to thinking about father's offer to help, got me to wondering again what father was afraid would happen.

Even before school let out, I watched Howard's house from my room a lot. I spied during time allowed me for Nintendo. I couldn't help looking during homework.

I saw the police come to search for evidence, the For Sale sign go up, people coming to see if they wanted to buy, when Eyewitness News came to take pictures, when newspaper cars and television trucks came from other stations.

Howard didn't have his red Mustang any more. I noticed it not coming or going. I asked mother. She told me Dr. and Mrs. Landis were upset with Howard for the disgrace he caused them. Howard would not go to Oberlin College that fall.

One time, right after school let out, Howard was on their deck, looking up at my window. I backed away so he couldn't see me. I was afraid Howard wanted to ask me why I was getting him in trouble.

Dr. Landis saw Howard looking up at my window. Dr. Landis ran at Howard and choked him. I almost yelled to mother who was downstairs, but Dr. Landis let go. Two times Dr. Landis smashed Howard in the face with his fist. Howard didn't hit back. He just put his hands up to stop being hit more. Dr. Landis kept smacking the sides of his head. Howard got a bloody nose. After that Howard never looked at our house.

Mr. Gorman and Dr. Hartenfells had ordered me to let them know immediately if Howard talked to me or even tried to. Mother had already made that rule. But I didn't tell about Howard looking at my window because Howard already got punished.

I missed seeing Howard. He never hurt me. We had fun. We talked about tracking dogs. Howard said he might be getting a dog only he didn't know who would take care of it when he went to college. Howard showed me Nintendo tricks. I liked him better than the children in my school and Howard liked me better than they did. Paw-paw and Mamsy were no fun at all, always making me do things, warning for cancer if I bit my nails and talking about eating balanced food.

If we got new neighbors I hoped there'd be a dog and somebody nice who was my age. Probably nobody would buy Howard's house. Not after all that happened. Paw-paw said it was because they wanted too much money. They sold the red Mustang, though.

I couldn't watch Howard finish mowing or do his trimming because we were having supper early. Mother and me had work to accomplish on the bicycle I got for Christmas, which I would be riding in the parade tomorrow. Tomorrow was the Fourth of July.

My bicycle was going to be really neat. It would win a prize unless they weren't fair. My bicycle had cardboard around it in the shape of a boat, painted so it looked like a boat with rowing oars. I would be George Washington crossing the Delaware. I'd have a tricorner hat, a wig, white knickers, white stockings and square-toe shoes with heels.

After supper we had to attach the mast on the handlebar and hoist the sail mother sewed. The sail didn't belong but it was red, white and blue and looked patriotic. I'd practiced so I could steer with one hand and hold the colonial flag.

"There," said mother as she adjusted the sail. She got her camera. I put on my George Washington clothes. With the kickstand down, I could balance myself. Mother took a whole roll of pictures, from front, back and both sides.

"If these turn out, Mamsy, Paw-paw, Granpaw, Granma and your father will want copies," she said.

I saw father when I rode past the Wendy's hamburger restaurant which was about halfway to the end of the parade. Father was with Mr. and Mrs. Gordon from the office. They waved but I couldn't wave back because one hand held the flag and the other held the handlebar.

I won first prize for my age. My picture would be in the *Canterbury News* next week. My trophy was a statue of a minuteman, half as tall as me. My name would be in gold on the base. Mitzy and Kevin and other kids came by after I was awarded it on the platform at the football field. "Your mother won that for you," said Mitzy. "Your mother should get the trophy." I didn't tell her she was rude or that I didn't want to come when she said how great her birthday party would be. I was invited to stay overnight. I would of traded my prize—or anything—not to have to go. I could be sick but I was scared to, after promising Mitzy to come. Mitzy could cause trouble. Luckily, I was going to Lake Erie with Mamsy, Paw-paw and mother two days after the birthday party.

Sergeant Lutz came by yesterday and asked about fishing with father. "It's nice that you have these two long vacations this summer," he said. Sergeant Lutz said not to worry about the trial. There would be time to get ready after I got back from Lake Erie.

11

WHEN MOTHER TURNED onto Mitzy's street, I saw the lights. In both corners of the front lawn there were floodlights like you saw during sales at shopping centers and at automobile dealers. The floodlights shot beams into the air, high above her castle-house. After it got dark it would be even better. A happy-face clown was waiting to open the car door and let me out. "Hello, Charles," said the clown.

Carrying my present, I walked beside the clown on a blue carpet with white stars, under a canopy which went from the curb up to the door where there was another clown. He was a sad clown and was pretending to wipe tears off his clown face. I wished I had a better present. All it was was a dumb board game which cost $6.95. Mother said we should not be ostentatious about birthday presents and I added *ostentatious* to my vocabulary book.

Out in back, they'd set up a giant table in the part that stuck into the middle of their moon-shape swimming pool. There was room at the table for Mitzy and her twelve guests. We sat on stools. The two clowns gave out balloons, pointed hats and blow-whistles. The children blew their whistles at each other. Heather got me right on my nose. They were all having fun but I felt miserable.

The two clowns were Mitzy's older brothers. That was how they knew my name. I hadn't seen Fred for a long time because he was going to Denison University. He must of been home from college for the summer. The sad clown was Karl who Coach Pepper Jordan wanted awful bad for the Ohio State football team. But Karl was going to Cornell because education was as important as football. Karl was the one who scared me. One time about a year ago he asked me why I had a queer for a baby sitter. I said I didn't know and got away from him. I didn't know if Mitzy told him something or how he knew Howard. I thought Mitzy got ideas from him.

The clowns cleared the table and Mitzy opened her presents. "That's nice, Large Charles," she said when she opened mine. She was being polite. Mine was the worst present. The best came from Heather who gave Mitzy a Sega cartridge. Mitzy went "oooh" and ran to hug Heather.

After presents, the happy clown did magic tricks with cards and coins. He was excellent. I couldn't tell how he did anything.

We all brought swimsuits and made a lot of noise when we jumped in the pool. It was hot and the water felt welcome. Color lights were ostentatious around the pool and patio.

At ten o'clock it was time for the other kids to go home. I'd felt a little better during the magic show and swimming but I was wishing I could go home with the other children; wishing so hard my stomach was aching. Mrs. Gerlach came out to say whose cars were waiting. I was surprised to see Heather leave. "Heather's grandmother died and the funeral is tomorrow," Mitzy told me. "So you're the only one who gets to stay all night," she said.

MITZY took the lamp off the table between our beds, "so we can talk," she said. She turned out the light.

My sheet and cover was jumbled from trying to get away from Moose who jumped on my bed, tried to lick my face and tugged at the blankets when I covered my head.

Moose leaped from my bed to Mitzy's. When he pawed Mitzy, she pushed at his head and rubbed his ears. Moose turned in circles and flopped at the foot of Mitzy's bed. "That's where he sleeps," she said.

"Moose could be a tracking dog," I said. "We could teach him. Tomorrow morning, maybe."

"Tell me everything you said Howard did." Mitzy wasn't interested in training Moose. "That's why I asked you to be my all-night guest," she said.

"I'm not allowed."

"Don't be silly," she said. "You have to tell in court anyhow."

"That's different," I said. I was thinking of running, being sick even if it would make Mitzy do something foolish.

"Please," she said. "Pretty please." She leaned out of her bed to get closer to me.

"I don't want to and you better not talk about it either. They'll try you like they're doing Howard. They'll interrogate you."

126

"Stop using big words," she said, not bothering to whisper. "What's terrogate?"

"You stop or you'll find out."

"Oh boy," she said. "I'm really scared."

"You are a simple shit," I told her.

She got quiet for a second. But I could hear her rolling on her bed. "You better tell me," she said.

I didn't answer.

"Okay then," she said, her voice getting louder.

Someone opened the door. It was Mrs. Gerlach.

"Mitzy, you and Charles must go to sleep," said Mrs. Gerlach. "I could hear your voices down in the family room."

"Charles was calling me names," said Mitzy.

Mrs. Gerlach turned on the ceiling light. She looked cross. Mrs. Gerlach stepped toward Mitzy's bed.

"Mitzy, I don't want to hear any more of that," said Mrs. Gerlach.

"He called me a simple shit," said Mitzy.

"You are asking for the switch," said Mrs. Gerlach. "One more word and you're going to get a blistering. Even if it is your birthday and even if Charles is here."

Mitzy didn't answer. Mrs. Gerlach stood beside Mitzy's bed looking down. Mrs. Gerlach looked as tall as the ceiling.

"I'm sorry, mommy," said Mitzy. "I didn't mean it." Mitzy's voice was different. My legs were shaking under the sheet. I was glad Mrs. Gerlach wasn't looking at me. I was even gladder that she came in the room when she did.

"You had better mean it. If I hear one more peep, you'll wish you hadn't."

"Yes, mommy," said Mitzy. "I promise."

Mrs. Gerlach leaned over. She pulled back the sheet and shook Mitzy. Hard. Mrs. Gerlach replaced the sheet and spread. "Not one peep," she said. She turned out the light.

127

She left the door cracked and I could see light from the hall.

Mitzy didn't say anything. Mrs. Gerlach was probably outside the door, listening.

I layed on the bed shivering, hoping Mrs. Gerlach had scared Mitzy bad enough to shut her up.

I didn't think Mitzy was asleep. I heard footsteps in the hall. They walked on by. "Charles," she whispered. "Your present stinks. It was the worst one."

SHE was on top of me, pulling off my covers. It was daylight. "Time to get up, Large Charles," she said, tickling me. I squirmed, kicking with my feet to get her off. She rolled me on my tummy and got hold of my hand. She twisted it, pushing it up. "Give?" She was giggling. Moose was growling. He had a corner of my covers in his mouth and was jerking his head from side to side.

"Let go," I said.

"Not till you give."

"I give."

"Really give?" she pushed my arm.

"Ouch," I said, trying not to yell loud enough for her mother to come.

"You're my slave," she said. "I can do anything I want with you. I can make you talk." She had me where I couldn't move. Then she jumped off.

I took my clothes to the bathroom where I changed out of my jammies. I flossed my teeth before I brushed them. Mitzy was in her jeans when I got back, ready to go downstairs for breakfast. She didn't know you were supposed to floss twice a day.

"Did we get a good night's sleep?" Mrs. Gerlach asked when we came in the kitchen.

"Could you call my mother?" I asked Mrs. Gerlach.

"Charles, is something wrong?" she asked.

128

"I have a pain in my stomach."

Mitzy made faces at me when Mrs. Gerlach hurried to the telephone. I didn't care. I had to get away.

I'd tell mother the same story. She'd probably have me examined by Dr. Merwin but that was better than staying there. Besides I didn't think you could x-ray pains in the stomach. I'd tell mother I had a wonderful time at the party and how sorry I was to come home early. I'd write Mrs. Gerlach a lovely note. I was better at lying than I used to be. When I was little I used to think grownups could always tell when you lied. They couldn't, not even Dr. Hartenfells.

Besides, we were going to Lake Erie and I wouldn't have to tell Dr. Hartenfells how I got sick at Mitzy's birthday party. I wouldn't see Mitzy for a long time.

"Did you get too much ice cream and cake?" mother asked when she picked me up.

"I don't know," I said. I felt like I might really throw up.

12

THE TRIAL WOULD start on Monday. Except for school and Sunday school, I had been staying in my room. I sat in my room and thought. I thought and watched Howard's house, looking for him to come and go. I hadn't caught new specimens for my insect collection or pursued my study of dinosaurs. I'd completed no extra credit projects for Ms. Trawick, my teacher for third grade. When I sat in my room thinking, I tried to figure a way to get out of the trial. There wasn't any.

The more I sat and thought the worse it got. I didn't see

Howard very often but I thought about him in his house. I remembered his room, all the things we'd done together.

Yesterday I told Dr. Hartenfells again that Howard didn't cause my sore places.

"If it wasn't Howard, how do you think it happened? she asked me.

"I don't know," I said.

"I see," she said. "You're thinking it would be better if you didn't say Howard hurt you." She smiled and held my hand.

I nodded.

She took the rest of our visit, which was all afternoon, telling me how she and mother and Dr. Rosalind Dean and Mr. Gorman and the judge and Sergeant Lutz would all be protecting me when we went to the courthouse.

"You won't be going in there alone," she said.

"We're like a team?" I asked.

She put her hands on my arms. "You are the smartest young man I've ever had the privilege to work with," she said.

Dr. Hartenfells didn't fool me. She lied too. It wasn't a team. I had to do it by myself.

I needed father's help. But we didn't get to see him last weekend and wouldn't this one either.

I asked mother if that was because of the trial.

"In a way," mother said.

I got dressed for Sunday school. At my desk, I looked out at the golf course and Howard's backyard. I'd wait in my room until mother said it was time to go.

I had a plan. After Sunday school, I'd find father in Fellowship Hall. I'd tell him it was a matter of life or death.

I didn't have any choice. Even if it made mother and father fight. Even if father wouldn't be allowed to come back to our house.

I couldn't sit in the courtroom and point at Howard. Even if mother and father never spoke to me again. That was what I found out from sitting in my room, thinking, looking at Howard's house and yard, watching for Howard to come and go.

My new Sunday school teachers were Mr. and Mrs. Carver. This was their first class since they had been on vacation the last two Sundays. They asked us to call them Don and Ellie. They had us tell our names and something we did this summer which God would like. Ellie went first to demonstrate. Ellie thought God was pleased when they were in the Grand Teton Mountains and instead of going to church on Sunday morning, they got up and hiked to a rock ledge where she and Don looked out over a valley, watching birds and listening to wind in the pine trees.

After Ellie and Don I got called. I mentioned a fish I took off my hook and put back into the French River, how it zipped away.

"Yes," said Ellie Carver. "Yes, yes, yes. God certainly liked that.

"And what is your name, sweetheart?" she asked, turning to the next boy who'd been jerking around in his chair. He was a hyper who maybe didn't get his Ritalin on weekends. I didn't hear what the other children said they did to make God happy because I was thinking of how to find father and wondering if my plan was a bad idea. Shouldn't I go ahead with the trial and do what I was supposed to? If they found out I lied, I'd be in worse trouble than Howard. Everybody in the whole world would know. I was shaking and my stomach hurt.

I had also been looking at the huge lump under the sheet, sitting on a table pushed up against the window. "We have a surprise for you," said Ellie Carver after the last child in our circle spoke. Don Carver pulled the table out to the middle of the room. Ellie whisked away the sheet. Most of the kids made oohs and ahs, but I didn't see anything special.

All it was was a hibachi cooker, with charcoals on top of sticks of wood. There was a blue oilcloth to keep the hibachi from hurting the table. There was lighter fluid. There was three boy dolls made of china and dressed in jeans and tee shirts. There was a sign taped on the base of the hibachi cooker. It said *Fiery Furnace.*

"We're going to tell you about three boys," said Ellie. "It's a story from the Bible."

"Then we're going to do an experiment," said Don.

"Do we all know what an experiment is?" Ellie asked.

We all nodded our heads.

"The experiment will help us think about the story," said Don. "It will make us ask questions. We'll take the rest of the morning—and maybe next Sunday too—to talk about our story."

The fat girl from last year clapped her hands and everyone was interested.

"The names of the boys in our story are difficult," said Ellie. "They are Shadrach, Meshach and Abednego." She pronounced the names slowly. The names of the three boys was scotch-taped to the china dolls. Shadrach was blue. Meshach was yellow. Abednego was green. Another doll, King Nebuchadnezzer, was red, and taller.

The story Ellie Carver told us was short and easy to understand and a lie. I kept looking at my watch. It was only fifteen minutes till time to find father in Fellowship Hall.

"Wow," yelled one boy and everyone was clapping and yelling. I jumped too. I didn't see Don light the fluid in the base of the hibachi. Flame shot up and the sticks caught fire. We all backed up but then crowded closer. There was smoke all over the room and Don had to unscrew the smoke detector on the ceiling by the door.

"Can you imagine a fire seven times hotter than this one?" asked Ellie.

Everyone shook their head, remembering how King Nebuchadnezzer's fire was seven times hotter than usual for his furnace. I didn't interrupt but I was going to ask Ms. Trawick or Mr. Shirley. I didn't believe anyone could make a fire that was seven times hotter than fire.

"So you see," said Ellie. "How brave those boys were. How great their faith in God. How God protects us."

Don dropped the three china boys into the fire and they sat in there with the fire burning all around them. Their names burned up though. King Nebuchadnezzer stayed on the blue oilcloth where he watched.

"Nobody but the real God could save you from a hot fire," said the fat girl.

"That is exactly right, Cynthia," said Ellie. Ellie and Don were looking around the circle at our faces. They were smiling.

"Was the king's fire hotter than the fire you built in the hibachi?" I asked.

"Oh my, Charles," said Ellie. "Much, much hotter. This fire only gives you a hint."

"How do we know they went completely inside the furnace?" I asked.

"The Bible tells us," said Ellie. "The fire was so hot that the men who put them in the furnace died although only their hands got in the fire."

"Would you put your hand in this fire?" I asked. "Or would Don?" The others looked at Don and Ellie.

"You believe in God as much as they did don't you?" I asked.

"Well, yes," said Ellie. Her smile didn't look natural. "At least I hope so."

"God isn't testing us," said Don. "He isn't asking me or Ellie to prove our faith."

134

"Could we get Reverend Ethridge to put his hand in the fire?" asked a boy.

"Yes, let's," said half the children. The others clapped their hands.

There was noise out in the hall. Sunday school time was over. I had to get to father.

"We'll continue our discussion next week," said Ellie. "I can see that all of you have questions." She told us that was good because Bible stories were supposed to make us ask questions. "We can't get answers until we ask questions," she said.

Don and Ellie made us form a circle, holding hands around the fire which was still hot with blue and orange flames between the burning charcoals and the china dolls still in there.

Don said a prayer for us to think about this week as we remembered the story of Shadrach, Meshach and Abednego.

I went for the door as soon as the prayer finished but Ellie grabbed me.

"Charles," she said, kneeling down to talk to me on my level, taking both my hands in hers. "I hate to see you leave without responding to your question."

"That's okay," I told her. If she didn't let go father could be gone. He didn't stay in Fellowship Hall as long as he used to. Sometimes he walked through and straight out to the parking lot. Don came over. Don and Ellie were worried about me, whether the story about the fiery furnace had troubled me.

"It was the best Sunday school class I ever attended," I said.

They let me go, thanking me for my questions.

I saw mother. She was at the table where they pour coffee. She had hers and was looking for me. Vivian was with her. I darted behind a group of people. I wanted to find father before mother found me.

I saw him. He was with Reverend Ethridge and two other ushers with red flowers on their coats.

Reverend Ethridge saw me coming. "Well, here's someone you'll want to see," said Reverend Ethridge. He touched father's arm.

Reverend Ethridge bent toward me, pulling in the stomach of his preaching robe. "Charles," he said. "You will be in our prayers this week. The Lord will give you the strength you need."

"Father. I have to talk to you," I said. I didn't mean to be rude to Reverend Ethridge.

Reverend Ethridge patted my shoulder and moved away. The other ushers went with him.

"I need help," I said. "Like we talked when we fished."

Father was looking at me till I said help. Then he looked over my head.

"Good morning, Babs," he said.

I turned my head. Mother was behind me and Vivian beside her.

"Charles, where have you been?" asked mother.

"I just got here," I said. "Our Sunday school class went overtime."

I hoped father wouldn't give me away.

Father looked at me hard, like he was trying to pass a secret code. Then he looked at mother. "The trial is still scheduled to start tomorrow?" he asked her.

Mother told him it was and that I would be with Mr. Gorman this afternoon for preparation. She wanted father to call her after lunch.

He said he would.

"I'll fill you in then," said mother.

Father stared at me again. "Charles, I'll stop by the courthouse tomorrow morning, before the trial starts." He turned to mother, smiling. "I know Judge Van Horn fairly well," he said. "I'll have a word with the judge."

Father got my message. He remembered what he said during fishing.

Reverend Ethridge was looking at us from halfway across Fellowship Hall. He came back over.

"It's a joy to see you two together and with Charles this morning," he said, looking at mother.

Mother put her hands on my shoulders. "Charles is doing better than I am," she said. "I draw strength from the way in which Charles is handling this."

"You two can be proud of this young man," said Reverend Ethridge.

"We certainly are," said father.

"Aren't we ever going home?" asked Vivian who'd been standing beside mother, watching and listening.

"Vivian, I expect this has been a strain for you as well," said Reverend Ethridge leaning forward to touch her shoulder.

"I have to testify too," said Vivian.

Reverend Ethridge nodded and kept his hand on Vivian's shoulder. He told her his prayers would include her as well as me. People with coffee cups in their hands were staring at us.

Reverend Ethridge was backing up. "Call anytime," he said, looking at mother, then father. "I'm available. I want to help."

Mother and father thanked him.

"I'll leave you two with Charles," Reverend Ethridge said. "Charles had something to say and I interrupted him."

Reverend Ethridge left. "Charles, what did you want to say?" asked mother.

"Nothing," I said. "I don't know what he meant."

Mother glanced at father, then looked at me.

"He's lying," said Vivian. She frowned at me. "Charles it's so obvious every time you lie."

"Stewart, do you know what Reverend Ethridge meant?" asked mother.

My heart was about to pound through my shirt. I was looking hard at father even if mother was watching.

Father shook his head. He said he had to leave but would call mother this afternoon like they said.

Mother didn't ask me more questions.

WHEN Sergeant Lutz came in the cruiser to take me to the courthouse, mother told him she had rethought the suggestion about protective custody. Mother asked me to wait in my room so she and Sergeant Lutz could talk.

I didn't know what was happening. This was the first I heard about protective custody. I checked my dictionary. I couldn't find it. I probably had it misspelled.

When mother came upstairs she told me she and Sergeant Lutz had made some decisions. They wanted to make the trial easier for me. Ms. Trawick had been telling mother how children were bothering me at school. Sergeant Lutz thought that Howard's father might try to talk to me.

Mother and Sergeant Lutz sat down with me at the table in the garden room. They explained protective custody. They wanted me to stay at Rosewood Center during the trial.

I'd have my own room at Rosewood Center. It sounded scary. Why did mother decide to get rid of me? The only good part was not having to go to school and see Mitzy till the trial was over.

Mother would come to visit every day. "I hate this worse than you," she said.

Mother hugged me. She was crying. She told me how proud she was of me.

"I hope this is worth the pain it has caused," she told Sergeant Lutz.

Sergeant Lutz hoped so too.

Mother went upstairs with me to pack my suitcase. She would bring anything we forgot or that I wanted after I got to Rosewood.

"Let's crank up the engine, push the buttons and roll," said Sergeant Lutz. "I'm going to give you the special treatment." We were in his cruiser and he'd made sure my seat belt was fastened. We were on our way to the Hall of Justice. Sergeant Lutz and Mr. Gorman wanted me to see where I'd be testifying. Then I'd be taken to Rosewood Center.

"I thought Mr. Gorman was coming too." I had to talk loud. We were going fast as a bullet. The sirens were screaming. Cars pulled over to let us by and people on the sidewalk looked at us.

"Gorman is waiting at the courthouse," said Sergeant Lutz. "I talked to him on the radio while you and your mama were getting packed."

BOOK II

13

THE KID IS panicked, thought Clay Gorman. He was about to blow, yet he sat straight in his chair, smiled and said, "Just fine, thank you." The kid didn't trust him, didn't trust his mother, didn't trust anyone. His hands were ice, he jumped when the door opened, his eyes darted to see who was coming down the hall, his legs and fingers fidgeted when he sat. Except when he caught you looking at him. Then you saw an adult in a child's body. He was smart, quick to pick up hints, full of words no eight-year-old used, even if the way he used them made it hard not to smile.

143

Handling sex-offense cases for the past year, Clay had seen scared kids. But none like Charles King.

It wouldn't take much for Charles to freeze when he stepped into the courtroom. Clay had seen that happen.

Fortunately the father was out of the way. Three times this morning, Sergeant Lutz said, Charles asked if anyone had seen his father. Charles kept looking down the corridor and had wanted the curtain in his room left open.

Clay had intercepted Stewart King III in the lobby just after leaving the judge, Charles and Sergeant Lutz. Clay had known Stewart King for several years but they'd had no contact other than Bar Association lunches and being thrown into the same foursome at last fall's golf outing. Stewart was big-firm, the grandson of the founder of King and Braxton, a lawyer who billed $250 an hour and knew all there was to know about proxy statements, stock offerings, securities law. Lawyers at King and Braxton didn't handle garbage.

"Where is Charles?" Stewart asked, briskly crossing the lobby when he spotted Clay.

"Can we go down to my office for a minute?" Clay suggested. Bart Mansfield, the lawyer for Howard Landis, was standing in front of the courtroom double doors, eyeing them.

In his cubicle in the prosecuting attorney's offices, Clay made his pitch. "Charles is under pressure. He's afraid you don't approve of what he's doing." Clay offered King a cup of coffee.

"I'm not sure it's my business," said Clay. "But I think Charles feels caught between you and Barbara."

Stewart King slumped in his chair, seeming to shrink inside his custom-tailored suit. His fingers twisted a tie with tiny horse stirrups on it. "You're right," he said.

Clay moved in with arguments.

It took fifteen minutes for King to rationalize his surrender. Now King was gone, back at his law firm in pursuit of billable hours.

Clay returned to the ninth floor. In the small room next to Judge Van Horn's chambers, Clay found Charles doodling on one of his *Yes and No* books. The curtain was pulled. A look at Fred Lutz told Clay that things were not going well. The kid had been crying. A hanky was lying on the table.

"We've got problems," said Lutz. Lutz looked at Charles.

"I've been lying," said Charles.

Clay slid into a chair at the end of the small table, putting himself between Lutz and the kid. For an eight-year-old to recant on the courthouse steps was no shocker. It happened.

"You were lying when you said Howard touched you where he shouldn't?" suggested Clay.

Charles nodded. He reached for the handkerchief.

"I expect Howard would be mad at you for doing that?"

Charles nodded and sniffled.

The recantation was the kid's excuse from the witness stand. It was a ploy Clay knew well. Take time with the kid, Clay reminded himself. Forget the clock and that Bart Mansfield wanted to talk about a plea.

There would be no plea bargain. Howard Landis was guilty. Hadn't the doctor found lacerations and swelling in the anus? There was blood on the underpants. Physical evidence didn't lie. The magazine and pictures had been found in Howard's room. Then two months ago, Bart Mansfield had made his mistake. He let Howard take the Penile Plethysmograph, the peter-meter test, as Sergeant Lutz called it. Howard Landis was a fat eighteen-year-old who got turned on by pictures of naked boys. The evidence was solid, as good as it came. The psychologist and the psychiatrist, two of the best in Columbus, were convinced.

"Charles," said Clay. "If you didn't have to look at How-

145

ard. If Howard wasn't in the courtroom when you answer questions, would that make a difference?"

Charles looked up. You could see him fighting not to cry again. "What about Mr. Mansfield?" he asked. "What about the judge? All those people?"

Clay smiled. "What if it was just you and me?" he asked. "Would that be better?"

Charles dropped his head.

"We know something happened to you." Clay put his hand on the kid's arm. "We know you hid the blood-stained undies. The doctor saw that something was done to your bottom."

"No." Charles squirmed in his chair, away from Clay. He stood up. "Howard didn't. It's a lie. They made me say it."

Clay glanced at the curtain-covered window. Anyone could be out in the corridor.

There was a knock at the door. Clay cracked the door. It was Shorty, Judge Van Horn's bailiff. Clay stepped into the corridor. Down the hall, a lawyer was telling a joke to three other lawyers. No sign that anyone had been eavesdropping.

"Judge is winding up," said Shorty. Clay looked at his watch. Only 9:50. "Judge wants you and Bart to talk," said Shorty. "I guess Bart told Judge there's a chance to work out a plea. Judge says take an hour if you need it."

"There won't be a plea," said Clay.

"Just telling you what Judge said." Shorty rubbed his nose. "Judge doesn't like this kind of case. Judge doesn't like dragging kids into the courtroom. Judge says you've got a nice boy in there."

"That's right," said Clay. "That's why we won't make a deal with a pervert."

"Well, what do I tell Judge?"

"Where is Mansfield?" asked Clay.

"Downstairs. Having coffee in the cafeteria."

Clay grinned. "If the judge wants me to talk, I'll talk," he said.

Clay went back in the room. The kid had his arms folded on the table and his head lying on his hands.

"Take Charles down to our office," said Clay. "Don't bug him. We'll put everything on hold till lunch." Maybe at lunch, thought Clay. Maybe with the mother. The mother was a determined woman. She understood what you had to do to stop the Howards of the world.

Charles looked up. His neatly parted hair was messed, his eyes red and his face blotchy. "You think I'm a baby, don't you?" he asked.

"No," said Clay. "I think you are a smart and brave little boy."

"I'm sorry for my tantrum," said Charles.

"We'll talk some more at lunch," said Clay.

"Does mother have to know about my tantrum?" asked Charles.

"Like I promised," said Clay. "Anytime you want what we say to stay between you and me, that's the way it will be."

Charles smiled, just a little. "Strict confidence," he said.

"You got it," said Clay. He put his finger across his closed lips as he backed into the corridor.

THE bearded guy who was bent over the table, making a diagram with bold flourishes of a felt-tip pen, would be Mansfield's shrink. On the other side of the shrink sat Rob Teater, Mansfield's bag carrier. They had the corner table. A paper plate with crumbs and a half-eaten glazed donut had been pushed aside.

Mansfield introduced Murray Lowenstein. The shrink put his charts into his attache case and left, saying he'd be on the ninth floor in defense counsel's room. "I can use the time to put finishing touches on my article for the *Journal of Child Abuse,*" he said, watching Clay's reaction through gold-rim glasses.

"You're going to lose," said Mansfield as Clay pulled out a chair. "Your boy won't hold up."

"You know something I don't?" asked Clay.

"I know your boy is tighter than a forty-year-old virgin," said Mansfield. "He's going to blow and your case blows with him."

"Is that all?" said Clay. He respected Mansfield. Mansfield was a personal injury lawyer, medical malpractice his specialty. Criminal defense was a sideline and he didn't indulge it without a fat retainer, money to hire experts. Mansfield was a war horse, the veteran of a hundred jury trials. His boyish looks, blow-dried mop of blond hair, mustache and horn-rimmed glasses masked a crafty litigator.

Mansfield sipped the coffee Rob Teater had fetched. Clay and Mansfield traded insults. The game was on, Mansfield probing to see what he could get in a plea bargain. It was a good sign. Mansfield wasn't so sure of his case.

This case was big for Clay. Not murder and not front page, but enough to rate daily coverage in the local section. You had rich people, successes in the community. The families were neighbors, living the good life in million-dollar houses on the fringe of the Canterbury Country Club. Readers without these advantages enjoyed learning how the eighteen-year-old son of Dr. Dwight Landis had sodomized the seven-year-old son of one of the Kings at King and Braxton.

For three years, Clay had been trying sex cases; child abuse, gross sexual imposition, rapes, contribution to delinquency. He was number one in the section. Not bad for a thirty-two-year-old. But he wanted murders, to bust white-collar fraud, maybe nail a big-name politician. He was on track to be prosecuting attorney when Flannigan retired after one more term.

There would be no plea bargain. As he sparred with Mansfield, Clay was looking for clues to Mansfield's defense. You gave things away when you inflated your cards to make a deal.

"The physical evidence is solid," said Clay. "Howard was the only one who had the opportunity."

"Was he?" asked Mansfield. You had to admire Mansfield's control over the facial gesture, his ability to make his eyes show disbelief.

"Maybe you skipped your homework," said Mansfield. "Did you forget the sister, the father and the fag teacher?"

He meant Donald Shirley, the second-grade teacher at the Canterbury School. The best defense was to put anyone but the defendant on trial. It could be other people, the victim, "heredity and environment" or sometimes even "society."

"I'll check with the boss," said Clay, pushing his chair back. "Let's put the jury in the box. We can talk some more tonight."

"Fair enough," said Mansfield.

Getting off the elevator, Clay saw Mrs. King. The mother was with a lady companion, seated by themselves outside the courtroom doors. She stood as Clay approached.

"We're ready to start," said Clay. "But I need to see you for a minute."

She followed Clay through the door that led to the back corridor. Clay stopped as soon as the door closed behind them.

"What is happening?" she asked. "No one has had the courtesy to—"

"I'll fill you in at lunch." Clay cut her off. "I need your help. Charles has the jitters. He's denying what he's told everyone." Clay held up his hand to keep Mrs. King from

149

interrupting. He had only a few minutes to tell the mother about the kid's denials, to explain to the mother how she could be helpful with Charles between now and lunch.

Shorty, the bailiff, came around the corner. "There you are," he said. "Judge wants to see you and Bart in chambers."

"Give me two minutes," said Clay. It would be enough. At lunch, Clay could decide whether to keep Charles as the first witness.

Before going into chambers Clay told Sergeant Lutz to put the kid and the mother in a room, alone.

CLAY stood in front of the jury box rail. He paused, seeking the eyes of each juror. Except for the cherub-faced pre-school teacher in number seven, he was satisfied. Eight of the twelve were women and five of those were mothers. There was a retired postal clerk, an insurance salesman and two blue-collar types. All looked at him expectantly, leaning forward in their chairs, eager to hear about the case.

The pre-school teacher should have been bounced. In answer to Mansfield's questions, she'd expressed concern about the vulnerability of teachers to sex abuse charges. She had been responsive to Mansfield, smiling and nodding, giving her promise to wait for the evidence, turning sober as she vowed not to convict unless guilt was proved to her beyond any reasonable doubt. You shouldn't have been squeamish, Clay chided himself.

There she sat, in the corner of the second row, her dimples creased by a smile, her short hair in an attractive perm. She looked at Clay with what seemed like trust. Maybe she would be okay.

It was 1:44, Tuesday, the second day. Seating the jury had taken longer than expected—even allowing for the questions Mansfield's shrink had designed.

"We are here," Clay began, "because Charles King, a seven-year-old boy, was sexually abused by the defendant. The defendant had the trust of the family. He was ten years older than Charles, one hundred thirty pounds heavier. The defendant lives a fantasy life of sick perversion. He took advantage of his size, age and position of trust to indulge his lust with Charles King. The defendant has scarred the boy for life."

"Objection." Mansfield had spoken from his seat, in a monotone, as if his purpose were only to have the court stenographer make a record of his position.

"Yes, that is improper." Judge Van Horn, reared back in his chair. His eyes closed and his hands clasped behind his head, he too sounded bored.

"We are not here to be vindictive," say Clay. "We are here because Howard Landis refuses to admit what he did. Howard Landis needs help. You can provide that help."

"Objection!" This time Mansfield was on his feet. "Your Honor," he said, more controlled. "The prosecutor's thirst to win overrides his respect for the law."

Judge Van Horn rocked forward. "Will counsel approach the bench," he said.

"This will not be tolerated," whispered the judge. "You are not going to turn this trial into a circus." The judge sent counsel to their tables and told the jury to disregard what Clay had said.

Fat chance of that, Clay thought. Walking slowly from his table to take his position in front of the rail, Clay was satisfied. He'd pricked Mansfield. You couldn't let the defense pretend they weren't being hurt.

Clay glanced into the gallery and was pleased to see newspaper reporters taking down his words. "The state will show you," said Clay, "a defendant who has never had a date with a girl, a defendant who lives in what any of us would consider a palace." Clay lowered his voice. "But within that palace there is the dark room where he holes up with his smut and his fantasies." Clay stepped back to counsel table and picked up a magazine. He returned to the rail and held the cover so the jurors could see the picture. "This is *Naked Boy,*" he said. He watched the jurors crane to look, then pull back in disgust. "This isn't pretty," said Clay. "I apologize for dragging you into this filth. But that's where this defendant takes us."

When he took the magazine back to his table, Clay was pleased to see Howard Landis mop his face with a handkerchief. The magazine had been found in a search of Howard's bedroom. The tip of Howard's shirt collar was turned up. His eyes looked wet and frightened. Clay hesitated, giving the jurors time to stare at Howard, to picture the defendant in his fat, slimy shame.

He held up Charles King's blood-spotted undies by the waistband. "These will be State's Exhibit One," he said.

"After you see the evidence and hear the testimony from that box," Clay angled his head toward the vacant witness chair, "you will have no doubt that Charles King was violated and that Howard Landis is guilty."

Clay returned to counsel table. He drank from his water glass. He had reached his wind-up. In the next five minutes he would prepare the jury for Charles. After talking to Frances Hartenfells last night, Clay had changed strategy. Charles had to testify live. A video tape would lack impact, even if the judge allowed it. If Charles testified by video, the jury would wonder, be more likely to accept the suggestion that he was lying or protecting someone. The jury had to see Charles squirm, identify with him. So Charles would testify but he didn't have to go first.

Clay walked to the rail. "The last witness you will hear on behalf of the state will be Charles King." He dropped his voice and rested his hands on the rail. He was close enough to smell Sen-sen on the breath of the retired postal clerk.

"Do any of you realize how terrifying . . ." Clay stopped, looked up at the high ceiling and started again. "I can't ask a question," he said. "So let me put it this way. An eight-year-old boy will come into this courtroom to face the pervert who violated him. You will see a frightened little boy, a little boy so ashamed of what was done to him he doesn't want to talk about it. Especially in front of a judge, reporters, spectators and strangers.

"I'm going to be even more frank with you," said Clay. "I don't know exactly what Charles will say. I don't think Charles himself knows."

The pre-school teacher and at least four others nodded. The jury was with him. He hoped he'd get the same feeling when he was up here during closing argument.

"This is what I think his testimony will be." At the far range of his vision, Clay saw Mansfield start to get up, then slide back in his chair. A good sign. Mansfield was afraid to object.

"I think Charles will tell you that when he was naked, Howard Landis touched him where he didn't want to be touched and that Howard Landis touched him hard and that Howard Landis kept on and on when Charles begged him to stop."

Clay again picked up the blood-stained undies, soon to be State Exhibit One. This time Clay spread the waistband with his fingers to show how small they were. "It is hard to talk about the painful things that happen to us," he said. "We say so and so has suffered a setback, that a loved one has passed away. Even adults do this. Charles will tell you he was touched. Touched hard in his bottom."

Clay stepped back. He took a breath. "Now," he said, "I'm not going to press Charles. I've spent too many hours with him and I know how painful it is for him to talk about what was done to him."

Again, Mansfield, on the verge of rising, reconsidered.

"We don't have to press him," said Clay. "You will know exactly what happened when you hear him. But even if Charles were not able to face the pressure of this courtroom, you would know what I mean when I say the defendant touched Charles hard in the bottom. You would know because Dr. Merwin will tell you how this little boy's bottom was torn; you would know because you see these undies."

"Ladies and gentlemen of the jury, you can't ignore the tearing, the swelling, the blood on these underpants. These do not lie. They tell you what the word *touch* means."

Back in his chair at counsel table, Clay looked at the clock. He had taken exactly twenty minutes. He sat at counsel table and drank from his water glass, waiting for Mansfield to speak.

"Make it easy for Charles," Dr. Hartenfells said last night. "Let us carry the load. This defendant is guilty and should be convicted even if Charles doesn't testify." She was right. Clay had won child abuse cases where the child was too young to testify and where the physical evidence had been less compelling. Let Mansfield try to dodge those blood-spotted underpants.

"THAT was quite a dramatic performance." Bart Mansfield stood in the middle of the open space between the witness stand, judge's bench, counsel tables and jury box—the "pit," it was called. Facing the jury box from the pit, Mansfield turned to look at Clay. Clay folded his hands on counsel table and waited. The jurors were not buying Mansfield.

They did not seem drawn to Mansfield's first argument. If Howard had been the sitter for three years, sometimes as often as three and four nights a week, why hadn't anything happened before? Why no complaint by Vivian, the eleven-year-old sister? "Vivian may be the most important witness

154

in the case," Mansfield told them. "I want you to listen carefully to her testimony."

The jury wasn't interested. Two were watching Shorty
Glecko fumble with papers which had been brought to the
bailiff's desk for the judge to sign during recess. Clay's
mind was only partly in the courtroom.

Clay was thinking how different the case looked now
than it had yesterday when he'd rushed to Rosewood after
court adjourned. Voir dire examination had not been finished. The kid was blowing his case—only Clay would be
the loser. Nobody cared about excuses when you lost a case
people were watching. That damned kid.

Frances Hartenfells was waiting in the reception area at
Rosewood. Called by Sergeant Lutz, she had seen Charles.

"What happened today is exactly what I would expect,"
said Dr. Hartenfells. Clay's feelings about the kid who was
destroying his case began to soften.

"Charles is caught in the abuse syndrome," said Dr.
Hartenfells. "That he would see Howard in the corridor
and freeze, withdraw, deny his accusations, throw a tantrum—all of it supports my diagnosis."

"You will testify to that?"

"Absolutely." Frances Hartenfells was a woman who
didn't back off, as blunt as the chop of her wedge-cut hair.
She sat across the narrow table in one of the Rosewood
visiting rooms, blinking her gray eyes, defying Clay to challenge her conclusion.

By the time she and Clay walked into the dormitory to
visit Charles, Clay was regretting his anger. Clay had no
kids, a choice he and Sheila had made in deference to Sheila's career as an accountant. But he could imagine. This kid
was being put through hell. A year of hell.

Bart Mansfield still wasn't getting through to the jury. So
what if Howard had made an old wagon into a race car,
painted it and given it to Charles? Or that Charles wanted

Howard to go with them to an Ohio State football game one Saturday when Vivian couldn't use the ticket? The jurors wanted to know what happened in the bathroom.

"I'll agree with Mr. Gorman on one point," said Mansfield. Clay gave Mansfield his attention. When Mansfield said he agreed with you, it was a warning.

"When Charles King walks in that door," Mansfield pointed, "and climbs into that witness box, you are going to see a frightened little boy." Mansfield stopped, looked at the ceiling and stroked his chin. "No," he said. "Frightened isn't the right word. You will see a panicked little boy."

The jurors were with him now, leaning forward in their chairs. No one was looking to see who was in the gallery or what Shorty Glecko was doing.

"You will ask yourselves," said Mansfield, "why is he panicked?"

It was bullshit but Clay was curious to hear Mansfield's answer.

Mansfield began to pace, across the front of the jury box. Head lowered, he appeared to be lost in thought. He turned and came back.

"Charles King is a smart boy," said Mansfield. "You will see for yourself when he testifies."

Mansfield stopped pacing and faced the jury. "Something a neighbor boy did would not create the fright, the panic you will see."

The jurors were focused on Mansfield's face as if nothing else existed in the courtroom.

"Let me fill you in on what Mr. Gorman left out," said Mansfield. "Did Mr. Gorman tell you anything about Mr. King? Mr. King, the father of Charles? Where he is now? Why did he leave his wonderful home on Country Club Way?"

"Object." Clay had to do it, break the mood.

"Sustained." Judge Van Horn's voice seemed to catch the

156

jurors by surprise. As one, their heads tilted to attend the judge in his elevated perch. "This is opening statement," said Judge Van Horn. "Questions to the jury are out of bounds."

"I apologize," said Mansfield. "Sometimes I get carried away."

"Proceed."

"What the evidence will show," said Mansfield, "is that this man, this father . . . was a violent man. He has had counseling and went in for treatment immediately . . ."

"Object!" Clay shouted.

". . . after this alleged incident in the bathroom," Mansfield had gone on, talking faster to get his words out while Clay kept shouting his objection.

"The court will take a recess," Judge Van Horn announced. The judge did not take his eyes off Mansfield as the jury filed out.

In chambers, Mansfield demanded the presence of the court stenographer. A tough nut, Mansfield, not one to wilt under judicial censure. In fact, Mansfield seemed up, energized by the spat.

Mansfield let the judge have his say. His face redder than usual, the judge neither sat nor removed his robe. Mansfield was flirting with being held in contempt of court, the judge threatened.

"May I explain?" asked Mansfield when the judge lost steam.

"I think you had better," said Judge Van Horn.

"The defense expects to prove that the abuse to Charles King came at the hands of his father," said Mansfield.

"You won't be allowed to call witnesses that weren't disclosed," said the judge.

"I don't intend to," said Mansfield.

Clay saw the strategy. It would depend upon Murray Lowenstein. The game Clay was playing with Dr. Hartenfells

157

could go both ways. Get a few facts, then have your psychiatrist give his opinion. "Yes, I am convinced that Charles was sexually abused by his father," the shrink would say.

That's what the jury was thinking right now. It didn't bother Mansfield to drag things out in chambers, to leave the jurors out there with their speculations.

"You see, judge," said Mansfield. "If we make a relevant issue of whether the father is the abuser . . . then every argument I've made is proper."

Judge Van Horn wasn't persuaded. But Van Horn had dropped into his chair. "I'm warning you, Mansfield," said the judge. "This had better not be a bluff. If you don't produce, I'll have your ass."

"I fully expect to produce," said Mansfield, not blinking at the use of the word *ass* by a man who never swore and ostentatiously turned his wine glass upside down before taking his seat at Bar Association dinners.

With the help of psychiatric opinion it might not be that hard for Mansfield to produce.

The realization ate at Clay. Stewart had sought counseling. The separation had come a week after the discovery of those spotted undies. Mansfield probably knew that Stewart had opposed involvement of his boy in the criminal process. Stewart had broken furniture, smashed up the King's garden room. All Mansfield needed was to raise reasonable doubt.

Another thing. Trials weren't won and lost on the basis of the truth. Only God knew the truth. Verdicts reflected what the truth appeared to be. Until you understood the difference between truth and evidence, you didn't belong in the courtroom. And Christ, the evidence here could be manipulated. Especially with the help of a shrink.

This would be a long night. The first step was to meet with the mother again. Sergeant Lutz could help. They had to go back a year, go over facts and times, day by day. They had to be prepared to cut Mansfield's nuts every time the bastard tried to put the blame on Stewart.

The preparation of Charles wasn't finished either. The kid's story had to be taken apart. See where Mansfield could find opportunities. Charles surprised you with what he knew and what he said. Fright and panicky retractions were only part of the problem. Greater was the risk that cross-examination might turn Charles into a witness against his father.

14

"THE STATE CALLS Dr. Frances Hartenfells." Clay glanced at
the clock. It was three. The jurors were back in the box
after the afternoon recess. Clay had them ready for
Hartenfells, set up by Owen Merwin with his description of
the swelling and inflammation. The teacher in number
seven had winced when Merwin told how Charles flinched
during Merwin's examination.

"Dr. Frances Hartenfells." Shorty Glecko opened the
double doors at the rear of the gallery and called into the
lobby. Along with spectators and reporters, jurors looked

160

to see who would come through the doors. It was like a tennis match with heads turned to await the serve.

She came in lugging a gray canvas bag which was half as tall as herself and bulged at the sides. Without the bag she would have looked elegant, navy blue over a white blouse, her blonde hair combed back to an attractive wedge. She placed her bag on the floor beside the witness box before raising her hand to be sworn.

Clay walked to the rear corner of the jury box. He would keep the jurors focused on the witness rather than himself. Hartenfells adjusted herself, took a sip from the glass of water which Shorty Glecko had put on the shelf in front of her.

Clay started slowly. He wanted the jury to absorb the credentials of his witness, degrees from Northwestern and Johns Hopkins, residency at Shepard Pratte, staff privileges at the major Columbus hospitals, special consultant to the child abuse care team at Children's Hospital, a prolific contributor to the medical journals.

"Tell us, Dr. Hartenfells," said Clay, "about the first time you saw Charles King."

"He came with his mother," said Dr. Hartenfells. "Very frightened, very embarrassed. Actually somewhat hostile." Hartenfells spoke in a deep voice for a woman. It was a voice that attracted and held attention.

"You say hostile, doctor?"

Before answering, Hartenfells looked at Bart Mansfield. Mansfield kept scribbling on his yellow pad as he had during the exposition of the doctor's qualifications. Slowly Hartenfells turned back to face the jury. "I have been called in on . . . perhaps two hundred cases of suspected abuse. This one stands out as vividly in my mind as any."

Clay, expecting objection, glanced at counsel table. Mansfield continued to scribble. Howard Landis, however, looked desperate, as if he had been abandoned by the law-

yers on either side of him. The jurors had been staring at
Howard since the trial began, trying to decide whether he
was capable of doing the things Clay charged in the opening statement. Howard was one of the main players, but
also an observer, forced to choose between looking away
or looking back when jurors checked his reaction to what
had been said by counsel, witness or judge. Since the first
morning, Howard had been restless, unsure of himself. But
now he looked panicked, as if he sensed the blow about to
come.

"Charles did not want his mother to stay with him," said
Dr. Hartenfells. "I always—in the initial stages—leave that
choice to the child. After his mother left, he refused to talk
freely, even about unthreatening subjects like his hobbies,
school, his classmates and playmates, the shows he likes on
television. He refused my offer of a treat. In fact it was not
until our third session that I was able to see progress in the
rapport-building process."

Dr. Hartenfells paused to scan the jury, taking in the
length of both rows. She was good. Her movement was
natural. She was drawing them in, all of them.

"Charles is exceptionally intelligent," she said. "The combination of intelligence and resistance made Charles clinically fascinating."

"In what way, doctor?"

"It was apparent that Charles was an abused child. In
addition to Dr. Merwin's findings and the results of the
colposcopic examination, there were the other signs—withdrawal, embarrassment, lack of trust. Yet here was a seven-
year-old of superior intelligence who was performing well
in school."

"Doctor, did you undertake to treat Charles?"

"The first step was to make him feel comfortable. I interested myself in his insect collection. I drew out his knowledge of dinosaurs." Hartenfells smiled and the jurors

162

smiled back. Mansfield had yet to look at the witness. Judge Van Horn leaned forward, resting his arms on the bench, as interested in the testimony as the jurors.

"How often did you see Charles?"

"Twice a week. That is still our schedule. Much remains to be done. The emotional trauma is deeply planted."

"Objection." Still Mansfield did not look up. He sounded like a recording.

"Yes," said Judge Van Horn, but he smiled as he looked down at the witness. "The court appreciates the extent to which you have become involved in the treatment of your patient," said the judge. "But here in court we are governed by certain rules, one of which is that you should not offer information beyond what is necessary to answer the question."

"I'm sorry," said Dr. Hartenfells. "I wanted to give as complete a picture as possible."

"That's quite understandable," said Judge Van Horn. Turning to the jury, he said. "You will disregard everything in the last answer after the testimony that the witness has been seeing the patient twice a week."

The retired postal clerk in number two and the woman in number nine seemed puzzled. The others smiled at Dr. Hartenfells.

"Did there come a time," Clay asked, "when you were able to ask Charles about the soreness which Dr. Merwin found?"

"After much hard work, yes." Hartenfells leaned forward, her eyes asking for understanding. "You see, I was dealing with a sensitive boy who had been severely traumatized," she said.

Mansfield stared at the witness. With his pencil between his fingers, he had lifted his hand from his tablet.

"Mr. Mansfield?" asked the judge.

"Never mind." Mansfield's pencil skidded out of his grip,

163

across the table and floor. Clay crossed the pit to return it to Mansfield. "As you were saying before we were interrupted," Clay spoke while resuming his position at the corner of the jury box.

"I think you want me to tell you about the afternoon we made the breakthrough."

"If you will, Dr. Hartenfells."

"Charles came in at four, after school. That is his usual time. His mother drops him off and picks him up at five although, typically, our sessions tend to run over.

"This was a Thursday and it had been raining. Charles was wearing a shiny yellow raincoat with his hood up. He did not remove the hood until his mother left and I closed my door. He noticed that water had dripped on my carpet and said he was sorry.

"I think I should describe my office. It might look to you like a brightly decorated elementary school classroom. It is fairly large. I have toys and gadgets, picture books, posters of animals, space vehicles, sports heroes, Indians. In one corner I maintain a well-equipped sandbox. I try to create an environment where any child will find something of interest. Charles had chosen to sit in one of the bean bag chairs which are in a corner of the room, on a braided rug. I always let the child choose and this is the area which has felt comfortable to Charles.

"For several sessions, I had been leaving four of my anatomically correct dolls on the braided rug, not directly between us, but along the wall. Charles had glanced at these dolls. However he asked no questions, showed no curiosity."

"Excuse me, Dr. Hartenfells," said Clay. "The jurors may wonder what we mean when we speak of anatomically correct dolls."

"Certainly." She came out of the witness box and loos-

164

ened the drawstring on her canvas bag. "I think you will understand if you see what I am talking about."

The jurors were leaning forward. She pulled out two large dolls, one a boy and one a man. Both were naked. The boy's penis was small but the man's stuck out grotesquely and was encircled in black synthetic fibers at its base.

She hesitated, then reached into the bag to withdraw a woman doll which had breasts with purple nipples and fuzzy hairs between the legs. All three dolls had pink, rubbery skin and the same vacant expression. "May we show these to the jury?" asked Clay.

"You already have," said Mansfield.

"Any objection, Mr. Mansfield?" asked Judge Van Horn.

"No," said Mansfield.

Holding the man and boy dolls in each hand, Dr. Hartenfells walked to the front of the jury box. "These are called anatomically correct dolls," she said. "They are a significant aid to the child in describing events that may be difficult or embarrassing to verbalize."

Dr. Hartenfells handed the man doll to Clay and demonstrated how the joints of the boy doll could move. She twisted the head, bent the knees, spread the legs and put the arms into various positions. When Dr. Hartenfells returned to the witness stand, Clay put the three dolls on the floor, behind the bailiff's desk. He did not want the jurors distracted.

"I believe," said Clay, "you were about to describe your breakthrough?"

Dr. Hartenfells nodded. "By this time Charles and I had built some rapport," she said. "He was able to talk freely about his Nintendo adventures and his hobbies. He looked forward to the glass of chocolate milk and the two pecan sandies I always put out for him on a small table next to his

165

bean bag chair. I noticed him looking more closely at the anatomically correct dolls as he sipped his milk.

" 'Would you like to play a game with the dolls?' I asked.

"Charles frowned. There was a ring around his mouth from the chocolate milk. 'Why would we play a game with those?' he asked.

" 'It is like Nintendo,' I said. 'We can use the dolls to make up a story.'

"Charles looked at me as if I were not very smart. 'I see no resemblance,' he said. I almost smiled. Charles will startle you with his words and the maturity of his expression. But I didn't smile. 'No resemblance to what?' I asked.

" 'Nintendo,' he said, and I could see that he was becoming defensive.

"I picked up the boy doll and slid onto the rug in front of Charles. I held up the doll. 'Does this resemble anything?' I asked.

" 'Me,' he said. I could feel my breathing quicken. I knew I had reached a critical point. I cautioned myself to let Charles control the direction of our conversation.

" 'Does this other doll resemble someone?' I asked, putting the boy doll on the rug and picking up the man doll.

" 'Howard,' he said.

The courtroom was quiet. Someone at the far end of the jury box had gasped. Clay glanced at Mansfield. Clay had expected Mansfield to object to testimony about what Charles had told Dr. Hartenfells. But Mansfield was remaining silent. What was the bastard's game?

"May I continue?" asked Dr. Hartenfells.

"Please do," said Clay.

" 'Can you tell me why the doll resembles Howard?' I asked.

" 'Because it has pink skin,' he said. 'It's pink and smooth like Howard.'

"I was trying to think where to go with his answers when

166

he blurted, 'Howard's weewee is more enormous than mine.' "

In the jury box heads were moving, though not in unison. Jurors tried to keep an eye on Howard while Dr. Hartenfells testified. Mansfield was afraid to object, but his legs jittered underneath counsel table.

Howard no longer looked as pink as the anatomically correct dolls. He had often reddened during the trial, but now his face was drained of color. His eyes seemed to cling to the American flag which was mounted to the right of Judge Van Horn's bench. He avoided looking at the jury, the judge, Clay or the witness.

" 'Howard is your babysitter,' I said to Charles." Dr. Hartenfells glanced at Howard.

" 'He was my babysitter,' Charles answered.

" 'That's right, Charles. He isn't any more. I wonder why that is?'

" 'Don't you know?' Charles asked. It takes a great deal of concentration to maintain trust with Charles. You can't lie to him. I could lose him instantly.

" 'Can you tell me?' I asked.

"Charles nodded.

" 'Would it be all right for you to tell me?'

"Charles nodded again.

" 'You liked Howard, didn't you?'

"Charles nodded once more.

" 'It wasn't your idea to have him stop coming to your house?'

"Charles shook his head.

" 'What did you like best about Howard?' I asked.

" 'Howard said I was like a little brother. He called me his best friend.'

" 'Best friends have secrets, don't they?' I asked.

"Charles nodded, so slight a nod you had to be watching closely to notice."

167

At defense counsel table, Howard's face remained pale and he was still staring at the flag. He sat rigidly, as if movement might betray him.

Dr. Hartenfells took a sip from her water glass. "I reminded Charles of secrets about myself which I had shared during our earlier sessions. I won't repeat those here, but I mention this because it may help you understand the situation. I have found that being honest about myself and sharing personal feelings is terribly important in building rapport with a child who has been subjected to abuse."

The school teacher on the jury was nodding, as were several others. Mansfield underlined the note he was writing on his yellow pad. If Mansfield thought he'd found an opening for cross-examination, he was going to get zapped. Hartenfells didn't make such comments inadvertently.

"I let Charles know," said Dr. Hartenfells, "that his mother told me there were secrets. Charles seemed to like my honest approach. I told Charles I'd rather hear his secrets from him.

"The anatomically correct dolls were on the braid rug beside me and he was still in his bean bag chair. I was sitting curled at his feet. As we talked he would glance at the dolls. He was doing that as he seemed to consider my question.

" 'We had secret games,' Charles said."

The courtroom was nearly as quiet as it had been on the Sunday afternoon when Clay and Sergeant Lutz took Charles up for his familiarization visit. Dr. Hartenfells's voice pierced the chamber as she described the games: horsey-ride and monster.

"We were well past the end of our hour," said Dr. Hartenfells. "Yet we were still on the surface. I knew—and I could see that Charles did as well—there was a dark area beneath. I instructed my secretary to reschedule my appointments.

168

" 'Did you ever see Howard without his clothes on?' I asked.

"Charles nodded.

" 'That's right,' I said. 'I believe you told me Howard had an enormous weewee.'

"Charles giggled as he nodded.

" 'Maybe you saw Howard without his clothes when you were playing horsey-ride or monster?' I asked.

"Charles shook his head.

" 'I bet Howard has seen you without your clothes more than you've seen him,' I said.

" 'Certainly,' said Charles. 'He assists with my tubby.' "

Dr. Hartenfells paused. "I wonder if I might have the boy doll?" she said, looking at Clay.

"I think you should mark it as an exhibit," said Judge Van Horn.

Clay took the boy doll, marked State Exhibit 7, across the pit to Dr. Hartenfells. She laid it, front down, on the shelf in front of her, handing her water glass to Clay.

"Did you use State Exhibit Seven in your conversation with Charles?" asked Clay.

"I did," said Dr. Hartenfells. "I asked Charles to pretend he was Howard and that the boy doll was himself. 'Show me how Howard assisted you with your tubby bath,' I said."

Clay saw it a second before he heard a gasp from the jury box. The reaction rippled through the gallery. Howard had fallen sideways, off his chair. Rob Teater, Mansfield's bag carrier, had tried to break the fall. Shorty Glecko and Mansfield were bending over Howard. Out of the gallery and through the rail which separated the gallery from the pit, came a well-dressed man with gray hair at the temples. It was Dr. Landis.

Judge Van Horn rapped his gavel. "It is four o'clock," he announced to the jurors, all of whom were craning to get a

169

look at Howard, who lay on his side on the floor. Their view was blocked by Teater, Mansfield, Glecko and counsel table. "The court will stand in recess until nine tomorrow morning," said the judge. "Mr. Glecko, will you escort the jurors down to the jury room."

Judge Van Horn was shaken. He had neglected to give the standard charge, to prohibit the jurors from talking about the case. He had not offered counsel the opportunity to request instructions. Slowly, the jurors filed out, turning at the door, trying to see what was being done for Howard.

Howard's father, kneeling beside him, loosened Howard's tie. A photographer's flash went off. "Get the hell out of here," Howard's father shouted. Judge Van Horn had come off the bench. Still in his robe, he stood behind Howard's head.

"I'm sorry, dad," Howard mumbled. "I don't know what happened." Howard was looking up, into the circle of eyes staring down at him. "All of a sudden I got lightheaded," he said. His father told him not to talk.

Clay, standing next to the judge, spotted Dr. Hartenfells putting her anatomically correct dolls in her bag. Clay went to her. "What does this mean?" she asked.

Clay didn't know. He promised to call tonight.

Howard was back in his chair. He seemed shaken but otherwise all right. Mansfield was talking to the judge. Clay left Hartenfells to join the conversation.

The judge asked to see counsel in chambers. Mansfield demanded a court stenographer. "We want to make a record," he said.

In chambers, the judge tossed his robe across the arm of a burgundy leather couch. The court stenographer had set up her stenotype machine in the middle of the room, in front of the judge's desk. Behind the desk, the wall was plastered with pictures from Judge Van Horn's golfing career, the most prominent being a shot of the judge and Jack

Nicklaus in a foursome from a Pro-Am event at Muirfield Village.

"We move for a mistrial," said Mansfield. "The jury was sent home thinking God knows what—and with no instruction."

"No instruction was requested," said the judge. "And no objection was made."

Shorty Glecko came in to say that Howard's father was taking the boy home.

"What was it?" asked the judge. "He just fainted, didn't he?"

"Yeah," said Glecko. "He seems all right now."

"You can't let the trial go on," said Mansfield. "We can't get a fair trial."

"I'll voir-dire the jurors," said the judge. "I'll do that first thing tomorrow morning. We'll find out whether the ability of any of them to sit impartially has been impaired."

"That's useless," said Mansfield. "You can't trust their answers after such a spectacle."

The judge saw that Mansfield was trying to bait him, to provoke a reaction that could be used on appeal. "I'll be in chambers an hour early," he said. "If you find legal authorities to support your argument, the court will be pleased to consider them."

Clay went straight from the courthouse to Rosewood. Charles seemed in reasonable spirits, an assessment supported by Sergeant Lutz. The two had gone with the K-9 unit on a search for drugs in an eastside warehouse. Charles had shown fascination with Rooster, the tracking dog. Sergeant Lutz had persuaded the boys to spend the afternoon demonstrating training techniques and Rooster's capabilities.

Back in the prosecutor's office, Clay called Dr. Hartenfells. They complimented each other on how well the day had gone. "Don't let Mansfield rile you," Clay warned. "He's trying to put error on the record."

Hartenfells laughed. She had a deep, throaty laugh.

After the call, Clay went upstairs to the county law library. As an assistant prosecutor, he had a key. He would stay long enough to assure himself that none of Mansfield's arguments were going anywhere. He called Sheila to let her know he would not be home. Sheila wasn't surprised. He had taken his suitcase. Often during trials, Clay used the shower and one of the beds in the prosecutor's office.

15

CLAY'S ALARM WENT off at 6:30. He felt as though he hadn't slept. He walked down the street to the hotel for a waffle, orange juice and coffee.

When he got to the ninth floor of the Hall of Justice, Clay found Judge Van Horn and Mansfield in chambers, each eating a creme-filled donut. A Jolly Pirate donut box sat on the edge of the desk. "Have one," offered Mansfield.

Clay opened his briefcase and took out copies of the cases he planned to rely on. He handed a set to Mansfield, another to the judge. Mansfield had already given a brief to the judge.

The judge made quick work of the legal authorities, reading Mansfield's brief first. "Let's hear what the jurors have to say," he said. Van Horn seemed more interested in the headline in the sports section of the *Columbus Dispatch,* which lay on his desk, folded, next to specks of icing from his donut. "Without Panetto, this could be a long Saturday," he said, referring to a knee injury suffered in practice by the Ohio State quarterback. Mansfield seemed loose, almost cocky, offering to take Ohio State with six points for a ten spot.

"Is Howard here?" asked Clay.

Mansfield smiled, then nodded. "Howard is feeling much better, thank you," said Mansfield.

Judge Van Horn questioned each juror. No, none had talked about the case or read the story in the morning paper. Yes, each could hear the case impartially. No, the fact that Howard had fainted would not influence them. Mansfield declined Judge Van Horn's offer to question the panel. When the judge overruled his motion for a mistrial, Mansfield whispered his objections to the court stenographer.

Throughout the interrogation, Howard sat calmly, blinking, returning the glances shot his way from the jury box. Warily, he watched Dr. Hartenfells enter the courtroom.

Dr. Hartenfells was wearing green today. On the way to the stand, she nodded to the jury. She put her canvas bag on the floor beside the witness box.

"Dr. Hartenfells," said Clay. "When we recessed yesterday you were telling us about the use of anatomically correct dolls to re-enact what happened when Charles got a tubby bath. How did Charles respond?"

"He didn't want to play that game. He was nervous, biting his fingernails. 'You are trying to find out how my bottom got sore,' he said. Then he began to cry. I had been seeing Charles for over a month—seven times, to be precise. This was the first time he cried.

"I told Charles he would feel better after he told me how he got sore. Charles kept shaking his head and crying. 'I hate you,' he said. 'I want to go home. I don't want to ever see you again.'"

The courtroom, though full of spectators, had become quiet. The jurors were alert.

"I was encouraged," said Dr. Hartenfells. "One of the difficulties with Charles lay in the tight control he kept over his emotions. I told Charles, 'You hate me because I guessed how you got sore.'

"Charles nodded. I handed him Kleenex. He couldn't stop crying.

" 'Nobody thinks you did anything wrong,' I told Charles.

" 'Yes, they do,' he said between sniffles.

" 'Who?' I asked.

" 'Mother,' he said. 'You. Dr. Merwin.'

"I let him cry. I put my hand on his knee. He brushed my hand away.

" 'Howard hurt me,' he said. His answer startled me. He simply blurted it out."

"Objection," Mansfield was on his feet. "We move for a mistrial," he said. "This violates the ruling made at pretrial that—"

Judge Van Horn slammed his gavel down. "This will not be discussed in the presence of the jury," he said. The judge declared a recess.

In chambers, the judge was angry. "The witness has been repeatedly describing what Charles said," the judge accused. "You raised no objection."

"I trusted the state to abide by the rules," said Mansfield. "I don't want to keep objecting, to make it appear that we are hiding evidence. I was willing to let some hearsay come in to show the procedures the witness used in her office. But this is highly prejudicial. It goes to the ultimate issue in the case."

"Mr. Gorman?" Judge Van Horn turned to Clay.

"The witness is a treating physician," said Clay. "We have supplied the court with authorities. A treating physician may relate statements given by a patient in order to obtain treatment."

"Bullshit," yelled Mansfield, not caring that the court stenographer was recording his words. "Charles King was not seeking treatment. He never wanted to be in that woman's office. If Charles is going to accuse my client, his accusation must be made from the witness stand. The accusation must be under oath. My client has the right to confront him and I have the right to cross-examination."

"The court has been doing its own research," said Judge Van Horn. "The court is not going to declare a mistrial. In fact, Mr. Mansfield, I will allow the answer to stand and I will permit Mr. Gorman to continue this line of questioning."

Clay winked at Dr. Hartenfells as he took his position at the rear corner of the jury box. During the recess, spectators had jammed into the courtroom. People stood along the back and side walls.

As Clay fed questions to Dr. Hartenfells, he kept looking down the two rows of heads. The jurors were absorbed. No need to rush. Dr. Hartenfells, referring to counseling notes, recounted her sessions with Charles week by week. Mansfield, the starch taken out of his argument, made objections to protect his record.

"Did there come a time," asked Clay, "when Charles trusted you enough to say how the tearing and swelling inside his anus occurred?"

Dr. Hartenfells asked for State Exhibit 7, the boy doll. Judge Van Horn granted permission for her to approach the jury box.

She held the doll by its stomach. She bent the arms and the knees. She spread the legs and turned the doll so that its

176

head pointed at Shorty Glecko's desk and the split between the pink bottom cheeks was aimed directly at juror number 3, the Bexley housewife. The eyes of every juror were fixed on the tiny anus.

Dr. Hartenfells cradled the doll, covering the anus with the palm of her hand. "Charles was able to show me what happened," she said.

She slowly inserted her index finger into the doll's anus. She twisted her finger. It was excruciating.

Clay, still at the side of the jury box, could read the pain in the jurors' reactions.

Howard could not watch. He was looking at the courtroom clock which had almost reached eleven.

"Is that how Charles described what happened to him?" asked Clay.

"Yes."

Dr. Hartenfells returned to the witness stand. You could feel the jury's relief. She put the boy doll in the canvas bag, with the other anatomically correct dolls.

Clay waited for the witness to adjust her dress and take a sip from her water glass.

"Dr. Hartenfells," asked Clay, "do you have an opinion, based upon your training, experience, your treatment of Charles King and upon reasonable medical certainty, whether Charles will be able to come into this courtroom and show us what happened to him in the same way he did in your office?"

"Object." Mansfield remained seated at counsel table. "This has reached the point of absurdity. The question does not involve medical science at all."

"Overruled." Judge Van Horn had been glaring at Howard since the demonstration at the jury box rail.

"I do have an opinion," said Dr. Hartenfells. "Charles will not be able to do this in a courtroom."

"Why not?"

177

"Even after nearly a year of treatment, he feels too much guilt. When he finished showing me, he threw the doll down on the floor. He kicked it. He begged me to stop asking questions. He cried and made me promise not to tell his mother."

"Why then would he have told you these things?" asked Clay.

"In my opinion he was able to share with me for two reasons."

"Yes?"

"First, we had established excellent rapport. Secondly, I could tell as the weeks went by that Charles was feeling more and more pressure to tell someone what happened."

Dr. Hartenfells looked out into the gallery. She turned to look up at the judge before facing the jury again. "In a courtroom he will not be able to expose such a vulnerable part of himself," she said. "I would not think anyone would ask him to do that." She stared at Mansfield.

"Mr. Mansfield, you may cross-examine," said Clay.

16

MRS. KING MADE Clay feel self-conscious, that his tie was slightly wrong, that he hadn't shaved since morning, that flaws could be found in his trial preparation or strategy. Yet she was never openly critical. She accepted suggestions.

She had dark hair that fell to her shoulders, a delicate nose between smoldering eyes. She was a woman you kept looking at. The way she held her head, the way she formed her words, making a little corner with the ends of her lips, the movement of her fingers and hands—everything was feminine. She looked different tonight, not quite so perfect.

"You wanted to talk?" he asked.

"Yes," she said. "I don't want to make a mistake." Her voice sounded cool and correct, as before.

She was to be the next witness. Maybe that was troubling her. A woman like Mrs. King would want to perform well.

She stirred her coffee. They were in the Family Circle Restaurant, the rear dining room, the one for nonsmokers. The dinner rush was over and half of the booths and tables had been vacated. It irked Clay that she was waiting him out, holding back the reason she'd asked to meet.

"The defense is going to make your husband . . ." Clay hesitated.

"Yes," she said. "He is my husband. Our divorce is not final." Her smile was almost unnoticeable. "Why don't you call him Stewart," she said.

"They are going to exploit the separation," said Clay. "Mansfield will try to show that your fights with Stewart are the cause of the symptoms Charles shows and that Stewart himself may be the one who abused Charles."

"It's probably a good tactic," she said. "Don't most child abuse cases happen within the family?"

"Mansfield has enlargements of the pictures you took of the garden room on the night of the fight," said Clay. "Otherwise nothing new has come up that would affect your testimony."

"They probably have found out a lot about Stewart," she said. "His drinking and the counseling he's had."

Clay nodded.

"Mr. Gorman," she said, pausing to take a sip of coffee and dab her lips with her napkin. "I'm not afraid of saying what I have to say in court."

"Good," said Clay.

"After the year I have endured . . . a failed marriage, an abused child, the difficulties in keeping a home together so that the lives of my two children don't get disrupted—Mr.

180

Gorman, it will take quite a lot for Mr. Mansfield to embarrass me."

"All right," said Clay. "You tell me. Why did you want to talk?"

She smiled, as if pleased that she had won. "My concern is for Charles," she said. "I can hardly bear the thought of his being exposed to your questions, let alone cross-examination."

Clay looked at her, not yet sure of her purpose.

"Charles keeps a great deal to himself," she said. "I am worried almost to the point of losing control."

"That would be hard for me to tell," said Clay.

She smiled again. "I'm sure that Charles would feel better if the case were dropped," she said.

Clay nodded, trying to ignore the hollow feeling in his stomach.

"Yet my mind tells me it is the wrong decision," she said.

Clay waited and she did too. They stared across the table at each other. This time he would wait her out. She motioned for the waitress to refill her coffee cup.

"Charles has become reclusive," she said as the waitress walked away. "He has no playmates. He doesn't go to his little friend Mitzy's house anymore. The last time he was there, he came home sick. He blames himself for what was done to him and it is destroying him."

"That isn't an unusual reaction," said Clay.

"I know." She sounded irritated. "Dr. Hartenfells has been most thorough in answering my concerns," she said. "I've read everything I could find that deals with the problems of child abuse."

"Then you are aware of the studies which show that children who face their molesters have fewer problems in later life."

"I'm trying to believe that," she said. "I'm praying."

Clay nodded. This woman would not accept a lawyer—a

prosecutor, no less—as authority on the psychology of her son.

"Charles was clinically depressed during much of the vacation we took at Lake Erie," she said. "I've received alarming reports from his teacher, Ms. Trawick. Charles avoids the children in his class. His nail-biting and thumb-sucking are worse than ever. He sits in his room and stares at the Landis house. I've seen him duck into our house to avoid Dr. Landis and Mrs. Landis. Charles no longer plays in our yard. And of course it distresses me that he wakes up screaming at night. He's had nightmares for the past month even if he doesn't remember them. I think they are too frightening for him to tell. And . . ." she stared at Clay, "I understand those nightmares have continued at Rosewood."

"I don't know," said Clay.

"Well, I do," she said. "They have heard screaming from his room."

"Dr. Hartenfells has talked to Charles about this?"

"Charles doesn't remember them."

"Everything you say, Mrs. King, underscores the severity of the crime we are prosecuting."

"Yes," she said. "But I want you to understand why it is difficult for me to accept logic and the psychological literature."

"I do understand."

"Mr. Gorman, this is tearing me apart," she said. "I am doing my best to follow the advice of Dr. Hartenfells, to have a positive attitude when I am with Charles, to be supportive."

"You have done that," said Clay.

"I don't know," she said. "I don't ask the questions I'm desperate to ask. Yet I feel as if I've pushed Charles, that I've made the vile things Howard Landis did worse."

"Everyone who is associated with the case," said Clay, "admires the way you've handled the situation."

"Thank you," she said. "That doesn't help."

"You haven't asked me to take a plea bargain."

"No."

"Then I'm still confused. Why did you want to talk?"

"You know Stewart, I believe?"

"Casually," said Clay.

"I want Stewart to make this choice." She looked as if someone were strangling her. "I want you to speak to him. If Stewart wants the case dropped, that will be my decision too."

"Aren't you avoiding your responsibility?"

She looked at Clay clinically, not smiling, not angry, not annoyed. "Whatever decision is made," she said, "Stewart and I must be together. Our disagreement is hurting Charles."

"Mrs. King, we are in the middle of trial. A trial that is going well."

"Stewart is in his condominium. He is expecting your call."

Jesus Christ. Of all the reasons for a cop-out, this was a first. Of Stewart's reaction, Clay had little doubt. King had been against the prosecution from the start. Clay considered trying to get Judge Van Horn to agree to a video examination of Charles. No, Clay had promised Charles to the jury. A change in the middle of a trial could cost him the case.

"What if I refuse?" asked Clay.

"Then I want the charges dismissed."

"And if I refuse to drop them?"

"Mr. Gorman," she said. "This is not the time to play games."

"I'll talk to Stewart," said Clay.

"When you do," she said, "you should know one thing

183

further. I have told Stewart I want a reconciliation. I want that whatever decision he makes."

Clay wished the cup in front of him held a martini.

"Don't misunderstand," she said. "I do not love Stewart. In fact, he disgusts me. But we owe this to Charles. Charles has his life at stake. That's unfair, but that's the way it is. I am not going to see him put in the middle. I will do anything to prevent that."

"Does Mr. King—Stewart—know your feelings toward him?"

"No." She answered quickly, aggressively. "That is a problem with Stewart. He has never known or made any effort to know my feelings toward him."

"You are certainly candid," said Clay.

She smiled. "In a crisis it is foolish to close your eyes to facts, Mr. Gorman. I also trust that you will exercise discretion in how much of my feelings you relay to Stewart."

"You have talked to Stewart?"

"I have told him I love him and miss him terribly," she said. "I am prepared to make those statements believable."

"I see," said Clay.

"Just so you understand."

"I think I do," said Clay.

"Is there anything else you want to know before you talk to Stewart?" she asked.

He shook his head. "Why did you choose me for this assignment?" he asked.

She sipped the last of her coffee. "Because you are a lawyer," she said. "To you this is a game to win or lose."

"I don't believe I quite follow," said Clay.

"Your feelings aren't involved. You don't really care about Charles."

"I still don't follow," Clay took a deep breath, determined to conceal his anger.

"If Charles is to testify, I want you to make sure that

Stewart supports the decision. I don't want Charles to think he has been forced to choose between us." She had spoken more softly.

Jesus Christ. Despite a great day in court, he felt whipped.

"Charles means everything to me," she said. "There is nothing I would not do for Charles. Or Vivian."

"He is fortunate to have a mother who loves him that much," said Clay.

She looked away. She was fighting tears. When her eyes came back, they were moist but as determined as before. "This is so unfair," she said.

"I know," said Clay. "But I believe in doing everything possible to hold the people who do these things responsible. I believe that is also best for Charles."

"If I didn't believe that," she said, "I wouldn't have been able to function this past six months."

Clay waved off the waitress who was, for the third time, approaching them to refill empty coffee cups. Mrs. King's eyes followed the waitress. Only two older women, in a booth on the other side, were still in this section.

"Even Stewart doesn't deserve this," said Mrs. King.

They had been here a long time. Fifteen minutes ago Fred Lutz had come into the entryway to the rear dining room. With a nod of his head Clay had backed Lutz off. Lutz would be in the car out front.

"I will be at the courthouse early tomorrow morning," said Mrs. King. "If we decide to go forward, I feel confident of my testimony. You don't need to worry about that aspect." She left, taking the separate check she had requested.

CLAY called Stewart King from the restaurant, using the wall-mounted phone next to the candy counter.

"Come on over," said King. "I'll tell security to send you up." King sounded friendly, as if Clay were an old fraternity brother whom Stewart hadn't seen for years. King had been expecting the call, grabbed the receiver before the second ring.

"We may have problems," Clay told Lutz on the ride to Waterford Towers. Lutz filled Clay in on how Charles was doing at Rosewood. Lutz pulled in under the veranda to drop Clay at the entrance.

The lobby of glass, wood and marble was elegant, but it did not prepare you for Stewart King's layout on the fourteenth floor. The antiques, oriental rugs and oil paintings would buy and furnish Clay and Sheila's split level in Worthington.

King, relaxed in slacks and a pullover sweater, offered Clay a drink from an opened bottle of Bushmill's Black Bush. A client had sent a case from Ireland. It was good liquor, smooth, mellow. This would be a place to relax, removed from the city whose lights glistened below.

They took chairs on either side of the fireplace. Without embarrassment, King recounted his split with Babs, his resentment of her control over the children and his attempts to retaliate. "You get into the control thing, using the children as pawns," he said. "It can be pretty ugly."

King poured himself another drink, his third since Clay had come. King appeared to handle liquor well.

"Tell me straight," said King. "You've worked with kids in these deals. God, that protective custody deal threw me for a loop. So does the courtroom, cross-examination, jurors staring at you—it's no place for a child. There ought to be a better way."

"You wanted to ask me something?" suggested Clay.

King placed his glass on the table. He leaned forward, clasping his fingers over his crossed knee. "How is Charles handling the situation?" he asked.

Clay stifled an urge to smile. He took a sip of liquor. "Charles is handling everything very, very well." He leaned forward and lowered his voice. "Don't take offense," said Clay, "but I think that of the three—mother, father, son—Charles is making the best adjustment."

King picked up his glass and gently swirled the liquid. "The boy wanted help. He sounded desperate when I saw him at church the Sunday before the trial started."

"He's better now," said Clay. "You once tried cases, Stewart. The hardest time is just before it starts."

King smiled and nodded. It had been a good guess. Most big-firm partners got exposed to trial work in their first years. It was part of the law-firm orientation process. Most moved on to lucrative specialties but they thought of themselves as former trial lawyers who could hop in the pit and wither a witness on cross-examination.

"Charles handles responsibility," said King. "Throughout this ordeal, his work in school has not dropped off."

"That," said Clay, "is unusual in these cases."

King seemed to be sifting his data. Clay moved in. "Charles will feel better after the trial," he said. "Confronting the molester in court is part of the healing process."

"That's hard to believe," said King.

"Check it with the professionals," said Clay.

"Babs made the same point," said King.

"Tell you what," Clay decided to gamble. "You talk to Charles yourself. We've been unfair, keeping him away from you. I misjudged your motives. I thought you were using Charles in your struggle with your wife."

"You weren't entirely off base," said King.

King asked questions, interested as Clay described what Charles had been doing at Rosewood, going out with the K-9 unit, taking pistol practice at the Police Academy range, bonding with Sergeant Lutz, keeping up with his schoolwork, even doing a report for extra credit.

187

"Your wife respects your views," said Clay. " 'Stewart is more objective,' she told me."

King refilled his glass. "Just a little," said Clay, holding his glass up.

"Ordinarily I don't drink this much." King smiled. "My drinking has never been the problem Babs imagined."

Clay nodded.

King turned in his chair. He was looking out the window, at the lights in the windows of the Franklin County Hall of Justice.

"Couldn't Charles testify by video tape?" asked King.

"He would still be cross-examined," said Clay. "It would be almost as hard for him and if he falters, the jury is not as likely to identify with him."

King nodded as if he understood.

"A video weakens our case," said Clay. "It greatly increases the chance that Howard Landis gets off. If Landis gets off, Charles will be damaged, maybe seriously. He will believe the jury has rejected him and his story."

"It looks like a no-win situation," said King.

"Do you want to sleep on it?" asked Clay. "We won't call Charles to the stand until next week."

What King wanted to do was talk about Babs. "A hell of a good woman," he kept saying. The two were still in love, missed each other greatly. King was not easy to live with. He worked long hours, sometimes took his pressures home with him, sometimes failed to be sensitive to the needs of his wife and two wonderful children. Fortunately, he had a wife who was great with kids. Babs deserved credit for Vivian and Charles.

"You can't fight the way Babs and I did," said King, "if there isn't a lot left in the relationship." He couldn't imagine living without her. Couples who never fought were those in whom love had died.

"This is all fine and dandy," said King, sweeping his glass

188

to indicate the apartment before pointing to a museum-quality vase on the side of the hearth. "But I want to be back with my family, back with the woman I love."

"She wants that too," said Clay.

It was ten-thirty when Clay called Sergeant Lutz to be picked up. The case would go forward. Stewart could be called as a witness, Stewart would encourage Charles to face his challenge, the Kings would resume life on Country Club Way as soon as the trial ended. Clay, as he rode down the elevator, could imagine Barbara King smiling her cool smile, confirmed in her selection of Clay as the man to get the job done. He could also imagine Bart Mansfield's expression when Clay told him that Stewart King would be a witness for the prosecution.

"I'M ready for a beer," Clay slid into the front seat of Fred Lutz's Ford.

"Chet's?"

Clay nodded. It was hard to find a neighborhood bar that hadn't been taken over by yuppies or fallen into sleaze. Chet's had been the same for forty years, or so Clay was told by the clientele, some of whom claimed to be forty-year regulars. It was a place to get out of the house, talk at the bar or drink by yourself at a table, depending on how you felt.

The crowd was larger than usual for a Thursday. The television, mounted just beneath the ceiling, at one end of the bar, was turned to the third game of the playoffs, the A's vs. the Red Sox in Fenway.

"What's the score?" asked Clay as Irving put two beers on the bar.

"Sox three to one, bottom of the eighth."

Clay carried the beers to the table where Lutz was sitting, in the corner, away from the television. Then he went to the telephone. It was in a narrow hall, between the doors to

Gents and Ladies. He let Sheila know he'd be sleeping at the office again.

"Have a beer for me," Sheila said as she hung up. Clay hadn't tried to cover the noise from the bar when Crews homered for the Red Sox. Sheila didn't get upset over shit like that.

"You're doing great with the kid," Clay told Lutz. "Keep him busy. Entertain the hell out of him."

"What do you think I've been doing?" Lutz knocked back his Stroh's and reached for his second bottle.

"Is the kid going to retract?" asked Clay.

"You tell me," said Lutz. "This boy grows on you. He's scared shitless, but he's a plucky little bastard. He's smart as hell and he asks the damnedest questions."

"Like what?"

"Like at the police academy. We'd just finished firing. I let him shoot my .22 backup. He asked me if I ever shot anybody."

Clay grinned. Lutz didn't like to talk about the night he'd answered an alarm from a Lawson's store. "What did you tell him?" asked Clay.

"I said I had to once."

"I bet that impressed him."

"That's when he asked me how it felt. How did I feel right after I pulled the trigger and knew I killed a man?" Lutz's expression changed. He was back in the Lawson's.

"Hey, Fred, you brought this up," said Clay.

"Yeah, well, here's what's odd. This kid is looking at me with those wide brown eyes. I mean, he really wants to know."

"He isn't your usual eight-year-old."

"It was spooky. Real spooky."

"Yeah," said Clay.

"Then he surprised me again. He asked if murder was the worst crime. I told him it was."

190

" 'For murder you get put in the electric chair,' the boy said.

" 'Sometimes,' I said. 'If it's a bad murder.' The boy is fascinated by the electric chair."

"You shouldn't have got him interested in that," said Clay.

"It wasn't me," said Lutz shaking his head. "Most kids are fascinated by Old Sparky. I've seen them on tours, running their hands over the oak armrests, fingering the straps, touching the mask that goes over your face, sitting in the chair and closing their eyes. But these questions Charles asked—they weren't kid questions. 'Murder is killing someone?' he asked.

"I told him it was.

" 'But you killed someone and that's not murder,' he said.

"I had the boy in the lounge at the Police Academy, drinking an orange pop I got from the machine. I explained justifiable homicide to him. He had lots of questions—good ones. We covered self-defense, protecting your house, war, police work."

"Sounds like he's cut out to be a lawyer," said Clay.

"Then he tells me that since killing people is the worst crime and since you don't always get punished for killing, would there be justifications for crimes not as bad as killing?"

" 'Charles, you're thinking about something besides murder,' I said.

"A kind of glaze came over his eyes. He kept looking at me, though.

" 'What is it?' I asked.

" 'Nothing,' he said.

" 'What do you mean, "Nothing?" '

" 'I mean I've asked all my questions,' he said. 'I understand your explanation.'

" 'What do you understand?' I asked.

191

" 'I understand there's reasons which excuse doing bad things.' Then he told me he liked to know about rules. He told me you couldn't play Nintendo unless you knew the rules. 'It's important for everybody to obey the rules,' he said."

"You're letting your beer get warm," said Clay.

"You spend a day with the kid and he'll surprise you," said Lutz. "Probably two or three times. So how the hell does anyone know what he's going to do when he gets on the witness stand?"

"That worries me," said Clay.

"But let me tell you something," said Lutz. "There's nothing you or me—or even Supermother, for that matter—can do to change that. That's just the boy's nature."

"But you like him?"

"Yeah, and don't ask me why. When I was his age I was looking to beat the shit out of kids like him."

"I'm going to hold the mother off," said Clay. "I don't want to put her on the stand right after Hartenfells."

"Because of what I told you about the boy?" Lutz looked puzzled.

"Hardly," said Clay, smiling. Clay had been mulling over his strategy. He would go with the short fact-witnesses next. The kid who'd been in Howard's cabin at Camp Agape would tell about Howard lingering in the shower, watching the nine-year-olds, making sure they were thorough in soaping themselves.

He'd put on the football player to give the jury a vignette of Howard as manager of the team, offering massages after practice, rubbing on the red-hot, ministering to sore muscles and cramps. After Hartenfells, the jury should be primed to draw the right inferences. That would take it past the weekend, possibly into Tuesday. Allowing for Dr. Dean, the mother and Stewart, Clay wouldn't get to Charles until next Friday.

Clay drained the last of his third beer. The Red Sox had won game three and gone one up in the playoffs. "I've got to get ready for Mansfield's onslaught," he said.

When he got to the prosecutor's office the daily copy was waiting for him. He would read Dr. Hartenfells's testimony, imagine himself as Mansfield, see what looked vulnerable to attack when Mansfield cross-examined her.

17

"DR. HARTENFELLS," MANSFIELD stalked the witness box. "You gave us a lengthy exposition of your credentials and degrees." Mansfield stopped about six feet from the witness and smiled. Hartenfells smiled back. She was wearing navy blue, a dress with puffs at the shoulder and a high collar. "Actually you are not so much a child psychologist as you are an expert in preparing children to testify in sex abuse cases." Mansfield glanced at defense counsel table where he had a stack of transcripts from other trials with slips of paper to mark parts of the testimony—presumably previous testimony by Hartenfells.

"Is that a question or your opinion?" asked Dr. Hartenfells. Most of the jurors laughed.

"Take it as a question," said Mansfield.

"I talk to children who have something they want to tell me."

"Is that how you describe your profession?"

Dr. Hartenfells looked, somewhat apologetically, at the jury. "It's as good a description as I can manage," she said.

"Did you say *want?*" Mansfield's voice rose. "Are we to understand that Charles King *wanted* to tell you the things you have related?"

"May I explain?" Hartenfells looked up at the judge.

"Answer the question first, then you may explain," said Judge Van Horn. Clay hoped the jury saw the look Mansfield had given the judge.

"Yes," said Dr. Hartenfells. "A child, Mr. Mansfield, can want, even feel pressure, to tell his story, yet experience embarrassment and pain in the telling."

"And you know that even if Charles acted as if he didn't want to tell?"

"That is where my training comes in. I should be glad to explain."

"Spare us, doctor." Mansfield smiled but no juror did. "I suppose you will claim that Charles wants to tell us here in court what happened to him, but that it will be difficult . . ."

"Far more than difficult, Mr. Mansfield."

"Would you say that Charles wants to tell these ladies and gentlemen—and the judge here—if we can help him overcome his embarrassment?"

"First, you make a false assumption. His embarrassment cannot be overcome. Not in a public setting. Nor do I believe that to be your purpose." Hartenfells paused. A snicker from someone in the jury box had triggered laughter in the gallery. Judge Van Horn rapped his gavel.

195

"Secondly," said Hartenfells, "Charles King does not in any way want to be in this courtroom. He is coming here because it is the law's requirement."

"Unlike yourself who are here because you are being paid?"

Hartenfells glared at Mansfield. Mansfield was making a mistake. "What is your hourly rate?" asked Mansfield.

"One hundred and twenty-five dollars."

"Not a service for the underprivileged?"

"There are many arrangements. My practice covers the full spectrum of society."

"I see," said Mansfield. "But in this case, which level of society's spectrum is footing the bill?"

"My fees are paid by Mrs. King."

"Mrs. King is paying for your testimony here in court?"

"Yes."

"Doctor, let's move to a less touchy subject." Mansfield turned his back and walked away from the witness box. In the middle of the pit he spun around. "Let's talk about coaching the witness," he said.

"Are you asking me if I coached Charles?"

"We'll come to that. Right now I want to know if you think it possible to coach a child witness."

"Content can be coached," said Dr. Hartenfells. "Affect cannot be."

"Is it possible to put that in terms someone like me could understand?" Mansfield grinned at her.

"I am saying that no one can coach a child when to show embarrassment, when to withdraw, to color, fidget, bite fingernails. You don't coach a child—or anyone else—to be depressed. That is what we mean by affect, Mr. Mansfield."

"But it takes someone like you to identify those things. I mean we lay people . . ." Mansfield swept his hand to indicate the jury ". . . could be fooled, because we lack your expertise?"

196

"If you are asking me whether my expertise is helpful where a child has been traumatized by sexual abuse, the answer is emphatically yes."

"I wasn't asking you that, doctor. I was asking about coaching and who can detect coaching."

"Mr. Mansfield," Hartenfells stopped. She turned away from Mansfield to face the jury. "There is absolutely no doubt that Charles King was sexually abused." She leaned forward, letting her eyes move from juror to juror. "And that it happened as shown to me with the anatomically correct dolls. Neither of those facts is the result of coaching."

"We are to take your word on this?"

"I can give you the results of Leland Gill's research, if you wish."

"If Dr. Gill has opinions, I'm sure the state will call him as a witness," said Mansfield.

"Didn't you tell Charles that the 'icky feeling would go away' if he told you what Howard did to him?" Mansfield asked, waving a transcript of Hartenfells's testimony from another trial.

"I would not have told Charles that because it is a lie," she said. "The icky feeling may never go away."

When Judge Van Horn declared the morning recess, Clay was able to enjoy his coffee. Hartenfells had nailed Mansfield. But Mansfield seemed insensitive to his defeat. Mansfield looked jaunty as he stood to resume the attack after recess.

His issue was testing. Charles had been given the standard tests—house, tree, person; kinetic family drawing, draw a person; red-flag, green-flag people; tell a story; Roberts Appreciation Test; sentence completion; the Wechsler Intelligence test. Most of the work had been done by Dr. Rosalind Dean, the sociologist who was yet to testify. But Hartenfells was familiar with the techniques and the results Charles had produced.

197

"You say those tests prove sexual abuse?" asked Mansfield.

"I did not say the tests proved the abuse," said Hartenfells. "I said that the results are consistent with sexual abuse."

"Ah yes." Mansfield looked up at the ceiling which formed a dome above the pit area, lighted indirectly from around the perimeter. *"Consistent with.* Those are the key words. Tell me," said Mansfield, seeming to address his question to the top of the dome, "Is there any trait you can identify—any trait we might find in any child, not just Charles—which would *not* be consistent with sexual abuse?"

Hartenfells hesitated. For the first time she seemed unsure about her answer.

"Take whatever time you need," said Mansfield. "We realize how hard it may be for you to think of something you would not offer as proof of sex abuse."

"That isn't the point," said Hartenfells.

"What *is* the point?"

The jurors, particularly the school teacher, were waiting to hear the answer. The mail carrier sneaked a look to see how Clay was reacting.

"The point is that no one factor may be taken in isolation. They must be read in combination."

"Read—that is, by someone such as yourself?"

"Yes."

"So as Mrs. King's hired witness, you can't tell us any one factor that we could look for in a child and say, 'Now, that indicates this child has not been abused'?"

"That is a silly question."

"Well, have patience with silly me," said Mansfield. Most of the jurors were smiling.

"I named a number of factors which are consistent with

198

abuse," said Hartenfells. "The opposite of those traits
would presumably be consistent with nonabuse."

"That makes sense." Mansfield walked across the pit to
the jury box rail, holding his hand to his chin as if lost in
thought. "My only problem," he said, turning on
Hartenfells, "is that you've named hyperactivity and you've
named depression and listlessness. Where do we find an
opposite in there?"

The jurors and the gallery laughed. At the edges of her
carefully groomed hair, Hartenfells had colored slightly.

"That's why I said you need to look at factors in combination. This isn't a game where you make black-and-white
pronouncements based upon any one factor."

"I see," said Mansfield. "Run through that house-tree-pic-
ture test for us. Let's see how we use that to prove sex
abuse."

"Charles was given a blank piece of paper," said Dr.
Hartenfells. "He also had colored pencils and an eraser. He
was free to move the paper any way he wanted."

" 'What kind of house should I draw?' he asked.

" 'You decide,' I said.

"The thing that was striking in the drawing Charles made
was the detail. Also his trees were animated. By that I mean
the limbs were arms and had fingers."

"That proves he was abused?"

"Consistent with abuse," said Dr. Hartenfells.

"Ah yes, consistent with. I suppose I could ask Charles to
draw us a house or a tree . . . or a person when he comes
in to testify. Then we could analyze his drawing?"

"I don't believe the courtroom is the proper setting for
such an experiment."

"Of course, no one could coach him in here."

It was not a question and Hartenfells did not answer. She
pushed at her hair, trying to hide her annoyance.

199

"Based on your experience, how do you interpret an animated tree in a child's drawing?" asked Mansfield.

"It is an indicator of psychosis. The trees Charles drew
were misshapen. I'm not saying Charles is psychotic. But
his drawings do show how deep-seated and damaging the
abuse has been to his psyche."

"Because he puts arms on his trees?"

"In part."

"That wouldn't just show us a child with a good imagination?"

"If you want to understand the test, I can refer you to
several studies. Langelier, DiLeo, Kappitz, Myers."

"Please," Mansfield held up his hand. "I wasn't asking for
a dissertation."

"And you aren't really interested in understanding any of
these procedures."

"Move to strike," said Mansfield. "It is not responsive.
Further, the jury will have to decide what the motives of
myself and the learned doctor may be."

"Sustained," ruled Judge Van Horn.

Mansfield had found his stride. Unhurried, he had Dr.
Hartenfells produce drawings, notes, test papers. He
marked them as exhibits before asking Dr. Hartenfells to
analyze them. He was no longer fighting the witness. As the
day wore on, past lunch recess and into the afternoon, the
conclusions she drew seemed increasingly farfetched.

Clay was worried about another of Mansfield's strategies.
Mansfield was going to subject Charles to some of these
tests in the courtroom. Then Mansfield would call upon
that fraud, Murray Lowenstein, to interpret the results. The
argument that the tests were not critical to the state's case
or to the opinions of Dr. Hartenfells would sound lame.
Additional preparation of Charles had to be undertaken.

"How much longer do you expect to take with your examination?" asked Judge Van Horn. It was three by the courtroom clock.

"The claims this witness has made are so far-ranging," said Mansfield. "Our task has only begun."

Van Horn sent the jurors out for afternoon recess.

Clay assured Dr. Hartenfells that she was doing fine. In the back hall, he ran into Shorty Klecko.

"What did you think?" asked Clay. "Mansfield seemed to be making points."

"Aw, hell," said Shorty. "He's blowing smoke. Your lady's holding up. Anybody that looks at that fat bastard can see right off he done it."

Clay felt better, even if he knew that Shorty Klecko was perfectly capable of telling Mansfield he'd blown the state's case out of the water.

When the trial resumed, every seat in the gallery was taken. Standees crowded against the walls. Word had spread. The confrontation between Mansfield and the icy broad with balls was worth watching.

"Dr. Hartenfells, there is one other matter you didn't cover with Mr. Gorman," said Mansfield. "I was wondering if the omission was calculated or inadvertent."

Clay objected. He would do more of that, try to nip the speeches. Judge Van Horn administered a gratifying rebuke to Mansfield.

"You have described a number of tests," said Mansfield. "In fact, you brought along the folder which contains this material."

"And I allowed you to look at everything in it."

"So you did." Mansfield walked across the pit and back. "So you did," he said again. "Some of that material was what Charles produced in the so-called Complete a Story test?"

"Yes."

"I was wondering why you left out the most complete story Charles wrote?" Mansfield waited for an answer.

"I can't respond when I don't know what you are referring to," Dr. Hartenfells finally said.

"You do recall a story about a praying mantis?"

"Yes, that was not part of the testing."

"Perhaps then it was more spontaneous. Less subject to hints dropped by the test administrator."

"I resent the insinuation. Furthermore, I know the integrity of Dr. Dean."

"But Charles did do the mantis story on his own?"

"Yes."

"Was that story psychologically significant?"

"Many things are significant, Mr. Mansfield. The mantis episode interested me. It confirmed some of my conclusions. It supports Dr. Dean's testing."

"But you didn't bring it to court? Didn't mention it during your lengthy responses to Mr. Gorman?"

"I considered it cumulative."

"What significance did you draw from the mantis story?"

"It is the product of an emotionally disturbed child. A sexually abused child, if you will."

"Isn't the mantis story about a predatory mother who eats her babies?"

"There is that element."

"Could that mean that Charles felt pressured by you and his mother to make accusations against the wrong person?"

"Mr. Mansfield, your interpretation is innovative. It suggests that you yourself would be an interesting subject for analysis."

The jurors laughed, the judge laughed and the gallery exploded. Mansfield grinned, bowed and swept his hand down in homage to Hartenfells. "Touché," he said. Suddenly the grin disappeared. Mansfield took two steps toward the witness box. "Didn't you testify that in evaluating a child's pictures or stories you look to see the sex of the predator—that such may indicate how a child views his world?"

"I did."

"The predator in the mantis story was female?"

"I don't believe Charles put himself in the mantis story. If you have it there, I would be glad to tell you what I see in it."

"Well, doctor," said Mansfield, turning from the witness. "Since you didn't bring it to court and evidently didn't want to discuss it, I think we will wait to hear Dr. Lowenstein's interpretation of the mantis story."

"As you wish."

"And," said Mansfield, pivoting to face the witness, "for the significance of your efforts to conceal it."

Dr. Hartenfells leaned forward to respond, reconsidered and adjusted her dress before taking a sip from her water glass.

"You were seeing Charles for therapeutic purposes," said Mansfield. "Rather than for the purpose of making a case for the state?" he asked when the witness did not respond.

"Yes." It was a good sign. Hartenfells saw the danger in trying to one-up the questioner.

"But you haven't told us how Charles felt about his parents getting divorced. Is this another little matter you have chosen to hide?"

"I don't believe the divorce has anything to do with the abuse."

"Perhaps not. But was Charles in any way upset by the fights his parents had?"

"He was devastated."

Great, thought Clay. The jury was impressed too. It was always best to concede a point you couldn't win.

"Devastated, you say?" Mansfield again turned his back on the witness.

"Yes."

Mansfield whirled. "Might a child who has been emotionally devastated show some of the symptoms you have related? Might such devastation reflect on these various testing procedures?"

"Yes, to both of your questions," said Dr. Hartenfells.

Mansfield bobbed his head in appreciation, covering any feeling that she had stolen his cross-examination.

"That devastation does not change my opinion," said Hartenfells. "Would you like to know why?"

"I would like to know why you have decided to be the boy's advocate."

"I don't believe that a desire to explain my findings makes me an advocate."

"It does when you haven't been asked a question."

Judge Van Horn pounded his gavel. Though no objection had been made, he ordered counsel to the bench.

"This has got to stop," Judge Van Horn whispered. "I expect counsel to ask proper questions. Mr. Gorman, I want you to tell your witness to answer the question—and no more."

Clay whispered the instruction to Dr. Hartenfells. Mansfield returned to his post in front of Shorty Klecko's desk. En route he picked up a transcript from the stack on counsel table.

"Now, Dr. Hartenfells, you pride yourself on being an advocate for the child." Censure from the judge had little effect on Mansfield. "I'm sure you told Charles," he continued, "that you would be his advocate here in court. You told us how you manipulated him by 'sharing' some secrets of your own and, believe me, doctor, I have no intention of prying into those. You gave Charles chocolate milk and pecan sandies, made promises that he would feel better if he answered your questions and you praised him for being

204

brave, intelligent and a good boy. You offered every reward you could conceive of to get the answers you wanted."

Mansfield had kept on, ignoring Judge Van Horn's gavel and his shout of "Mr. Mansfield, Mr. Mansfield," from the bench. The judge was fuming.

"Let me rephrase," he said.

Judge Van Horn glared at him. It was hard to read the jury. They liked the show. Their attention had shifted from Howard to the battle between lawyer, judge and witness. But there were things Clay could say about this at closing argument. He added to the notes on his legal pad.

Mansfield tossed the transcript he had been holding. It slid across counsel table until Rob Teater grabbed it. Mansfield picked up the daily copy from yesterday's testimony.

"You testified," said Mansfield, opening the daily copy to where he had it marked, "about something you described as a diagnostic play session?"

Dr. Hartenfells nodded.

"This was your session with the anatomically correct dolls. Your breakthrough session?"

Dr. Hartenfells nodded again.

"During that session, you sensed something terribly dark?"

Again she nodded.

"In most child abuse cases," asked Mansfield, "isn't the abuser a member of the family?"

"Often that is the case."

"If a father is the abuser, that would be pretty dark?"

She nodded.

"Wouldn't the hesitancy, the hostility and embarrassment you observed be *consistent with*"—Mansfield drew those words out slowly—"the father being the abuser?"

"Yes."

Mansfield was firing the questions. Wouldn't all of the testing show the same results? Testing helps in detecting abuse, but isn't it true that it doesn't identify the abuser? If Charles were protecting his father, might he not use Howard as the cover? Did she know that the father was in counseling? That the father had a history of losing control? A drinking problem? That the father had been thrown out of the house by Mrs. King well before the date of the breakthrough session with the anatomically correct dolls?

For fifteen minutes, Mansfield had been pressing his point and Hartenfells had responded only by nodding.

"I believe you testified," said Mansfield, "that Charles extracted a promise from you to maintain the confidentiality of what he told you."

She nodded.

"Specifically, you promised not to tell his mother."

She nodded.

"Have you kept that promise?"

Again Mansfield had stunned the witness. Her coloring and hesitation gave the jury her answer.

"I suppose you thought," said Mansfield, "that his mother should know things, that other considerations outweighed the promise you made to Charles?"

Dr. Hartenfells nodded, but she looked bad. The jury did not like this.

"Have you considered," asked Mansfield, "that the reason Charles didn't want his mother told was that he was protecting his father; that Charles was lying about Howard?"

"Yes . . . I mean, no. I mean, I considered many possibilities, but no, I do not agree with you."

"Of course," said Mansfield, "when Charles kicked the anatomically correct doll and said he hated you—those acts are also *consistent with* the father theory we are considering."

"No."

"They aren't?"

206

"Well, perhaps consistent," she said. "But you overlook so much."

"What have I overlooked?" Mansfield, all innocent, waited for her answer with his mouth open.

"It is important to pay attention to the affect shown by the child; to the way he relates events as well as to what he says."

"Yes," said Mansfield. "We recall your lecture on that point. Is that what you say I overlooked?"

"Yes. It was the behavior of Charles when he finally was able to tell me how his anus got swollen and torn."

"What behavior are we talking about?"

"His nervousness, blushing, his intense anger after he had spoken."

"Anger directed toward the doll and toward you?"

"Yes. That is what we call misdirected anger. Anger felt for the horrible thing done to him. It was aimed at the doll and at me because we were there to receive it."

"Anything else?"

"Yes. The way Charles reacts when I mention Howard Landis. He absolutely freezes. He is a fluent boy but he is reduced to being literally unable to speak. He was terrified when he came to court last Monday and saw Howard."

"You know that?"

"I was told about it."

"Move to strike," said Mansfield.

"We will supply the evidence to connect the answer," said Clay.

"Motion overruled," said Judge Van Horn. "Subject to the state's production of connecting proof."

"Doctor, you said Charles talked reasonably freely about the games he played with Howard. Horsey-ride and monster, I believe?"

"*Reasonably* freely, yes. He was embarrassed, felt some

207

guilt. But I sensed there was more, something far darker. And there was."

"I see." Mansfield stroked his chin, and looked at the floor. "Suppose," said Mansfield, "I were to ask Charles about the part his father played in tubby baths. Or perhaps whether his father had anything to do with the physical damage to his anus." Mansfield looked up. He saw, as did Clay and probably the jury, the fear in Dr. Hartenfells's expression. She saw what was coming and she didn't know how to answer.

Mansfield moved in. "I take it you would not expect to see Charles freeze; we'd see none of the symptoms you relied upon in concluding that my client is guilty?"

"In a courtroom anything is possible," said Dr. Hartenfells.

"Doctor," said Mansfield, "please keep your voice up. We all want to hear your answer."

"I would not trust any reaction in a courtroom setting," she said. "No competent psychiatrist would."

"Yet I believe you said you relied upon a reaction by Charles when Charles saw Howard here at the court-house?"

"That was not in the courtroom. Anyone should be able to see the difference."

"Wouldn't it be fair," Mansfield asked, "to let these ladies and gentlemen of the jury make their own assessment? See how Charles reacts to these questions?"

"As I said, Mr. Mansfield, I don't think that would be fair at all. Worse, it would be unreliable."

"You, of course, are a better judge than these ladies and gentlemen?"

Mansfield waited, but Dr. Hartenfells did not answer. She saw the trap. And there were traps beneath the trap. Clay's problems with Charles had multiplied. If Charles took the stand, the risks were enormous. But if Charles didn't testify, Mansfield had his closing argument.

"I guess you'd prefer not to answer," said Mansfield. "I guess we'll just have to wait until Charles takes the stand."

Mansfield looked at the witness for a moment. He walked back to counsel table and thumbed through his yellow pad.

The ice lady was furious. The jurors were staring at her. Mansfield was in no hurry to cut short this opportunity for her to fidget as she waited for his next question. "No further questions," he finally said. "We will have to wait for Charles."

18

I WAS SITTING at the desk in my room at Rosewood Center, waiting for mother. I had been looking up vocabulary words. I would finally be going to the Hall of Justice tomorrow morning to do my testifying. It had been two hours since Sergeant Lutz told me I would go into the courtroom tomorrow morning. Mr. Gorman would come after supper to go over the questions one more time. But they promised mother would eat supper with me first.

Almost every night since the trial started two weeks ago, someone—Sergeant Lutz or Mr. Gorman—had quizzed me about things father did. Howard's lawyer had played dirty in the trial. They explained to me the extra questions were because of Howard's lawyer trying to make the jury think father caused my sore places.

Howard's lawyer would try to make me ashamed. He might ask in tricky ways about father's fights with mother. If I made mistakes, Howard's lawyer might get away with blaming father.

I was sitting at the desk because I'd been checking words to add to my notebook. I thought that might make me forget about having to testify. It didn't.

Mother was late. She'd come, though. She'd come every night since I'd been at Rosewood. Instead of adding more words to my notebook, I was thinking of how to protect father. I had decided it was all right to lie. Everybody had been lying. Besides, I had told the truth and they didn't believe me. Besides that, I thought father might come back to live with us if I did good as a witness. Most important, I had no choice.

The trouble was, I kept thinking about how my sore places really got caused and worrying that I might give myself away when I got scared in the courtroom. What if Howard's lawyer tricked me and I blurted out what Mitzy and Heather and me did. It made me shiver. I wasn't smart enough to keep up with a tricky, dirty-player lawyer and I couldn't practice this part without telling mother or Mr. Gorman or someone.

I was thinking about that morning again. I'd thought about that morning so many times I could remember everything. At first, before mother found my bloody undies, I sort of hoped we might do it again. It had been exciting and we never got our chance to do Mitzy. But I didn't feel that way anymore. It had caused so much trouble. It was my punishment for what we did and I was going to be punished worse before the trial finished.

211

My room was freezing cold. The eyes of Abraham Lincoln's picture on the blue block wall starred back at me from above my desk. It seemed like Abraham Lincoln knew about my lying and about how my undies got bloody. But I knew that was ridiculous. Abraham Lincoln was only a picture and didn't know anything. He was dead long ago.

If God knew everything that happened like people said, he was making me pay for what I did. For lying, too. And for making father have to leave mother and our house.

I was pretty sure God did know everything. I didn't want to think about what happened at Mitzy's house but I couldn't stop the thinking. God made it come into my mind —all the time. The more I tried to forget or keep it out, the more it came. God had to be doing that since I couldn't do anything to stop it. No one else could, either. It just kept coming back and back.

Heather Knowles had been in the back seat. I hadn't known Heather was going to Mitzy's too. Heather was also in the second grade gifted section, but she was Mitzy's friend and not mine. Mitzy's mother was driving us to Mitzy's house where we were to stay overnight.

Heather stole things from stores and took money from her mother's pocketbook. I knew because Heather told me and once Heather showed me a twenty-dollar bill she got from her mother's purse. Her mother must of been dumb not to know her money was being stolen. Heather's mother was divorced. I never saw Heather's father and didn't know where he lived. Heather was tall for her age and pretty.

That night, I slept in the guest room by myself. Heather and Mitzy slept in Mitzy's room. If Heather hadn't come I would of slept in Mitzy's room.

When we got up on Saturday morning, Mrs. Gerlach told us she was going next door to make change at the table for the neighbor's garage sale. Mitzy took a plate of brownies her mother made and we went downstairs to the rumpus room. The rumpus room was a long room with wood panel walls and beams in the ceiling. There was a davenport and chairs around a stone fireplace at one end and a pool table at the other.

Moose yawned, rolled on his side and stretched. Stretched out, he was a long dog. His stomach heaved the way dogs did when they slept. Mitzy helped herself to a brownie, bit into it, and set the plate on the davenport. "When I told Heather you were coming," Mitzy said to me with her mouth full of chocolate brownie, "Heather wanted to know if we could get you to play our game."

"I did not," said Heather. "That was your idea."

"Well," said Mitzy to Heather, "you said you wanted to. Do you or don't you?"

Heather had on black pedal-pusher pants and she was sitting cross-legged in front of the fireplace. She looked at Mitzy, then at me, then at Moose, then back at Mitzy.

"Moose won't tell," said Mitzy.

"Ask Charles," said Heather. "See if Charles wants to."

They were looking at me. I saw how bad they wanted me to do it. I was excited. I knew some of Mitzy's games. But I was nervous because they might gang up on me. "What would be the rules?" I asked.

"We draw marbles out of a can," said Mitzy. "If it's your color, you get to ask for a piece of someone's clothing."

"That's not fair," I said. "You two could always want mine."

"Okay, then," said Mitzy. "I got a better idea. Each of us will be one color. Heather, you be blue. Charles is red and I'm black. We put the marbles in a can and shake them up. Whosever marble comes out has to take something off. We'll put the marble back after each draw so the number in the can is always the same."

Heather looked at me. "Go get the can," she said to Mitzy.

I didn't say anything. I knew the game would be to take

213

off clothes. But I wondered how long Mrs. Gerlach would be gone and whether she might come back for some reason. Mitzy ran upstairs. She had on yellow shorts. Her legs were skinny but tan and had hard muscles. I watched her, hoping she'd be the one who lost. She was taller than me but not so tall as Heather. Mitzy's hair was as black as mine. It was tied in a yellow bow and bounced as she ran up the steps. Mitzy came back with a large coffee can, out of breath.

"Here's the other rule," said Mitzy. "Whoever loses all their clothes first is the loser. The winners get to decide what they want to do to the loser and they can do anything they want."

"Anything?" I asked. We were sitting on the braid rug, between the davenport and the fireplace, with stuffed chairs on either side of us. I felt extremely excitable. The fireplace hadn't been used since last winter and smelled of stale ashes. Heather was breathing loud enough for me to hear. Her stomach went in and out under her tee shirt. She had tiny blond hairs on her legs, below the pedal-pusher pants.

"Anything," said Mitzy, who was putting three marbles of each color in the can.

Each of us was allowed seven pieces of clothing: shoes, socks, shirt, pants and undies. We'd take turns drawing marbles and the person who picked had to turn their head away and not peek. I picked first and got a black marble. Mitzy, grinning, put the toe of one sneaker to the heel of the other and pushed it off. Moose opened and closed one of his eyes.

As we played, the ceiling would groan and make funny sounds. Creaky noises came from the laundry room on the other side of the wall, behind Heather. I'd lost my sneakers and socks. So had Mitzy. But Heather had just lost her pedal pusher pants and was down to her undies. Except for

Heather and Mitzy's giggles, nobody had said anything the last two draws. Mitzy's turn came next. She reached in. The can was on the floor between us. She turned her head so it faced the davenport and pool table. She closed her eyes. She pulled out her hand which was clenched into a fist. Slowly she opened her fingers, dropping a blue marble on the rug. Mitzy looked at Heather. I did too.

Heather stood up. She had long legs for her age. Her rear end was round and stuck out, stretching her undies. She took the waistband of her undies and then quickly yanked them down and sat on the stone hearth of the fireplace. She put her arms around her knees which were clamped tight together. I stared at her. Mitzy's game had been a good idea. Moose got up, stretched himself and yawned. Moose trotted to the steps and squealed. He went up the steps, came back and squealed again.

"C'mon," said Mitzy, grabbing me by the arm. "We'll let Moose pee and at the same time decide what we're going to do to her." Mitzy put on her sneakers but didn't tie the laces. "Hurry up," she said as I put my socks on and tied my sneakers.

I went upstairs with Mitzy and Moose. Sunshine was streaming through the kitchen windows. It felt funny, like times when I'd come out of a movie in the afternoon. Mitzy opened the door to let Moose out. Mitzy followed Moose into the yard and was gone forever.

"I had to wait for him to pee," said Mitzy, dragging Moose back in by the collar. "We couldn't leave him stay outside."

"We better quit," I said.

"Quit?" She looked at me. "We're just getting to the fun part."

I was glad it wasn't me waiting down in the basement, sitting on the fireplace without any clothes. Mitzy explained how she also ran next door, that her mother was

215

busy making change for the garage sale which had zillions of buyers. "We've got all day," she said.

I had to go to the bathroom. When I came out, Mitzy asked me, "What should we do to her?"

I hadn't thought. I'd been sure Mitzy would decide. "Let's spank her," I said.

Mitzy looked at me. She was considering my idea. Her eyes looked wet and seemed to be burning. I saw that Mitzy liked what I said. But from the pucker of her mouth I saw she thought we could think up something better.

"I know," said Mitzy. "Let's fuck her."

"Fuck her?" I'd heard that word and knew it was a terrible word. It was what my father had shouted at mother. "Fuck you," he yelled during one of his temper tantrums.

"You know," said Mitzy. "It's what your daddy does to your mommy in bed."

"What?"

"Don't you know anything?" asked Mitzy.

I just stared at her.

"It isn't that bad," said Mitzy. "When girls grow up, they like to get fucked. It feels good."

"How do you know?"

"Because I do, stupid. Didn't your mommy tell you you got made when your daddy stuck his penis in her?"

"What's penis?"

Mitzy looked at me like I didn't know so many words after all. "The thing he pees with," she said.

"I don't believe that," I said. Mitzy lied too much.

"Well, it's true and I asked mommy if she liked it when daddy stuck his penis into her and mommy said she did. Only she said it was something you didn't get to like until you get bigger."

"I wasn't made that way," I said. "Not by father peeing into mother."

Mitzy was nodding her head like yes-you-were. "I found

216

out from my brother," she said, "that what mommy told me about is called fucking." That scared me. I knew Mitzy's brother was a bad person.

Mitzy pulled out a drawer. She found a wooden spoon with a long handle. It looked like the ones mother used to serve tossed salad. "We'll fuck her with this," said Mitzy.

Mitzy went down the steps first and I followed. Mitzy had the wooden spoon behind her back, so Heather couldn't see it.

"What took you so long?" asked Heather. "It's not fair."

"You lost, Heather," said Mitzy. "We can take all day if we want." Mitzy, still keeping the spoon behind her, pushed me with her other hand. "Tell her what we're going to do to her," said Mitzy.

We were standing in front of the davenport, looking down at Heather, who was still sitting on the stone fireplace. Heather had goosebumps on her arms and legs.

"It was your idea," I said to Mitzy.

"Don't be a baby," said Mitzy. "We agreed and you have to tell her."

"Heather, we decided to fuck you," I said. The way Heather looked at us and the way her knees shook when I told her got me excited. Probably she knew about fucking.

"Get down on the rug, Heather," said Mitzy. "Lie on your back and spread your legs." Mitzy brought out the spoon and waved it in front of Heather.

"No," said Heather who couldn't stop looking at the spoon. "Not with that. Only a finger is fair."

"You agreed," said Mitzy. "You aren't allowed to chicken out."

Heather glanced at Mitzy, then stared again at the spoon which Mitzy was slapping against her leg. Heather slid off the hearth onto the rug. She laid on her back with her eyes closed.

"Spread your legs," said Mitzy.

Heather did spread them, but not much.

"Here," said Mitzy. She put the spoon on the davenport. "We'll have to do it for her." Mitzy grabbed one ankle and had me take the other. We pulled Heather's legs apart until she yelled, "Stop." Mitzy told me to hold Heather by the shoulders. Mitzy picked up the spoon. The handle end was sticking out. Heather was squirming. "Sit on her tummy," said Mitzy. I sat with my knees apart so I could watch what Mitzy was doing.

Heather screamed.

"Don't be a sissy or I'll do it really hard," said Mitzy.

Heather was crying. "Please stop," she kept saying.

"Stop wiggling so much," said Mitzy. "That way it won't hurt. It'll feel good."

Heather had her legs stiff and slightly off the floor. She was crying but not loud. Mitzy told me to get off Heather's stomach.

"You push the handle in and out," said Mitzy.

I took the spoon. It went in a little way.

"You have to push harder," said Mitzy.

I got the end in.

"Now pull it back. Then go back and forth," said Mitzy. "We'll fuck Heather ten times."

"She's bleeding," I said. I saw a spot of blood on the handle.

"Okay, that's enough," said Mitzy, who pulled the spoon out. It wasn't in as far as I thought.

Heather was lying on the rug, sniffling. Her legs were still spread. Her skin was damp and smudged from the dirty rug and where I sat on her. Mitzy ran upstairs and came back with paper towels, some dry and some wet. Mitzy wiped Heather and then cleaned the end of the spoon. There wasn't much blood, only a spot. The basement smelled funny. Mitzy's polo shirt was damp, sticking to her.

Heather sat up and then scooted herself up on the hearth. Mitzy handed Heather her undies. Heather put them on.

"That wasn't fair," said Heather.

"It's fun," said Mitzy. "You'll see when we do Charles. That'll make everything fair."

"I'm not playing any more," I said. I was watching Heather and I was scared. We could of been in trouble.

"You don't have a choice," said Mitzy. "We each have to take a turn or it wouldn't be fair. The game was to see who went first. If we don't finish, Heather might get mad and tell. Isn't that right, Heather?"

"Yes," said Heather and she sounded a little better. She'd put on her tee shirt and was rubbing herself where the spoon handle went in. She put on her pedal-pusher pants. I didn't think Heather was hurt as bad as I thought.

"Take your clothes off," said Mitzy. She was looking at me. "Then you and Heather can do me."

When I got my clothes off, Mitzy said, "We have to fuck him in the rear."

"I know that," said Heather, who didn't seem to be hurt any more.

Mitzy made me get on my knees on the rug, cross my arms and put my chin on my hands. My rear end was sticking up.

"Yuck, he's smelly," said Mitzy.

"We can wash him," said Heather.

"No," said Mitzy. "We don't have time."

"Ouch," I screamed when the wooden handle started in. Mitzy had the spoon and I thought she was trying to hurt me. It felt like she was tearing my skin. I couldn't see but I had to be bleeding. Moose growled. He got up and started licking my face. I tried to move my face but that made it hurt worse.

"Now you do it," Mitzy told Heather. "But wait a second. Someone could hear him."

That scared me and I stopped yelling. It would of been terrible if someone had found us. Mitzy wadded my polo shirt and stuck it into my mouth.

"Push the handle in farther," said Mitzy. "He hasn't been fucked yet."

I was trying not to move because when I did it felt like I had the whole handle inside me. Finally they quit. I rolled on my side. My polo shirt was messy. I was having trouble breathing. I felt back there for blood but all I got was a smelly finger. Heather giggled.

Mitzy was cleaning the spoon. She looked at me and said, "Next time, you better wash first or we'll whip you with a coat hanger till you bleed." She looked like she wanted to do that. I didn't say anything, hoping she wouldn't. I was lying on the rug trying to catch my breath. My rear felt like the handle was still stuck inside.

"Look, he's shivering," said Heather.

"Heather, you were braver," said Mitzy. "You didn't need a shirt in your mouth." Mitzy was inspecting the spoon handle. She was smelling it. "I won't have to have a gag," she said.

They laughed. "C'mon, Charles," said Heather. "It's Mitzy's turn."

Mitzy was slipping down her shorts. I just laid on the rug. I hurt too bad. I didn't think I could move.

We heard the door open upstairs. "Hurry," said Mitzy, who yanked her shorts up and picked up the paper towels and the spoon. She put everything behind the firewood box, between the box and the wall. Heather was smoothing out her hair. I heard Mrs. Gerlach walking on the floor, right above us. "She's going to the bathroom," said Mitzy.

I got my clothes on. I finished tying my sneakers and Mitzy placed the marbles on the floor by the time Mrs. Gerlach opened the door at the top of the stairs.

"My goodness," said Mrs. Gerlach. "Is something wrong with the brownies?"

I looked at the plate. Only one had been eaten.

"We got interested in marbles and forgot," said Mitzy. "We've been having a tournament and Charles is winning."

"That's wonderful, Charles," said Mrs. Gerlach. "I hate to break up such a good time, but Charles, your mother called."

"We didn't hear the phone," said Heather.

Mrs. Gerlach smiled. "We have a remote extension," she said. "I took the calls at the Vogels'."

"Mommy is on the telephone all the time," said Mitzy. "We have an answering machine too."

Mrs. Gerlach patted Mitzy's head and straightened a hair that had fallen into Mitzy's eye. Mrs. Gerlach looked at me with a friendly smile. "Your mother will be picking you up for lunch in twenty minutes," she said.

"Could Charles come back after lunch?" asked Mitzy.

"I know," said Mrs. Gerlach. "We like having Charles visit us at our house, don't we?"

Mitzy nodded as Mrs. Gerlach straightened a few more of her hairs.

"We'll invite Charles again real soon," said Mrs. Gerlach.

My rear was sore. I was afraid Mrs. Gerlach would be able to tell when I walked. But when mother's Volvo pulled into the drive, I remembered to thank Mrs. Gerlach and Mitzy for a lovely time and for inviting me.

Vivian was in the car with mother. She sat there while mother got out to speak to Mrs. Gerlach who had come out with me. Mitzy and Heather were watching from the window. Mother thanked Mrs. Gerlach for "having my Charles" overnight.

"We were delighted Charles could come," said Mrs. Gerlach. "Fritz and I are looking forward to being with you and Stewart on Friday."

My rear felt funny. I crawled into the back seat and leaned forward into the space between the front seats. "Is Mitzy coming with them on Friday?" I asked.

"No," said mother, who was backing out the drive, waving with one hand to Mrs. Gerlach. "Friday will be for adults. But you and Vivian may have dessert with us."

"Why did I have to leave early?" I asked. My rear was hurt bad. I wondered what Heather was doing to Mitzy.

"You and Vivian are invited to a party," said mother. In the driver mirror she was looking at me and smiling. Vivian had turned her head and was staring out the window at some kid who was ripping down the sidewalk in his Big Wheel.

"What kind of party?" I asked.

"It's the fall picnic at Central Community House," said mother. "I didn't know until this morning that you and Vivian were invited."

Central Community House, the Symphony, Tremont Presbyterian Church and the Junior League kept mother almost as busy as father at his law firm. I knew that all my toys and previous clothes went to Central Community House for unfortunate children to have.

"This will be a nice opportunity for you and Vivian to make friends with some new boys and girls," said mother. "It is important to have friends from different cultures."

I shifted my bottom on the seat. My underpants were sticking and I was sore. I didn't want mother to see me squirm and ask questions. I was sticky-sweaty thinking about it.

"Do you feel all right?" In the driver mirror, mother looked worried.

"I'm fine," I said. "We were running around a lot."

In the mirror, I saw that my answer was good enough.

"There will be hotdogs and ice cream at the party," said mother. "Then some games which will be a lot of fun."

"How long do we have to stay?" asked Vivian who was still looking out the window.

"Vivian," said mother. "I don't appreciate your attitude."

"I just asked how long," said Vivian.

"It was awfully nice of Helen to think of you and Charles," said mother. "I want you to thank Helen as soon as we get there. We don't want anyone to think we are prejudiced."

Vivian didn't answer.

"Will you do that?" mother asked.

"I will too," I said.

Mother smiled at me in the driver mirror. "It's important to be polite and thank the people who do nice things for us and invite us to parties," said mother. She was looking at Vivian when she said that.

We stayed at the picnic until five. Mrs. Helen Nakamura made sure that we and the two girls my age who came with their mothers played in games with the black boys and girls.

"Thank you for inviting me to your party," I told Mrs. Helen Nakamura. "I had a wonderful time."

Mother stood beside me. "Beautifully done," she said to Mrs. Nakamura. Mrs. Nakamura and mother were overjoyed that so much clothing got donated to the picnic. I thought only white people gave clothes but each black child brought clothing or a can of food they didn't need. The donations would be given to very unfortunate families. I wanted to get home so I could go to my room and check my bottom. It still hurt and I wanted to see if you could see anything.

When we got home, father was in the leisure room. The game between Ohio State and the Southern California Trojans was in the second quarter, out on the West Coast. Mother fixed supper and set up trays so we could watch television and eat at the same time. Father was eager for

223

me to see the game so I didn't get a chance to check my rear end.

Father got excited watching Ohio State on television. He yelled at the players, stood up suddenly for long runs or passes, cussed the referees and sometimes the coach. Father had played football in high school and he was a football expert.

At half time I went upstairs. There was blood, and some poo too, smeared on my undies. In my bathroom I got up on the toilet seat and bent over so I could see myself in the mirror. I didn't see bleeding. I washed myself and that hurt. I started to bleed a little and dabbed myself with the washcloth. I wished I hadn't started the bleeding up. If mother came in, it would be disaster. I would of killed myself to keep her from finding out. I heard footsteps in the hall. I put on new undies and went into my closet to hide the ones with blood spots. The footsteps went past my door.

I pulled down my new undies. I didn't see any spots. I'd be careful how I sat and not to run. I was still sticky and sweaty. I had to get back downstairs. When the second half started father would wonder about me.

The game wasn't too exciting. The Trojans were ahead ten to seven when we got home and nobody had got any points since. In the fourth quarter, father started yelling. "Take it to the bastards, right up the gut," he shouted. Ohio State was marching in for the winning touchdown. "Suck it up, big guy, and hang in there," he yelled at our giant screen. An Ohio State lineman who was lying on the Astroturf was being examined by guys in white pants and red polo shirts. The player was helped up and wobbled around for a minute before going to the sideline.

When the game ended it was after nine and I was sleepy. Ohio State had won fourteen to ten. Though I was allowed to stay up until 10:30 on Saturday night, I told mother I'd like to go to bed. Mother said she had to call Reverend Ethridge. Then she would come upstairs to say goodnight and read me a story. Mother was chairperson of the Long Range Planning Committee. I didn't know if the call she had to make to Reverend Ethridge was about the Long Range Planning Committee. I was too tired to listen in.

When I took off my clothes, I didn't see spots on my new underpants. I thought the bleeding had stopped. But I was more scared than when I left Mitzy's house.

When mother came in my room, she asked if I learned any new words that could be added to my vocabulary notebook. I shook my head no. Mother sat in the chair next to my bunk and read a story about Indians from a book that had the large gold John Newberry seal. After the story, we looked up the words *prejudice* and *cultures*. We wrote those words in my notebook. Mother left.

I heard a knock on my door. I jumped. I was sure someone would catch me checking to see if there were blood spots on my jammie bottoms. Then I saw Abraham Lincoln with his eyes staring down at me. I was in my room at Rosewood. Abraham Lincoln's eyes followed you wherever you went in my room at Rosewood. So he was always looking at me.

The knock was the guard with mother. My hands were cold and I felt dizzy when I stood up. I'd felt awful since I came to Rosewood.

"How is my Charles doing?" mother asked. She kissed the side of my face. She looked worried. Her face and hair looked different but I couldn't remember how. The guard left us alone and closed the door.

"I put seven new words in my notebook today," I said.

19

"CALL YOUR NEXT witness." Judge Van Horn looked down over his bench at Clay. It was three-thirty on Thursday afternoon, the second week of the trial.

Clay stood behind counsel table. "Our next witness," he said "will be Charles King. However, Charles must be brought to the courthouse. We were not sure when we would reach him. The state requests a recess until tomorrow morning."

"Will this be your final witness?" asked Judge Van Horn.

"It will, Your Honor."

"The defense has no objection," Mansfield stood as he spoke.

"Very well." The judge rapped his gavel, sent the jury home and summoned counsel to chambers.

MANSFIELD loosened his tie, threw his coat over the arm of Judge Van Horn's sofa and slouched into the corner chair with one leg stretched and the other hooked on a padded arm of burgundy leather. Rob Teater delivered a Coke from the machine in the basement. Mansfield popped the can and drank thirstily. Mansfield betrayed no sign that the trial was going against him or that his attempt to blame Stewart King had been hurt by Stewart's strong performance on the witness stand.

"I want to question the boy in camera," said Mansfield.

"On what grounds?" asked the judge, who sat on the corner of his desk, still wearing his robe. "I understand the boy is intelligent. The court has heard testimony from younger witnesses."

"A witness under ten is not presumed competent," said Mansfield. "We're not satisfied the boy appreciates the meaning of the oath."

"All right," said the judge, who had removed and was wiping his glasses. Howard Landis was guilty. No trial judge in the state had fewer reversals and Van Horn was proud of it. On close calls, Mansfield would get the judicial nod.

"You may question the boy in chambers," said the judge. "But you aren't entitled to a deposition. Your questions will be limited to competency."

"Of course," said Mansfield.

CLAY met Lutz and Charles for breakfast at the Rosewood cafeteria. The kid wasn't eating. In front of him sat three pancakes swimming in syrup, bacon and a tall glass of watery orange juice. He looked all right, his brown oxfords shined by Sergeant Lutz for inspection. He wore corduroys, coffee brown like his eyes, and a plaid shirt.

"Did you sleep okay?" asked Gorman.

Charles nodded. "Father and mother won't be in the courtroom, will they?" he asked.

"They are witnesses and might have to testify again themselves," said Clay. "But I can ask the judge. He might grant permission."

"No," said Charles. "I can do this by myself."

In court, it would be bang, bang and out. In fifteen minutes, the kid could identify Howard, describe monster and horsey-ride.

Then the zinger—who caused the sores? All the kid had to say was, "Howard." When the kid said, "He touched me," Clay would ask if Howard touched him hard enough to hurt him. Get a yes and turn the kid over to Mansfield. The case had gone well enough to survive anything Mansfield might accomplish on cross.

"HELLO, Charles," said Judge Van Horn. "We've met before."

"I remember," said Charles.

"I don't know what Mr. Gorman has told you, but I'm a nice guy," said the judge. "Just because I wear a robe and am a judge shouldn't scare you."

Clay wondered why in the hell Van Horn had robed himself. The court stenographer was set up in the middle of chambers. Charles sat in a straight-back chair next to her stenotype machine.

Howard was outside, in the care of Rob Teater. "The defendant has a right to face his accuser," Mansfield had claimed.

"This doesn't involve accusation," said Judge Van Horn.

"The inquiry will be limited to the qualification of the witness."

The judge opened the center drawer of his desk and pulled out a Halloween-size Baby Ruth bar. Shorty Klecko delivered it to Charles, who saw that he was expected to eat it and did.

"Do I seem like a nice guy to you?" the judge asked.

"Yes," said Charles.

"You aren't afraid of me, are you?"

"No," said Charles, but his hands were shaking.

"Good," said the judge. "Here's what we're going to do. I'm going to ask you a few questions and then Mr. Mansfield may ask a few more. I want you to stop me—or Mr. Mansfield—if there is anything you don't understand. Is that a deal?"

"Okay," said Charles.

The judge pulled a second straight-back chair up beside Charles. He sat with his robe flopping onto the kid's legs. "Tell me, son," he asked, "do you know the difference between a lie and telling the truth?"

"I think so."

"If I told you my robe was orange, would that be the truth or would it be a lie?"

"It would be a lie, if you mean the one you have on now," said Charles.

"Very good," said the judge. "I can see that you are exceptionally bright."

"I am in the third grade gifted section at Canterbury School," said Charles.

Mansfield was lounging on the couch, but he was watching the kid closely. After answering each question Charles would glance at Mansfield. Mansfield smiled at the kid. A dirty bastard, Mansfield, to play games; but Charles seemed to be handling it.

Charles had come into chambers after talking to his

mom and dad in the small room. They'd spent a half hour together. Mom and dad came out with their arms around the kid. Both hugged him and said they'd stay at the court-house while he testified even if they weren't allowed to be in the courtroom.

"When the trial's over and I get caught up at school we're taking a family vacation to Disney World." Charles told Clay. "They asked me where I would like to go and I said Disney World." The kid sounded better than he had at breakfast.

"What happens to someone who tells a lie?" asked the judge.

"That depends," said Charles.

"What does it depend upon?" Judge Van Horn was frown-ing, peering at Charles over rimless glasses.

"It depends on how major the lie is," said Charles. "Some are worse than others."

"I see," said the judge.

"I might say I liked someone's present when I didn't," said Charles. "That wouldn't be as major a lie as some oth-ers."

The judge cleared his throat and asked Shorty Klecko to get him a glass of water. "Trying to shake off a cold," he explained.

"We understand what you are saying," the judge told Charles. "But what if you were asked in the courtroom if you liked a present someone had given you? What if you said you did when really you didn't?"

"Any lie in the courtroom would be major," said Charles.

"So," said the judge, "you think the seriousness of a lie depends not only on what it is about but also where it is told?"

Charles nodded. "Also who it is told to," he said.

The judge arched his eyebrow but asked no question.

"It's worse to lie to mother or father than to a playmate," said Charles.

"Why is that?" asked the judge.

"Because you don't get punished for lying to children."

"What about to a judge and a jury in a courtroom?"

"That would be deplorable."

"Very, very good, Charles," said the judge. "The court believes this witness has a better grasp on telling the truth than most adults. Clearly the young man understands the oath and clearly he will be able to relate what events he has observed." The judge coughed, cleared his throat and drank from his water glass. "Oh," he said. "I should make one further inquiry. Charles, what do you think would happen to you if you told a lie in the courtroom?"

"I would be punished," said Charles.

"How?"

"I don't know the exact punishment. It wouldn't be the electric chair, but I think it would be worse than anything that's been done to me in my whole life."

"Well," said the judge. "It's perfectly obvious that we have a qualified witness. Mr. Mansfield, you don't have questions, do you?"

Mansfield stroked the back of his head. He looked up at the acoustical tile ceiling as if weighing his decision. "Yes, Your Honor," he drawled. "A couple of little ones."

"I told you," said the judge, not hiding his irritation. "This is not to be turned into a deposition. The court will hold you strictly to the subject of competency."

"Naturally," said Mansfield.

"I don't see what you could possibly ask," said the judge. "But I guess we'll find out."

"Might I take your place?" asked Mansfield.

Without answering, the judge gathered his robe and settled into the high-back chair behind his desk. He reared back, took off his glasses and closed his eyes. Mansfield moved into the empty chair, facing Charles.

"I'm a nice guy too," said Mansfield. "I like kids."

Charles frowned.

"Don't you believe I'm a nice guy?" asked Mansfield.

"No," said Charles.

"Why do you say that?" Mansfield smiled and bent forward.

Charles leaned away. "I promised not to lie in the courthouse," he said.

Mansfield chuckled. The judge laughed and it was the first that Clay had seen Cheryl, the court stenographer, smile at anything a witness said.

Charles was not enjoying his victory. The kid was keeping his voice up, just as Clay had told him. He was listening carefully to the questions. His answers to Judge Van Horn had been fine. But he was holding himself rigidly in his chair, as if perched on the lip of a cliff. His feet squirmed. Twice he started to bite a fingernail but caught himself. His hands clutched the sides of his chair bottom. His face was ashen.

"You did lie to Dr. Hartenfells, didn't you?" asked Mansfield.

The kid's eyes darted to Clay.

"I take it you did not consider that a major lie," asked Mansfield.

"Objection," said Clay.

"Yes," said the judge. "We are not going into everything this young man has said to anyone. The issues are whether he can appreciate the oath and whether he is capable of describing the things he has seen and heard."

"With all due respect, if the boy is a liar, that is relevant to the competency issues," said Mansfield.

The bastard's tactic was evident. Mansfield knew the kid

232

would be found competent. The idea was to terrorize, to set the kid up without having to look nasty in front of the jury.

Clay needed to talk to Charles before he went into the courtroom, reassure him he didn't have to hide anything he had said to Dr. Hartenfells. Clay faulted himself for not anticipating, not covering that better.

Mansfield toyed with the kid, probing the difference between imagination and reality, asking whether Darth Vader was real, whether the kid's report on a praying mantis had been imagination. Was there a difference between imagination and lying? The judge was disgusted but allowed it because Charles was giving answers that demonstrated competency.

"Do you go to Sunday school?" asked Mansfield.

Charles nodded.

"Do you believe in God?"

"Yes," said Charles. Clay could see where this might go. It would be unfair to an adult. If the kid got asked if God was real, Clay would stop it.

"Does God punish you if you lie?" asked Mansfield.

"I think so," said Charles.

"You think so," said Mansfield. "Does that mean you aren't sure?"

"I don't know everything there is to know about God," said Charles.

Clay didn't have to object. "This has gone far enough," said Judge Van Horn. "The court has given you the widest possible latitude. Do you object to the competency of the witness?" The judge had risen and stood behind his desk with his hands clasped behind his back.

"I do object," said Mansfield softly. "Furthermore, I object to not being permitted to finish my inquiry."

"We're going into the courtroom," announced the judge. "The jury has been waiting since nine. We are going to finish the state's case today and get this trial moving. The court has a heavy docket and other cases which must be tried."

"Very well, Your Honor," said Mansfield.

"It will be the ruling of the court that Charles King is competent." The judge looked at Clay. "The record more than supports the ruling and I require no argument from counsel."

Everyone stood except for the kid, who seemed glued to his chair, still holding the sides as if he were about to fall. The kid's whole body, not just his legs, was shaking.

"Charles," said the judge. "Mr. Klecko will take you into the courtroom and show you where to stand. He will give you the oath as soon as the jury is seated."

The kid's eyes begged Clay. But Shorty Klecko had the kid by the hand. Let it go, Clay decided. If he talked to Charles now, Mansfield would pounce, ask the kid in court what Clay said to him, maybe rattle him even more.

Clay watched them leave, the kid's head coming up to the middle of Shorty Klecko's back, Klecko moving along with his bow-legged sway. There came a point with any witness at which the preparation ended. Charles was on his own.

20

WITH PEOPLE IN the spectator seats the courtroom looked different. "Wait here," Mr. Klecko told me. He left me standing between his desk and the flag. He hurried through the spectators and out the doors to the lobby.

Mr. Gorman didn't tell me they knew everything I told Dr. Hartenfells. If I admitted I lied, Mr. Mansfield would ask millions of questions. The judge would punish me. "Son, you'll have no problem in my courtroom as long as you tell the truth." That was what the judge said two weeks ago and I remembered.

Mr. Klecko was coming back, followed by a line of people. It was the jury. They saw me standing by the flag. Mr. Gorman winked at me from his table. Why didn't he do something?

I saw Howard. He was sitting between Mr. Mansfield and the other lawyer. I didn't want to look. I didn't want to look at anybody. I wished mother was there. And father. I hadn't wanted them to hear me. That was dumb. I wished she was there. I wished she was right beside me.

I had to save father. I had to keep my secret. I had to do everything perfect. I had to follow the rules.

"How we doin'?" Mr. Klecko asked. The jury people were standing in front of their chairs.

"Fine," I said.

Mr. Klecko picked up a wood hammer. Three times he pounded it. "Everyone please rise," he said. The jury people were already standing. Mr. Gorman, the spectators and everyone else stood up. They were looking at me. I was standing underneath the bench. It was too tall to see the judge but he was up there somewhere.

"The Court of Common Pleas for the County of Franklin, State of Ohio, is now in session." Mr. Klecko shouted like the master of ceremonies at Circus World in Florida.

I was surprised by another bang. It came like a firecracker from up where the judge was. "Please be seated." It was the judge's voice. The jury people sat. They were still staring at me.

Mr. Klecko nudged me on the shoulder. "Come with me," he whispered. He might of said that before he nudged me but I was thinking about what I told Dr. Hartenfells.

I had seen Dr. Hartenfells through the glass in that room where Sergeant Lutz took me, the room where I sat and talked to mother and father this morning. Why was Dr. Hartenfells at the courthouse?

I walked beside Mr. Klecko, out into the middle. I could

see the judge's head from his glasses up. His bench was taller than me. The lawyers and Howard were behind me and the spectators behind them.

Mr. Klecko asked me to raise my hand. He touched the one. "Do you solemnly swear that the testimony you are about to give will be the truth, the whole truth and nothing but the truth, so help you God?" His voice was loud, like he was talking to everyone and not me.

I swallowed. Mr. Klecko was looking at me. Everyone else too.

I nodded.

"You will have to say yes," said the judge. "So that the lady with the machine can record your answer." The judge had leaned forward. I saw his face, the collar of his shirt and the top of his robe. He was smiling. I looked up at him and said, "Yes."

"Very well," he said. "Please take your seat in the witness box."

Mr. Klecko put the booster on the chair. He helped me get on it.

I looked at the judge's rimless glasses so I didn't have to watch the jury people who were straight across from me. I didn't look at Howard either but I couldn't help seeing him when I checked to see what Mr. Gorman was doing.

Mr. Gorman was standing. He walked toward me and put his hand on the shelf in front of me. He smiled like everything was perfect. There was a glass of water on the shelf which I could drink if I got thirsty.

"Now, Charles," said Mr. Gorman. "I'm going to stand over there." He pointed to the end of the jury box. "I want you to speak nice and loud so we can all hear. I want you to look at me. Okay?"

I nodded.

He walked to that place. I remembered I was supposed to say yes instead of nod, but nobody corrected me.

When I looked at him, I had to see the jury people. Lots of them smiled. I smiled back and their smiles got wider. Also I couldn't help seeing Howard. He was looking down at the table in front of him. He was wearing a blue tie.

"Tell us your name?" Mr. Gorman asked.

"Charles Bateman King."

"Where do you live?"

"Two thousand seven hundred Country Club Way."

Mr. Gorman asked the easy questions. All I saw was his face and his mouth moving. If I watched him I didn't have to see the jury people or Howard or Mr. Mansfield or the spectators.

"Do you know Howard Landis?" he asked.

"Yes."

"Do you see Howard in the courtroom?"

"Yes." I looked quick to make sure.

"Where is he?"

I looked at Howard. "He's sitting between his lawyers," I said. "Right there." I pointed at him and looked back at Mr. Gorman. I saw Dr. and Mrs. Landis too. They were over by the wall, under the clock. It hadn't been so hard to point to Howard as I thought. But I had to do it once more.

Mr. Gorman asked the questions we practiced. He asked about Howard babysitting, the games we played, Nintendo, horsey-ride, monster, the pictures Howard took of me. I told what his camera looked like. It was a Polaroid One Step Flash. I was able to answer and keep my voice loud.

"Do you remember when Dr. Owen Merwin examined you and found sore places?" he asked.

"Yes." Five more questions to go.

"How did you get those sore places?"

I knew what I was supposed to say. This was the important part. Then I was supposed to look at Howard and point at him again. The water glass fell off my shelf. It broke. I must of accidentally hit it. Mr. Klecko was coming

238

toward me. I stared at the shelf where the glass was. I thought the judge said something but I wasn't sure. It was as quiet as when I came that Sunday.

"Charles." I heard my name. Mr. Gorman had said it. "Did you hear my question?" he asked.

I shook my head.

"I want you to tell us how you got your sore places," he said.

Mr. Gorman was standing beside me. I was crying and shaking. I didn't know what happened or what I had said. Mr. Gorman put his hand on my shoulder. "It doesn't matter that you spilled the water glass," he said. I saw Mr. Klecko taking the pieces away in a dustpan.

"I'm sorry," I said.

"We only have a few more questions," he said.

"I know," I said. "Five more." I remembered that. I had been telling myself, five more to go. It was still quiet. Mr. Gorman hadn't liked me saying how many more questions. He was smiling but a bad look had passed through his eyes.

"Can you tell us how you got the sore places on your bottom?" he asked.

"Howard," I said. I had to make up to Mr. Gorman for my mistakes. Four more to go.

"What did Howard do?"

"Touched my bottom."

"Did he touch it hard or easy?"

"Hard."

"Did it hurt?"

"Yes." There was only one more. Mr. Gorman stayed standing beside me. I could look at him without seeing the jury people. I didn't have to talk loud because it was so quiet.

"Is the person who hurt you in the courtroom?"

"He's sitting over there," I pointed to Howard. Howard

looked at me. He was pretty far away but he seemed more afraid than mad. "You did it, Howard," I said.

Mr. Gorman touched my shoulder. He didn't like me saying we had five more questions but I think he was pleased by how I did after that.

"You may cross-examine," he said.

Mr. Mansfield got up slowly. During those last questions, since the glass fell and broke, I had forgot Mr. Mansfield would be allowed to ask questions. I was thinking too hard about doing it right and how many questions to go. Mr. Mansfield walked up to me and put both hands on the shelf. He stared at me. Only he didn't say anything. He just looked at me. Then he turned and walked away. He knew about me telling Dr. Hartenfells I lied.

"Charles," he said. "You'd rather not be here, wouldn't you?" He sounded friendly and he smiled. But I knew what he was going to ask. He was going to ask why I didn't want to be here.

"It's a strenuous challenge, but I want to be here," I said.

The jury people were looking funny at me. They weren't smiling. They knew I just lied, but I had to.

"That answer doesn't sound like the eight-year-olds I know," he said.

"Object," shouted Mr. Gorman. I had forgot Mr. Gorman was still here.

"Sustained." The judge's voice from on top of me was a surprise.

"I know lots of words," I said. "I have been keeping a vocabulary notebook for three years." I didn't look to see who laughed. But there were several. I hadn't said anything funny.

"Charles." Mr. Gorman sounded like mother got when she criticized me during evaluation time. "When the judge says sustained that means you don't have to say anything until another question is asked."

I felt my face get red. Mr. Gorman had told me that lots of times. "I'm sorry," I said. "I forgot that rule."

"I'll take account of the age of the witness and give a better instruction when I make rulings." The judge leaned forward. He was smiling down at me. He wasn't mad at my breaking the rule.

"Since you know words, do you know what the word *rehearse* means?" asked Mr. Mansfield.

"Yes," I said. "It's what you do when you are in a play or play an instrument. Like my sister Vivian rehearses her violin two hours every day even on vacation."

"Very good, Charles." Mr. Mansfield was looking at the floor and walking across in front of the jury people. "Did you and Mr. Gorman . . ." He stopped to look at Mr. Gorman. Then he stood in front of Mr. Gorman so I couldn't see him. "Did you and Mr. Gorman rehearse the answers you gave here this morning?" he asked.

"Was that against the rules?" I asked back.

I saw some of the jury people smiled. I felt wet in my pants. I thought I had peed.

"You did rehearse with Mr. Gorman?"

"Yes, we did, so many times I can't remember them all."

"That's how you knew when there were only five questions left to answer."

I nodded, then remembered to say, "Yes."

Mr. Mansfield was pulling one of those dolls out of a huge bag. "Have you seen this before?" He walked toward me, carrying the doll, the one with the enormous weewee.

I nodded.

"It belongs to Dr. Hartenfells, doesn't it?"

"Yes."

"Did you get mad at this doll and kick it?" he asked.

I didn't know what to say. I hadn't got mad at the doll. I got mad at Dr. Hartenfells for making me answer questions.

"Charles," he said. He had that doll in front of me. Part of it was touching my shelf. "Why did you kick this doll?"

"I don't remember."

"I see," he said. "Do you remember telling Dr. Hartenfells you lied about saying Howard hurt you?"

"Father never did anything to me," I said. "Father would never hurt me."

He took the doll away. He put it on his table. He was looking at the jury people. Why didn't anyone say something? I wanted to get away from there.

"Did you think I asked a question about your father?" he asked.

"Yes," I said. "You're trying to get father in trouble."

"How could I do that?" he asked.

I didn't want to answer. I looked at Mr. Gorman, then up at the judge.

"Son, you must answer the question." The judge wasn't friendly to me like before.

"I don't know," I said.

"You love your father?" asked Mr. Mansfield, looking at me.

"Yes."

"You don't want him to get in trouble?"

I shook my head. They didn't make me say the answer. Mr. Gorman wouldn't look at me. He wouldn't help me.

"Charles, did you admit to Dr. Hartenfells that you lied about Howard Landis?"

Everyone was looking at me. They all knew. I couldn't do it. I saw those dolls and Howard and the judge and Dr. Landis. "Please," I said.

"Please what?" Mr. Mansfield asked.

"Please don't."

"You said you wanted to be here, to answer questions. You said something about a strenuous challenge."

I didn't answer.

242

"What is the strenuous challenge?" he asked.

I couldn't keep looking at people. I couldn't help crying. I rubbed my eyes.

I heard the loud bang. When I looked, Mr. Gorman was standing in front of me. "Is it over?" I asked.

"It will be pretty soon," he said.

"I don't want any more questions," I said. My pants were wet. Mr. Mansfield was watching and he was close enough he could hear us.

"Can I see mother?" I asked.

Mr. Gorman nodded. He lifted me out of my seat and put his arm around me. We walked to the same door I came in through. We went into that small room and Mr. Gorman pulled the curtains. Sergeant Lutz stood like a guard by the door.

"Now listen carefully," said Mr. Gorman. He sat me on the table and pulled up a chair. I was higher than him. "You've only got to answer a few more questions," he said.

"I can't," I said. "He knows I lied."

"It doesn't matter," said Mr. Gorman.

"Is it all right to say I lied?"

"Yes," he said. "Anything you say will be fine."

"Anything about anything?"

"Yes," he told me.

"But won't that hurt father?"

He shook his head. Why was he lying to me? Why did everyone lie?

"I'm more scared than I've ever been," I said.

"Good," he said. "Isn't that why you told Dr. Hartenfells different things?"

I nodded.

"You told her things because you didn't want to come to court."

I nodded.

"If you say that you are telling the truth, aren't you?"

243

"I think so," I said.

"Good." He slapped my leg. "That's what you say. You say you tried to get out of coming to court because you were scared."

"But I said in there I wanted to be in court."

"It doesn't matter," he said. "Don't worry about anything you said."

The door opened. It was mother and father. Father picked me up and hugged me. Mother had been crying. I could tell from her face.

"He's doing well," Mr. Gorman told them.

"Do I have to go back in there?" I asked. Mother didn't answer. She was looking at Mr. Gorman. So was father.

"I can talk to the judge," said Mr. Gorman. "But I would like to see Charles try again."

"What about it, Charles?" asked father. "Can you try one more time?"

They wanted me to do it. I saw how important it was to them. Specially father. When I said I would, father hugged me again.

THE jury people were sitting in there, waiting for me. So was Howard, Mr. Mansfield, the judge and thousands of spectators. Mr. Klecko helped me climb on the booster in the witness box.

"Charles, do you sleep in your underwear?" Mr. Mansfield was staying in his chair. That meant I had to look at Howard. Also I had to talk louder.

"No," I said. "I sleep in my jammies."

"You don't wear undies under your jammies?"

I shook my head.

"After your tubby bath, is that when you usually put your jammies on?"

"Yes." I was glad he'd stopped asking about lies and about father.

244

"Were there other times Howard saw you without your clothes?" he asked. "Or was it just when he helped you with your tubby bath?"

It was hard to think. So many people were staring at me. "It was only when he gave me a tubby bath," I said.

He was going to a table behind Mr. Klecko's desk. He got a sack. He put his hand in the sack. He had those undies, the ones with blood on them, the ones I hid and mother found.

"If Howard hurt you when he gave you a tubby bath," he said, "why wasn't there blood on your jammies instead of here on these undies?"

"I don't know," I said. Howard was staring at me, smiling a little, like he was glad to see how scared I was.

"You were telling the truth when you told Dr. Hartenfells you lied about Howard, weren't you?"

"I don't know," I said.

"Did you blame Howard in order to protect someone else?"

"I don't know."

"Who are you protecting, Charles?"

"I hate you. You aren't fair. I hate you and I hate Howard and I hate Dr. Hartenfells."

I heard Mr. Gorman shouting. I heard the judge. I heard noises from everywhere. I put my hands over my ears and put my head down on the shelf in front of me.

21

It was an obvious point to have missed, how blood got on the underpants when the kid was saying he'd been reamed after his nighttime bath. And then the kid sitting there, mumbling the word *father* over and over, jerking his head, looking around the courtroom as if he were being abducted, not hearing the judge or knowing where he was, dropping his head, crying into his hands. If it had been an adult, the case would be destroyed.

But the jurors seemed to be on his side. The machinist glared at Mansfield. The teacher looked ready to go to the kid, cuddle him. Two jurors had handkerchiefs in their eyes, another reacted with disgust at seeing Howard Landis smirk. One hundred percent pure, grade-A hate. At the door, the two secretaries looked back as Shorty Klecko herded the jurors out and down to the jurors' lounge. If they could, those two would give Howard Landis a death sentence. Clay was less sure of Judge Van Horn. Gaveling the courtroom to order to declare a recess, the judge had stared at the kid with the hard eye he laid on a defendant when about to impose sentence.

Clay needed to take a leak. The judge waved him into the private bathroom. The judge had his robe off and a cup of coffee in hand. A lawyer was in chambers with an entry to be signed.

"I'm playing Muirfield tomorrow," the judge told the lawyer. "Let's hope the weather holds."

"How you hittin 'em?" the lawyer asked.

Clay closed the bathroom door. The kid was unscrewed. But Dr. Hartenfells would be able to explain, probably turn the kid's collapse into support for her opinions. As a rebuttal witness she could explain that retraction was the last of five stages of a child victim's response to sex abuse. Clay flushed the toilet and came out.

"Your Honor," Clay began. "We may want to complete the examination of this witness on video tape. *Maryland* versus *Craig* gives us the authority to do that. This boy simply cannot face his molester in a public courtroom."

"The problem isn't his molester," said Mansfield. "It's being exposed as a little liar."

"Clay," said the judge. "I don't know if I can allow a switch in the middle of a trial. I'll consider it."

Maybe Van Horn hadn't turned against the kid. Clay didn't want to shift to video anyhow. At this point, the effect on the jury could hurt.

"I think Dr. Hartenfells should talk to the boy," said Clay. "We would like her input on how best to proceed."

"Ha-ha-ha," Mansfield brayed. The judge wanted to know if the psychiatrist would be used further as a witness.

"Probably," said Clay.

"I don't know," said the judge. "The boy's on the stand." The judge spun a mounted silver dollar that someone had given him as a joke to decide cases, one of many trinkets and mementos on his desk.

Shorty Klecko, red-faced, breathing hard, came in. "Mr. and Mrs. King are in with the boy," said Klecko.

"There's nothing wrong with that," said Clay.

"Sergeant Lutz sent me for Mr. Gorman," said Klecko. The way Shorty looked at Judge Van Horn indicated there was more than he was able to say.

Judge Van Horn walked to his window. He stood, looking down at the street and straightening his tie. "Clay, you talk to those people," he said.

"They want the case dismissed," Shorty Klecko whispered as soon as Clay stepped into the corridor. When Clay opened the door to the small room, he found Charles cradled in his mother's lap. Charles, with dead eyes, looked at Clay. Stewart King stood behind his wife with his arms folded in front of his jacket.

"It isn't worth it," said Mrs. King. "I didn't realize."

"Charles may not have to go back in." Clay was playing for time.

"How?" asked Stewart. "The cross-examination isn't finished."

"Mr. Gorman," said Mrs. King. "You have no appreciation of how I feel."

"We'll consider your feelings, but—"

"Mr. Gorman. I want the case dismissed."

You couldn't push. But Clay asked the questions. Were

248

they comfortable with letting Howard Landis off? Would it be any better for Charles in school? When he saw Howard in the yard? Wouldn't they like to consult Dr. Hartenfells? Dr. Dean? Maybe someone else?

Stewart King had said nothing. But he eyed Clay critically, a firm-jawed executive, skeptical, analyzing a business proposition. "I'll talk to the judge," said Clay.

Mrs. King nodded.

Clay needed help from the judge. But Clay was not going to dismiss. The choice was not Barbara King's. Clay could win with Hartenfells. Without the kid. In fact, Clay regretted having mentioned the possibility of continuing on video.

In chambers, Clay told the judge and Mansfield what the Kings wanted to do.

"I think I can persuade my clients to drop their claims," said Mansfield.

"What claims?" asked the judge.

"Malicious prosecution. Libel, slander." Mansfield helped himself to a coffee refill.

Clay glared at Mansfield. "I hope you can stand yourself when you look in the mirror," he said.

"Relax, Clay," said Mansfield. "This isn't the only case you'll ever try."

"I saw what you did to that boy in chambers before he went in. There's a kid across the hall who's been molested."

"But by whom?" asked Mansfield. "That's what we don't know."

"We know," said Clay. "But what makes me boil is that you're the guy who twisted the knife."

"Save it for the jury." Mansfield ripped the tops off of two packets of Sweet 'n' Low. He tapped the contents into his coffee.

Judge Van Horn watched the exchange from behind his

desk, expressionless, as if his mind were playing a treacherous hole at Muirfield. Mansfield walked in front of Clay to toss his Sweet 'n' Low wrappers in the waste basket.

Clay swallowed his pride, asked Mansfield if a plea could be worked out.

Mansfield chuckled. "Nice try, Clay," he said.

"Judge, we need some time," said Clay. "Let me talk to the Kings."

"I object," said Mansfield. "The state isn't entitled to this indulgence. The trial should go forward."

"No," said the judge. "I think we'll handle this a bit differently."

"How?" Clay and Mansfield asked the question together.

"I'm going to talk with the boy," said the judge.

"Clay and I will be present, of course," said Mansfield.

"No, sir," said the judge. "Just me and the boy."

Mansfield objected. He spouted reasons to the court stenographer. "At least the court stenographer must make a record of the conversation," said Mansfield. "It could be sealed and opened if necessary on appeal."

The judge shook his head.

Clay didn't like what the judge was doing either. But he said nothing.

"With all due respect," said Mansfield. "This is outrageous."

"The court has its responsibilities as well as counsel." It was all the explanation Judge Van Horn gave.

"Shall I bring Charles in?" asked Clay.

"No," said the judge. "Let's have Shorty do that, after he sends the jury out for lunch."

When Klecko left, the judge shooed Clay and Mansfield out. "I'd like a few minutes to myself," he said.

It was quarter to twelve. Judge Van Horn suggested that counsel have lunch, return at one-thirty.

Klecko came out of the small room, holding Charles by the hand. Charles saw Clay, but his eyes were as dead as before. The kid had his mother's hanky clutched in his other hand.

22

CLAY FOUND FRED Lutz outside the small room where Charles had been with his parents before being taken into Judge Van Horn's chambers. "I want to talk to the Kings," said Clay.

"Good luck," said Lutz.

"What's the problem?" asked Clay.

"They're not speaking. He blames her and she thinks he should be with the judge and Charles, using the weight of his law firm, pushing his so-called friendship with Van Horn."

Clay opened the door. Mrs. King sat, her chair turned away from the table, facing the still life of fruit. Stewart stood beside the table, his arms folded. Both had looked to see who opened the door.

"Mr. Gorman, I can't believe this is happening," she said.

"Can I speak with you privately?" asked Stewart.

"Why don't we all get a bite to eat?" said Clay. "We've got a problem and I'd like you both to talk with Frances Hartenfells. She needs to be part of the solution."

"I am not leaving this room until Charles returns," said Mrs. King. "I want this case dropped."

"You may not be doing the best thing for Charles," said Clay.

"You care?" Mrs. King's eyes blazed.

"You can't reason with her," said Stewart.

"Frances Hartenfells has been through these situations," said Clay. "It is never easy. But the kids who hang in there come out better."

"Mr. Gorman," she said, "your interest is in winning a case. Don't insult me by pretending otherwise."

"I am interested in seeing a child molester stopped," said Clay. "I also want to make this as painless for Charles as possible."

"Painless!" She shrieked the word. This was not Barbara King of Country Club Way. There was a smudge in the makeup at the corner of her eye. Her strand of pearls was caught on the collar of her blouse. "Mr. Gorman, we have nothing to discuss until my lawyer arrives." She spoke slowly and softly, as if to re-establish her composure.

"Fine," said Clay. "I'll check back later."

FRANCES Hartenfells was waiting in the prosecutor's office on the fourth floor. The problem of no blood on the pajamas caused Hartenfells no concern. "It isn't important," she said. "We don't know exactly when or how or how

253

many times the boy was abused. We may never know precise details. The experience was too traumatic. It is smothered in guilt. What is clear is that Charles is telling the truth when he says Howard hurt him. Everything that has happened adds confirmation."

Hartenfells seemed eager to take on Mansfield in front of the jury, to explain the boy's collapse. Unconsciously mouthing the word *father* was a cry for help, she said. Yes, the boy was protecting someone. He was protecting himself.

"But what if Charles can't go back?" asked Clay. "The kid is in bad shape. His mother isn't helping. The cross-examination isn't over. I don't know what Judge Van Horn will do."

Hartenfells smiled. "The judge is your problem," she said. "But I'll talk to Barbara King. I like her."

"So," said Clay, "I do, too. At least I thought I did."

"No, you didn't," said Hartenfells. "You only thought she was your ally."

"It doesn't matter," said Clay.

"I think," said Hartenfells, "that Mrs. King has no motive other than the best interest of Charles. She wasn't prepared for what an eight-year-old must face in one of these." Hartenfells brushed a loose hair into place. "You and the judge . . . and her husband are making it impossible for Mrs. King."

Hartenfells left in search of Barbara King. If the judge could be persuaded, Clay was thinking, it might work out better if Charles didn't return to the witness stand. Hartenfells would pick up the pieces as a rebuttal witness. Clay's case was solid.

"GET the court reporter," said Judge Van Horn. "I want this on the record."

Mansfield sat on the judge's couch, fingering and then

chewing an unlit cigar, not saying much, waiting along with Clay to hear from the judge.

The boy, along with his mother, Dr. Hartenfells and Sergeant Lutz had been taken to Riverside Hospital. Dr. Merwin would meet them there. The boy had thrown up. He was running a fever. "He's a basket case," Judge Van Horn reported. Beyond that the judge wasn't telling what had happened in chambers.

The summons to Judge Van Horn's chambers had come to Clay's office at 12:45. When he got there, Shorty Klecko told him Charles had been taken to the hospital ten minutes ago. The judge and the kid would have had fifteen, maybe twenty minutes together.

The jury, according to Klecko, had not been sent home. Jurors were in the lounge, watching television, working crossword puzzles, reading magazines or the newspaper, from which the page-nine story, "Landis Trial Nears End of Second Week," had been cut out.

"You boys," said the judge, "are going to spend some time in the books this weekend."

Balancing his yellow pad on his leg, Clay made notes. The judge had asked Dr. Russell Rothermich to examine Charles. Rothermich, a professor of clinical psychiatry at the Ohio State medical school, was en route to the hospital. "I want to know whether the boy is capable of returning to the courtroom," said the judge. "If he is, I want to know when."

"Will Dr. Rothermich question Charles about the abuse?" asked Clay.

"That's not the purpose," said the judge. "But if Dr. Rothermich acquires relevant information, he will be available as a witness—for the state or for the defense."

"Send the jury home," the judge told Shorty. "Have them back at nine on Monday."

A lot could happen over the weekend. Still, this felt like a reprieve. It gave Clay time. It could also mean that the judge was thinking of going forward without Charles.

The judge was considering five options. Resume on Monday with Charles back on the stand. Let Charles finish on video tape. Resume the trial but excuse Charles from further examination.

"You can't," Mansfield interrupted. "That makes a mockery out of the sixth amendment."

"I don't know what I can or can't do," said the judge. "We'll all be burning a little midnight oil this weekend."

Option number four was to strike the boy's testimony, instruct the jury to disregard everything the boy had said and go forward with the trial.

"With all due respect," said Mansfield, "that one is absurd."

Judge Van Horn smiled. Mansfield was rolling his cigar in his mouth, biting into the tip, as uneasy as Clay. But the judge was feeling none of the tension. Behind rimless glasses, his eyes were alive. He outlined the arguments and counterarguments to the options. "This one may end up in the big court in Washington," he said.

His last option was to declare a mistrial, set a new date in November and start over.

"That's the only way to go," said Mansfield. "After what's happened, there is no way my client can get a fair trial with this jury."

"Would you waive a claim of double jeopardy?" asked Clay. Clay hated retrials but it was something he had to consider.

"We can't answer that," said Mansfield. "I'm not sure jeopardy has attached."

"Maybe not, but you don't mind trying to snow the court," said Clay.

The judge squelched the argument. He was more interested in the "complexities of these novel issues," which would be his to resolve.

"For the record," said Mansfield, "we renew our objection to the ex parte questioning by the court of the accusing witness. At least we are entitled to have you summarize what was said."

"I'll take that under advisement." The judge smiled.

"We need to know, at least in general," pressed Mansfield, "to preserve our rights on appeal."

"You have made your record," said Van Horn. The smile seemed mirthful, as if the judge relished the game.

Van Horn sent Shorty Klecko to get his law clerk, a young lawyer the judge shared with three others on the common pleas bench. The judge wanted his clerk to get cracking. Issues of "big-court-in-Washington" dimension would not keep the judge from his Saturday round at Muirfield.

STEWART King stood by the window, looking at the Riverside Hospital complex from Dr. Owen Merwin's office in the medical building. His wife sat, twisted to face the door, listening to Dr. Rothermich with her back to the others in the office. Neither of the Kings had spoken since Clay came in.

Charles was in the hospital in a private room on the seventh floor, paying no attention to the game between the Bengals and the Houston Oilers which his private-duty nurse was watching on television. Lutz, who had been in the kid's room until Clay came, would check on Charles if the meeting dragged. The kid was running a temperature of 104 degrees, had been delirious, mumbling incoherently until drugged to sleep. "A nasty virus," according to Owen Merwin. It could go into pneumonia. "It probably took hold faster and hit him harder because of the strain he's been under."

The meeting was the result of a call from Judge Van Horn. Mansfield would get his interview with Dr. Russell Rothermich tonight.

Dr. Rothermich was holding forth, his phrases emphasized by puffs on his pipe. The smoke spread in front of him, leaving a haze over the Thank You for Not Smoking sign on Merwin's desk. As it spread, the smoke glinted in the slant of late afternoon sun, but Barbara King had voiced no objection.

"The boy has repressed memory of the time he spent in the courtroom. He is incapable of answering questions directed to the abuse he suffered." Rothermich sucked on his pipe stem, held the smoke and let it out. He was at ease, wearing no tie, his tweed jacket patched at the elbows. "For these purposes," said the doctor, "I assume the existence of an abuse."

Barbara King turned to look at Rothermich.

"Don't misunderstand," said Rothermich. "My assignment was to assess your son's ability to continue functioning as a witness. Judge Van Horn described the boy to me as a basket case. The description fits."

Rothermich detailed his findings, how Charles had responded with silence and blank expression to questions about the trial, how Charles mumbled "I don't remember," when asked about damage to his anus or when the question mentioned Howard Landis. Toward the end of the interview, Charles had not spoken other than to moan or call for his mother. Rothermich demonstrated a flapping movement with his arms and hands extended, a movement Charles made when he talked.

"The boy is not feigning," said Rothermich. "He has suffered a localized and somewhat irregular amnesia. Much material is being repressed."

"But it is part of his unconscious," said Hartenfells.

"Of course," said Rothermich.

Mrs. King coughed and fanned away the fringe of smoke which had reached her. Hartenfells asked Rothermich to extinguish his pipe, which he did, taking pains to scrape the bowl and clean the stem before fitting the pipe behind a maroon handkerchief which protruded from his jacket pocket.

"Unconscious material is the source of complexes," said Hartenfells. "It must be dealt with or it becomes destructive, perhaps psychosis-producing."

Dr. Rothermich pushed his shell-rim glasses up his nose, let his fingers drop to his chin and contemplated his colleague. "Treatment is indicated," he said. "I do not regard the courtroom as part of the cure."

"Nor do I." Hartenfells looked at Rothermich as though he were a slow learner.

The dislike Hartenfells and Rothermich felt for each other was hardening. Maybe they came from different schools of psychology. More likely, Clay suspected, Rothermich resented the gender of his colleague and Hartenfells knew it.

"Let me put this simply," said Rothermich. "With or without Charles—whether the trial continues next week or is started anew a year from now—I believe the continuation of court proceedings will do Charles grave psychological harm." Rothermich raised his arm, as if his pipe were still in his hand. "I further believe," he said, "that the boy is deeply disturbed."

"It seems to me," said Hartenfells, "that you are offering opinions beyond those requested of you by Judge Van Horn."

As the argument went on, Clay's thoughts drifted to the research he had done before coming to the hospital. There were arguments for letting the trial go forward without Charles. Dr. Rothermich's diagnosis of the boy's present condition could be helpful.

The bickering between the psychiatrists was wasting time. Everyone agreed that Charles could not return to the stand on Monday.

Judge Van Horn was the problem: how to persuade him to continue the trial without further participation by Charles. Clay was chafing to get into the law library and finish his research, because there would be no second chance if the judge declared a mistrial. Barbara King would never allow Charles to go through another trial.

"Please, doctor." Rothermich raised his hand. "I don't believe you have been listening."

"I'm listening," said Hartenfells. "I don't like some of what I've been hearing."

"Let me listen to you, then." Rothermich smiled.

"A stranger doesn't ask an abused child questions without building rapport," said Hartenfells. "It took me nearly two months to reach the place where Charles and I could explore the violation he suffered. Even now, almost a year later, Charles and I haven't gotten to the bottom of it. Here you confront the boy in the midst of a traumatic trial."

"That would seem," said Rothermich, "to confirm my point."

"The point is that you have not seen Charles long enough or in the proper setting. Your diagnosis strikes me as hastily formed."

Barbara King had again turned toward the door. During the squabble between the psychiatrists, it seemed to Clay that she was not listening, that her pain had taken her away from Dr. Merwin's office. Abruptly, interrupting Dr. Rothermich's response, she stood.

She walked in front of Dr. Merwin's desk to join her husband at the window. "Stewart, have you been listening?" she asked.

Stewart nodded, but kept looking out the window, as he had for the past hour.

"What do you think?" she asked him. She did not touch him. Clay couldn't tell whether she was asking a question or making an accusation.

"You and the doctors decide," said Stewart. "This has been your show from the start."

Barbara King stood, looking at the side of his face. She had winced, hearing his answer. She waited to see if he would say more. Her eyes wet, she looked at Frances Hartenfells. "Doesn't Charles pay a price if Stewart and I keep fighting?" she asked.

"You mustn't be so hard on yourself," said Hartenfells. Rothermich and Merwin nodded their agreement.

"I am going back to be with Charles," said Mrs. King. She left. Stewart followed her.

CLAY and Lutz set their trays at the end of a table next to the windows. The hospital cafeteria was a cheery, high-ceiling room with tables of orange-red, blue and yellow gleaming under fluorescent lights. It was Sunday night, not crowded, and they were able to find a place where there'd be no eavesdroppers.

"Jesus Christ," said Lutz. "I've been through a lot of shit, people coming apart during interrogation, finding bodies— one that was stuffed in a storage locker for over a week. I had to tell a mother her kid was burned to death in a fire. Like I say, lots of shit." He kept shaking his head. "But that bit up in the doctor's office . . . Jesus Christ, Clay, my skin is crawling."

"I think we can still make the charge," said Clay.

An elderly couple with trays in hand were moving toward them, eyeing seats at their table though the cafeteria was huge and nearly empty. Clay stared at the pair and they changed course. Clay lowered his voice. "I found a case," he said, "where a witness died in the midst of cross-examination. In that case, the trial judge let the testimony stand. That decision was affirmed on appeal. I don't want a mistrial. We've got them beat no matter what Mansfield does."

"It's not the goddamn trial," said Lutz. "I'm thinking of the kid."

"He'll be okay," said Clay. "After this is over, the kid can get back to . . . look, he's eight years old and he was doing all right before this happened. He's bright. There's money. The shrinks will pull him out."

"Yeah," said Lutz. "You weren't in the room with him. If they hadn't knocked him out with drugs, he'd have gone berserk when his mother left."

"She's back there now," said Clay. "She is telling him he won't have to go back in the courtroom."

"Yeah," said Lutz.

"Look," said Clay. "Therapy isn't our job. Leave that to those who are qualified. Our job is to convict a molester." Clay buried his hashbrowns in ketchup and took a forkful. He was hungry.

Lutz would not be put off. The kid was convinced his father had been taken to jail. Once, when a nurse went by in the hall, the kid had mistaken the rattle of her cart for shots from an automatic riffle. The kid wanted his mother in bed with him. Once the kid asked if he would be allowed to visit his father in jail. Then when the drugs were taking effect and he was drifting to sleep the kid suddenly sat up in bed and stared at the cover on his feet as if it were some wild animal.

"You're not listening," said Lutz.

"I am," said Clay, "but I'm wondering if I should call the judge. Or wait until tomorrow morning in chambers."

"You want my pie?" asked Lutz. "My appetite's not as good as yours."

"I'm going down to the office," said Clay. "There's no

need for you to hang around the kid tonight. Take the night off."

JUDGE Van Horn was hard to predict. Sometimes he seemed eager to talk to one side without opposing counsel being present. At other times he went into an ethical snit, angry with the assumption that he would consider an ex parte communication.

At ten, Clay decided to risk it. He had his legal authorities lined up. The judge answered the phone himself. "Clay," he said, sounding cheerful. "Dr. Rothermich just left the house. I asked him to drop by after he met with your adversary."

"I've come up with some pretty good law," said Clay. "I wonder if we could get Mansfield, meet with you in chambers a hour early tomorrow morning."

"We could do that," said the judge. "But I'm fairly well convinced I should declare a mistrial."

The problem was more serious than ethics. The judge had made up his mind.

"If it's a mistrial," said Clay, "it's double jeopardy."

"No," said the judge. "I'll make Bart waive his claim of jeopardy."

"Howard Landis will walk," said Clay. "We can't put the King family through another trial."

"I don't make the facts, Clay. The King boy can't go on. Even Mansfield isn't fighting Rothermich's findings. At least not very hard."

"Of course not," said Clay. "Mansfield wants a mistrial." Clay was kicking himself for waiting to make the call. Mansfield had gotten to the judge first.

The judge did not respond. Clay felt awkward. The whine on the phone sounded like the judge was whistling through his teeth. Clay waited.

"I don't know what to make of the boy," said the judge.

Quickly, Van Horn told what had happened in chambers. "I'm not even sure he heard me. He just sat there, staring at me." Van Horn thought Clay should negotiate a plea for one count of gross sexual imposition and one count of corruption of a minor. "Make Mansfield take one year of actual incarceration."

"He won't buy it," said Clay.

"I think he might," said the judge.

"What do you know?"

"Come in tomorrow morning," said the judge. "Tell Mansfield to be there an hour early. You can reach Mansfield at his office if you call now." The son of a bitch gave Clay the number for Mansfield's private line.

"By the way," said the judge. "Don't assume that I told Mansfield I think I have to declare a mistrial." The judge chuckled and hung up.

MANSFIELD had laughed too when Clay proposed a guilty plea and two years actual incarceration.

"We have Landis on corruption and on gross sexual imposition without Charles King's testimony," said Clay.

"Prove it in court," Mansfield replied.

MANSFIELD put two packets of Sweet 'n' Low in his coffee. He talked about Ohio State's big win over Oklahoma. He asked the court stenographer how her son was faring on his high school cross-country team. They were waiting for Judge Van Horn to arrive. Mansfield was posturing. He was nervous, less cocky than last night on the phone.

"Sorry to keep you waiting," the judge said, hanging his coat on a hook inside the door to his private toilet. The judge lectured them on the inadequacies of the traffic arteries serving downtown Columbus, how that mess was going to hurt the mayor's gubernatorial ambition.

"Let's see your law," the judge finally said. He took inch-thick briefs from Clay and Mansfield. He asked everyone to leave his chambers so he could "focus."

In twenty minutes, hardly time enough to skim the two briefs, the judge summoned everyone back. Van Horn had Clay's brief in hand, with pages rolled under. The page now on top was marked by the judge's green high-liter.

"We get paid for making the tough calls." Van Horn, smiling broadly, looked at Mansfield first.

"I'm going to let the boy's testimony stand," said the judge. "I'm persuaded by Clay's authorities. Bart, you've had a substantial cross-examination."

"Substantial cross-examination isn't enough," said Mansfield.

"The situation is parallel to the one where a witness dies in the middle of a trial," said the judge.

Clay listened as Mansfield's arguments were rejected. Why don't I feel better, he wondered. He was getting what he wanted. The judge was going to bring Dr. Rothermich down to court, ask a few questions in chambers for the record. Dr. Rothermich would be open to cross-examination by Mansfield. Mansfield was fighting to stay in control. Whatever had been said between Mansfield and the judge last night, Mansfield now thought he was being sandbagged.

Judge Van Horn wanted to know if Clay was ready to rest the case for the prosecution.

"We need to ask Dr. Hartenfells a few more questions," said Clay.

"Well, get her down here," said the judge. "We're going to get this show on the road."

Claiming he had to ask Judge West to cover a probation revocation, the judge followed Clay to the room across the hall where Clay had planned to make phone calls.

"Cut your deal," said Van Horn.

"If I don't?" Clay put down the telephone receiver. "Are you going to make a different ruling?"

"That's my business," said the judge.

Get it wrapped up and get away. Get back to the office and into something new. Clay was sick of them all: Van Horn; Mansfield; sweaty Howard Landis; the shrinks; the parents; Fred Lutz, the cop with a squishy backbone; even the kid.

By noon it was done. Mansfield, despite his bravado about reversal on appeal, couldn't gamble on a twenty-year sentence.

SHORTY Klecko brought the jury up so the judge could thank them for their attention and willingness to serve. "By performing this duty, you have contributed importantly to the resolution of the case and to the cause of justice," Judge Van Horn told them from his bench. The jurors would receive Christmas cards from the judge and a solicitation from Van Horn's campaign committee when he ran for re-election in three years.

The jurors stared at Howard as the judge announced that the defendant's not-guilty plea had been withdrawn; that it had been changed to a guilty plea to a lesser charge; that the defendant would receive a jail sentence. Some jurors looked puzzled. Shorty Klecko would fill them in. The jurors filed out for the last time.

Except for Dr. and Mrs. Landis, a few reporters, a lawyer waiting to see Judge Van Horn and a handful of spectators, the gallery was empty when the judge asked Howard Landis to stand. "Do you wish to make a statement before sentence is pronounced?" The judge asked.

"The defendant waives the right to make a statement," Mansfield spoke for Howard, who nodded his agreement.

The judge imposed sentence of one year actual incarceration on each count, the sentences to run concurrently. He committed Howard to the custody of the county sheriff to be taken to the Franklin County jail where he would be held pending transfer to the State Correctional Institution.

"Your Honor," said Mansfield. "The defendant has been staying at home. I am fearful of the situation at the county jail. I would request that he remain at home until he is taken to the S.C.I."

"Your request is denied," Judge Van Horn swiveled in his chair and stood to leave.

"Your Honor," said Mansfield. "At least order him to be kept in segregation. You know what happens in the county jail to a nineteen-year-old convicted on a sex-abuse charge."

"Request denied." The judge disappeared through the door behind his bench.

Mansfield walked to Clay's table. "Jesus Christ," said Mansfield. "Can you help me, Clay? What difference do three more days at home mean?"

"That wasn't part of the deal," said Clay.

"I'm asking, Clay, as a personal favor."

"It won't be any worse for Howard than it was and is for Charles King."

Mansfield turned. Clay watched him move across the pit on his way to explain the situation to Dr. and Mrs. Landis who were standing under the courtroom clock. A deputy sheriff had snapped handcuffs on Howard and was taking him out.

THE next morning, Clay felt less jilted. He didn't need a verdict or a splash in the newspaper to tell him he'd tried a hell of a good case. Clay lingered over coffee with Sheila, watching an extra segment of "Good Morning, America." He and Sheila had blown a hundred dollars on dinner and wine. Afterward in bed, Clay realized how much he'd missed her.

On his way to the office, Clay got the news on his car radio. Howard Landis, the son of a prominent Columbus physician, had committed suicide last night, hanging himself by his belt from a water pipe in a cell at the Franklin County jail. Jesus. Clay no longer felt like going to work.

23

CHARLES KNOWS. BUT Charles is keeping his secrets. Howard killed himself because Charles lied. They didn't tell Charles Howard killed himself until Charles went home from the hospital.

Father is home, living in mother's house. Father came to see Charles every day in the hospital. Father will remain at mother's house forever. If Charles hadn't lied, father would not have come back.

If a nasty virus hadn't infected Charles, everyone would know that Charles lied. They would have made him tell his secret. The judge suspected Charles all along.

They tell Charles the trial is over, that the jury people have gone home and will never return. They are trying to trick Charles. They are using Dr. Hartenfells. She still asks Charles questions. They still want to make Charles tell his secret.

If they find out, Charles must go to jail. It will be worse than Rosewood. Because Howard got killed, they might fry Charles in the electric chair.

Charles must return to the third grade gifted section in the Canterbury School. If Charles does not return, or if Charles fails to accomplish his tasks, they will know.

The only person who can save Charles is mother.

CHARLES must go to school this morning. Charles feels sick but he isn't telling. In yesterday's weekly review, mother gave Charles only one assignment. Go to school and do the work assigned by Ms. Trawick. Charles must not let mother down.

Charles got up early, flossed and brushed his teeth, put on his plaid Canterbury school pants, remembered his belt, buttoned his white shirt and put a clean handkerchief in his pants pocket.

At breakfast, Charles ate toast with a runny egg. There was also bacon. Charles drank a tall glass of orange juice. Charles wasn't hungry but he made himself eat because mother was observing. Mother watched as she pretended to be interested in Vivian's excitement about a quartet of Professor Botti's most promising pupils which Vivian joins after school tomorrow afternoon.

Charles ate too much. If he vomits, mother will keep him at home. Mother would not rebuke Charles but she would be disappointed.

Charles puts on his Gore-tex parka and his mittens. He will carry his backpack containing books and school supplies. The mittens and jacket prevent mother knowing that

270

Charles has hot, sticky hands and that his chest is thumping. Charles leans against the island in the kitchen. Charles feels dizzy but the countertop keeps him steady. Charles would like to remove his parka. It is smothering him, choking him, making him feel like vomiting.

Mother yells for Vivian to hurry. Mother will take Vivian and Charles to school this week. After that we'll have to see about Charles rejoining the car pool.

"How do we feel?" asks mother, who smoothes down a flap on one of the parka pockets.

"Fine," says Charles.

It is early when they arrive at the Canterbury School but Ms. Trawick is in her room, expecting Charles and mother. This morning, Charles will not wait for the school bell on the playground with the other children. Ms. Trawick is delighted to have Charles back.

"You may be a little nervous," says Ms. Trawick, "but you will be fine. We have an interesting week planned."

"Charles is nervous but he will be fine because this will be an interesting week," says Charles.

Ms. Trawick looks peculiar. She tries to hide her look by walking Charles to the window to show him the new solar energy experiment. Ms. Trawick suspects Charles.

After hanging his Gore-tex parka in the cloakroom, Charles returns to the window. He watches children assemble on the playground. Mother and Ms. Trawick whisper in the far corner.

"Charles, I am going to leave now," says mother. She walks toward Charles.

Charles hears her coming but he keeps looking out the window. Mother pats Charles on the shoulder. She places her arm around him and squeezes. "I'll be waiting for you in the parking lot at three-fifteen," she says.

Charles keeps looking out the window. He sees Mitzy. Mitzy is waving at Charles. She is coming to the window.

"There's someone who is glad you're back," says mother. "It will be good to see your old friends."

Charles nods. His head is pounding so hard it would blow apart if he tried to talk.

"Bye-bye, sweetheart," says mother. She kisses Charles on his neck.

"We've rearranged our tables. Let me show you where yours is." Her hand is still on his shoulder but her voice has changed. Mitzy is making faces at the window. Suddenly Mitzy runs away, back to some children by the swing. Those children stop playing to look at Charles.

She has taken Charles by his arm and is leading him to a table. It isn't mother. Mother disappeared. It is Ms. Trawick who has Charles. How long has mother been gone? Charles sits in his chair at his desk and puts his backpack in front of him.

Charles wants to run. His legs won't move. He can't get up. He is dizzy. The room and posters and blackboard and windows are spinning.

"Your mother told me how hard you have worked to keep up while you were away." Ms. Trawick has both her hands on his shoulders. Hearing her voice made the room stop spinning. She knows that Charles is shaking, but she does not criticize. She rubs his back, across his shoulders. She will help Charles meet his challenge. Mother has assigned Ms. Trawick to protect Charles.

Charles pulls out the drawer to his table. His water color set, extra tablet, magic marker pencils and scissors are there. So is *Fascinating Footprints*, a book about fossils. "Charles forgot this," says Charles. He takes out the book. "It is overdue at the library," he says. The book is shaking in his hands.

Ms. Trawick reaches for the book. "Don't worry about that," she says. "I'll take care of it."

Charles lets go of the book. If he wants, Ms. Trawick will

arrange for Charles to keep the book longer. Charles shakes his head. He takes things out of his backpack and arranges them in his drawer. He folds his backpack and places it under the table, out of the way of his feet.

Ms. Trawick sits in the chair at the next table. She tells Charles what she has planned for today, starting with the pilgrims. Each month is a different part of history and she is doing pilgrims because Thanksgiving comes this Thursday. As mother stressed, this is merely a three-day week.

The bell clangs. Ms. Trawick goes to her desk. They are yelling, making commotion in the hall. Mitzy comes in first. They stare at Charles. Charles looks down.

"Hi, Charles. See, my table got moved. I'm sitting next to you." Mitzy pushes her chair in close.

"Why didn't you wave when I came to the window?" she asks.

Get away from here, Charles screams, only no one hears. All of them are crowding around, telling Charles they're glad he's back.

Ms. Trawick asks everyone to take their seats.

"We're going to start with a game this morning," says Ms. Trawick. "We will go around the room, each person telling the class something about the pilgrims which no one else has mentioned. If you can't think of anything when it is your turn, you are out of the game. This will be a nice review for Charles. Now, let's start with Heather. We'll let the winner of our game take our pilgrim stockade and our pilgrim people home on Thanksgiving."

"Home to keep?" asks Kevin.

"Home to keep," says Ms. Trawick. The children clap their hands and are told to remain quiet.

The game will be fun. Charles asks if he may play. "Of course," says Ms. Trawick. "If you would like." She smiles at Charles. She is grateful that Charles wishes to participate.

It is easy for Charles to win because mother supplied him with two books about the pilgrims. Other children did not have that advantage.

The cramps and vomit feeling have gone away. Ms. Trawick called on Charles several times. Charles has made interesting contributions. When recess came, Ms. Trawick saw Charles sitting at his table writing in his tablet, pretending he didn't hear children invite him to the playground. Ms. Trawick scolded the bothersome children and told Charles he would not be required to take recess. At noon, Ms. Trawick sat at the table in the lunchroom with Charles. She stimulated the other children to imagine situations of today where something similar to the Mayflower Compact might be required.

If there weren't the children, Charles would not be disturbed by school. He would enjoy the challenges offered by Ms. Trawick. The children are dangerous, especially Mitzy. Too bad Mitzy didn't get killed instead of Howard.

Charles doesn't look at Mitzy's face but Charles can see her blue knee socks and plaid skirt. Out of the side of his eye he sees her white blouse. He knows she is looking at him. She has been looking at him all day. She is trying to give him something. She pushes a note into his hand.

Ms. Trawick didn't see. Ms. Trawick is writing decimal-point multiplication problems on the blackboard. Charles puts his hands under his table. The note drops on the floor. If Ms. Trawick looked, she would see. His face is hot and red. Charles keeps his eyes on the back of Ms. Trawick's head, but he knows children are watching him. He bends and tries to find the note with his fingers.

He jumps in his chair. It makes a thunderous noise but Ms. Trawick does not turn around. Down on the floor, someone touched his hand. It was Mitzy, giving him the note again. Charles crumples the note and puts it into his pocket. Mitzy giggles.

Ms. Trawick whirls around. She stares at Mitzy but doesn't say anything. Ms. Trawick orders Mitzy to come to the blackboard and solve the first multiplication problem.

Charles puts his hand in his pocket. The note is there. Other children know it is there. Charles feels dizzy. Ms. Trawick, Mitzy and the blackboard are miles away.

The afternoon recess bell rings. The children run out the door.

"Charles, are you feeling all right?" It is Ms. Trawick standing above him, in front of his table.

Charles nods.

Ms. Trawick puts her hand on his forehead. "Would you like to go to the nurse's room and lie down?" she asks.

Charles shakes his head. He can hear the children out on the playground. He looks out the window. Mitzy is in the middle of a bunch of them. She is telling. Now they all know.

"Well, you just sit here and rest," says Ms. Trawick. "I have to go to the headmaster's office for a minute," she says. "If you aren't feeling better when I come back, it might be best for you to lie down in the nurse's room. You have done very well today." Ms. Trawick smoothes his hair with her fingers and tells Charles she knows how hard coming back to school is, especially the first day.

Charles is trapped. It is only a matter of time. Charles pulls the note out of his pocket. He gasps for breath. Someone has their hands around his throat. They are choking him. He opens the paper.

Dear Charles,
I'm glad to see you back in school. Please be my friend again.
I missed you awful much.
Love,
Mitzy

There is a row of x's in red across the bottom. Charles shoves the paper back into his pocket.

"Charles, your shirt is wet and you are shaking." Ms. Trawick has her hands under his arms. She is pulling Charles up out of his chair. Charles holds on to the table. She pries his fingers loose. She is too strong.

"Charles must finish his day," says Charles. "Charles is not allowed to leave."

CHARLES is lying on the cot in the nurse's office. Charles wonders how he got here. Mother is sitting on a chair beside him. Mother looks worried. Ms. Trawick is standing at the end of the cot, looking down. The nurse is next to her. The nurse and Ms. Trawick are smiling at him.

"Do you feel a little better now?" asks the nurse.

Charles remembers the note. He pushes his hand into his pocket. It isn't there. His belt is unbuckled. Somebody loosened his pants.

"It's all right," says Ms. Trawick. "Charles, you haven't done anything wrong."

Charles rolls his head back and forth, looking at their faces. Then he sees the note. It is lying on the nurse's desk, behind mother. They found it when they searched him.

Their faces are drifting away. All Charles sees are dots on the ceiling. It is no use trying to escape.

24

CHARLES DOESN'T REMEMBER everything. But Charles knows he would be in jail if mother hadn't been there.

Fortunately, some good comes from a misfortune. At last mother realized the danger to Charles. But mother does not know that Mitzy and Dr. Hartenfells are the enemy.

It is June. If Charles were at Canterbury School he would be graduating from the third grade.

Charles does not miss Canterbury School. His scores from the Educational Records Bureau Comprehensive Tests place him in the upper first percentile for his grade in verbal aptitude and mathematics. Mother is pleased. After explaining percentile, which was an easy concept to grasp, mother shared the wonderful results with Charles.

Charles is being tutored by Mr. Thornton. Charles is in an approved home study program which fully qualifies under Ohio law.

Charles likes his home study program. Charles likes Mr. Thornton. Mr. Thornton doesn't ask questions about the trial, if Charles has playmates, if Charles feels bad because Howard is dead, what scares Charles, how Charles felt while father was in his high-rise condominium, none of those kind of questions. Mr. Thornton is enthusiastic about knowledge. "Be curious in everything," he told Charles. Mr. Thornton is teaching Charles to speak German. When his other assignments have been completed, Charles rewards himself by listening to German language tapes which Mr. Thornton secures from the language laboratory at Ohio State University. Charles and Mr. Thornton have conversations which mother, father and Vivian can't understand.

Mr. Thornton comes for one hour each day, in the morning at eight. Afterward Charles tackles his assignments by himself in his room. After supper each night mother reviews the work and asks questions from teaching manuals Mr. Thornton has provided to accompany the books Charles is using.

Mother resigned from her church committees and does not attend Junior League meetings. She is working as hard to protect Charles as Charles is to master his assignments. She knows the danger to Charles when mother isn't with him.

Father is much better. He has had no temper tantrums. No cross words have been said between mother and father. Even Vivian has been nice to Charles. Family dinners are enjoyable. Because Charles is doing his assignments, Charles is allowed to play Nintendo every night in the hour before bedtime. On his birthday Charles will receive his own computer.

When mother has to leave the house, Charles locks himself in his room. Mother said it was okay for Charles to protect himself.

Charles doesn't have to leave the house except when he goes to Dr. Hartenfells, or on errands with mother or to events with father. Father took Charles to every Ohio State basketball game and twice to see the Cincinnati Reds play games in Riverfront Stadium. Charles has been excused from church attendance.

If Charles does his assignments, maybe the visits to Dr. Hartenfells will stop. "We'll see," said mother when Charles asked. "Dr. Hartenfells is helping Charles a great deal," mother said. Mother doesn't know. Charles goes twice a week and each time it feels as bad as the day Charles went back to Canterbury School after being away for the trial.

Charles is in his room, listening to a German language tape to keep from thinking about his upcoming visit to Dr. Hartenfells. Charles must go to see Dr. Hartenfells as soon as mother returns from the supermarket.

THOSE dolls are still there. The one with the enormous weewee is on top. They are the first thing Charles looks for when he comes in. They are lying in the corner by the bean bag chair where Charles used to go to be questioned.

"We will have fun today." Dr. Hartenfells smiles at Charles. "No questions," she says, taking a step toward Charles. "I promise," she says.

Charles holds tighter to mother's hand. But he knows mother won't stay.

"We're going to play a new game," says Dr. Hartenfells.

"Doesn't that sound interesting?" asks mother.

"No." Charles says. He is getting tricked again. When he is able to spend his hour with Dr. Hartenfells without becoming upset he will be making progress and coming closer to the time when he won't have to visit her so frequently. Mother told him that on several occasions. But he can't help himself. "Please stay," he asks mother. "Just this once." He grabs her legs, slides to the floor and holds on.

"Your mother will be outside waiting for you when we finish," says Dr. Hartenfells. "I'll help you say goodbye."

Dr. Hartenfells pulls Charles across the rug, away from mother. Dr. Hartenfells wraps her arms around Charles and holds him against her.

Mother leaves quick, without saying anything. She is angry at Charles.

"Let's play in the sandbox this afternoon." Dr. Hartenfells leads Charles by the hand to that corner. It is a spacious sandbox, painted yellow. In it there are trucks, cars, many Fisher-Price people, assorted jello and cookie molds. There's a sprinkler can of water outside the sandbox. You can see the remains of sand shapes made from the molds.

"Let's sit here," says Dr. Hartenfells. On top of the sandbox sides there is a wide yellow shelf for sitting. "Let's take off our shoes, wriggle our toes into the sand and get comfortable," she says.

"Wriggle our toes into the sand and get comfortable," says Charles as he takes off his shoes and socks. He will be careful with her today. She is treating Charles like a kindergarten baby. She will have new tricks.

"I'm going to tell you a story," says Dr. Hartenfells. "Listen carefully. After I finish you may want to change it or you may want to tell me a story of your own."

She's looking at Charles with a smiley face and eyes, pretending she's another child. She looks stupid in her dress, with her toes pushing her nylon stockings into the sand. She waits for Charles to speak.

280

"Charles can change your story or, if he wants, Charles can make up a story of his own," says Charles.

She pulls her dress up above her knees and slides off the seat into the sand. She takes the people, trucks, molds and stuff out of the sand and sets them on the shelf. With her hands she smooths the sand. Right in front of Charles she draws a square. "This is a school," she says. "So we need children and a teacher." She selects Fisher-Price people and sticks them in the sand, inside her square.

"This is Phillip," she says, wiggling the one with an orange head and a blue cap. "Phillip is excited to be in school today because it is Sally's birthday," She holds up Sally. "Sally is Phillip's playmate and friend. In this school there is a celebration when a child has a birthday. There will be cake and ice cream. The children will sing happy birthday to Sally. That will happen in the afternoon, the last thing before school lets out for the day."

Dr. Hartenfells identifies the teacher.

"Phillip is excited because he made a jigsaw puzzle to give Sally," says Dr. Hartenfells.

In the school of Dr. Hartenfells it is against the rules to buy presents in the store. Children give presents which they make themselves. Phillip pasted a picture on plywood and cut out the pieces to make the puzzle for Sally. But he left it at home. Phillip felt awful when he got to school and remembered.

Dr. Hartenfells looks at Charles, showing with her face how awful Phillip felt.

"The teacher called Phillip's mother," says Dr. Hartenfells. "Phillip's mother will drop the present off at the school office in time for the party."

Everytime the door opens, Phillip looks to see if it is someone with the present. Afternoon recess has passed and it still isn't there.

It's time for the party. Still the present hasn't come. "You can imagine how worried Phillip is." Dr. Hartenfells stops talking. She is studying Charles.

"Charles can imagine how worried Phillip is," says Charles.

Dr. Hartenfells uses the molds to make tables out of wet sand for the children to sit at while they eat cake and ice cream. She describes what the children and teacher do. They sing happy birthday to Sally. Phillip's present still hasn't arrived.

"There is a knock at the door," says Dr. Hartenfells as she raps her knuckles against the side of the sandbox. "What can that be?" Dr. Hartenfells has asked a question but she didn't break her promise. She doesn't expect Charles to answer. She keeps rapping on the sandbox, turning her head and searching around the room with her eyes. "What can it be?" she asks.

It is someone from the office. Phillip's mother called. She had car trouble. It isn't serious but she can't bring the present.

The teacher tells Phillip that Sally will like her present just as much tomorrow. Maybe more, because she won't be getting any besides Phillip's.

"Charles," says Dr. Hartenfells. "Now it is your turn. You may change anything in the story that you think would make it better."

Charles shakes his head.

"You may ask questions about the story," says Dr. Hartenfells.

"Charles is allowed to ask questions," says Charles.

"Yes," says Dr. Hartenfells.

"Charles understands the story," says Charles. "Charles doesn't need to ask questions."

"Maybe Charles has a story to tell me," says Dr. Hartenfells. "I remember so well your praying mantis story and I understand you are writing some stories for Mr. Thornton."

"Charles is writing stories for Mr. Thornton," says Charles.

"Could you make up a story using our sandbox people?" she asks.

That was a question and she promised not to ask questions but Charles tells her the story of Phillip and Sally. He is pretty sure he puts everything in, gets it exactly right. "Phillip will bring the jigsaw puzzle to school tomorrow," he says. "Phillip will give it to Sally on the playground before the bell. Sally will like the present."

"That is a wonderful addition," says Dr. Hartenfells. "You must tell me how Phillip felt."

Charles is thinking. Dr. Hartenfells didn't ask a question. But ordering Charles what to tell is the same as questions. She is breaking the rules. Charles feels dizzy.

"Phillip is glad the story is over," says Charles.

"I imagine it's nice for Phillip to have a friend like Sally," says Dr. Hartenfells.

"It is nice to have a friend like Sally," says Charles.

"People need friends," says Dr. Hartenfells.

"People need friends," says Charles.

"Charles had a friend like Sally," says Dr. Hartenfells. "Her name was Mitzy."

Dr. Hartenfells tells Charles that she and his mother want Charles to have friends. Friends are important and Charles needs to be with children his own age. "You can have playmates even if you study at home instead of going to school," says Dr. Hartenfells. "Next week Mitzy will come with you. Your mother has talked to Mitzy and her mother. I thought it would be a good idea for Mitzy to come with you a few times. You, me and your friend Mitzy will play together and have fun."

"Mitzy will play together." Charles can barely hear the words he mumbled. He can't breathe. Mitzy told.

"Yes," says Dr. Hartenfells. "You don't need to worry," she says. "Mitzy wants very much to see you, to be friends again, to play together. She is looking forward to coming with you."

Everything is blurry. Charles looks for the door. Charles is trapped. Eyes spy on him through the wall. Mitzy is there. So are Mr. Gorman, the judge, Howard, Mr. Mansfield and all the jury people. Vicious animals too. Charles puts his head in the sand and tries to bury himself.

Charles is lying on a couch, looking up at mother. He is still in Dr. Hartenfells's room. He doesn't remember what happened.

Dr. Hartenfells is standing beside mother. "We had a good session today," Dr. Hartenfells tells mother. "Perhaps we tried to accomplish a bit too much at the end. But some very positive things happened. I think we are headed in the right direction."

Mother bends down. "It's time to leave," she says. "Mother is pleased to hear that you did well today. We'll have time to stop on the way home so that you can get a new Nintendo cartridge."

CHARLES puts his pillow over his head. The spider is after him again, the one that changes size. It is huge. Its red eyes glow at Charles, right through the pillow. The spider's mouth is bloody and there is blood on its tentacles. The tentacles are twisting above Charles and under his bed.

Since father came home, Charles has been sleeping in his own room. Mother said it would be better that way. Mother does not know that eyes watch Charles at night, waiting for a chance to take him away; that bloody arms reach for him. Mother allows Charles to keep the light on when he goes to sleep but sometime during the night the spider turns it off. Charles is in the dark, surrounded by terrible creatures. Charles puts his pillow over his head to keep from seeing and to keep from making noise.

If he cries the spider will attack. If he makes any sound, those tentacles will grab him.

Charles will not call for mother. It is against the rules for Charles to sleep in mother's room. It was because of Charles that father had to go to the high-rise condominium. Charles won't make such an enormous mistake again.

The spider is shrinking. Charles lifts his pillow. It is gone but invisible eyes are watching him. Charles is choking. He is shaking. His covers are on the floor and his jammies stick to him. He will have to yell. He is trying hard but he can feel himself screaming. The spider is coming back.

Charles crawls out of bed. He takes a blanket and his pillow. Charles will lie in the hall, outside the door to mother's bedroom. Charles moves without making a sound. This is what Charles does when he knows he can't last any longer. The spider will not come after him out in the hall because the spider is afraid of mother.

Charles wraps the blanket around himself. His pillow is against the bottom of mother's bedroom door. The hall carpet is thick, soft as a bed. Charles is still shivering but he feels better.

There is light coming from the crack under the door. Charles did not notice this at first. Charles hears voices. The voices are mother and father.

"Maybe Dr. Hartenfells is right," says father. "Maybe this is more than you can handle. Maybe six months at Harding Hospital is the right thing to do."

"I don't know," says mother. "I no longer trust my judgment."

"We can afford it," says father.

"But it will devastate Charles," says mother. Mother is crying. No one is talking.

"He has kept up with his schoolwork." Father's voice is soft. Charles has to put his ear to the crack between the carpet and the door. "It isn't hopeless. Isn't Dr. Hartenfells optimistic?"

"It's hard for me to stay optimistic," says mother. "Charles has taken over my life. He's dragging me down with him."

"Let the Hardings try," says father. "They are qualified to . . ."

"And of course I'm not." Mother raises her voice. She's angry.

"Don't take it that way," says father. "You've done all you can. No mother could have tried harder."

"I'm sorry," says mother. "I'm on edge."

"At least," says father, "you'll get a rest. Your life will return to normal. You'll be in better space when Charles comes back."

"This isn't fair to Vivian," says mother. "We've missed her last two recitals. She says she understands, but can she?"

"Look," says father, "I know this is tearing you apart."

"That damn vocabulary book," says mother. "I got him started but I wish I'd never seen it."

"It's probably good that he is grounded to something," says father. "He works hard at his studies. That may be keeping him from losing touch with reality."

"It's bizarre," says mother.

Their voices go on and on. Mother wants to get rid of Charles. Mother hates Charles. Mother has been lying worse than anyone.

When Mr. Thornton comes in the morning for tutorial hour, Charles tells him that he wants to put new words into his vocabulary notebook. Charles needs help because he doesn't know how to spell the words and can't look them up in the dictionary. The words are *bizarre* and *devastate*.

Charles is shaking and his stomach is in a knot. It gets

worse when he hears the definition of *bizarre*. But Charles does not run. He records the word in his notebook.

Mr. Thornton finds *devastate* for Charles.

Charles throws the dictionary at the window. The glass breaks. Charles grabs the vocabulary notebook and rips the pages to pieces. Mr. Thornton is chasing him, trying to catch him. "Charles hates mother," screams Charles. "Charles wants her dead. Charles is leaving and Charles is never coming back."

25

I HAD BEEN living their lie. It had been twelve years since
the trial, ten years since I got out of Harding Hospital and
three years since I last saw my psychiatrist, Dr. Matt Johnson. Matt Johnson told me I might someday want to tell
someone besides him what really happened. He encouraged me to do so if I ever felt like it. He wondered if it
might feel good to tell Howard's parents. I had often
thought about his suggestion. But until the two letters came
yesterday, I didn't feel like telling anyone. It would be too

complicated. It was safer and easier to live their lie, to put "that unfortunate period" in my life behind, as mother had advised.

I was sitting in the reading chair by my window, considering the best way to respond to the two letters I got yesterday. I was away from the people in my life, a junior at Bowdoin College, living in my own apartment. My apartment was one of three on the second floor of a converted seventy-year-old frame house which bordered the campus on a tree-lined street. The trees were now icy and bare, giving me a clear view of the library and the walks which led to it. It was the middle of February and sub-zero raw.

I was sitting in my reading chair looking out my window at the students making their way over the ice-packed sidewalk to the library, their heavy collars pulled up and scarves across their faces as they leaned into the wind which buffeted my window. I was furious.

Except to go to the library after I received the two letters, I had not left my apartment. That wasn't especially unusual because my apartment had a kitchenette, bath, bedroom and a nice-sized sitting room which I had filled with bookshelves, my computer, all my peripherals, file cabinets and desk. I had saved a niche in the corner for my reading chair, side table and television. So I had everything I needed and did not go out except for classes, library visits, to do research in the laboratory and to replenish supplies. My needs for supplies were scheduled on computer programs to minimize outside trips. I was fortunate to have these conveniently located, well-equipped quarters. I had lived in a dormitory my freshman year with an absurd roommate who had no serious intentions with regard to his studies. That place had been a lunatic asylum.

It was most unusual to receive on the same day two letters which would take me back to the trial, disrupt my academic routine and produce a rage which was severely challenging my ability to control myself.

I had opened the letter from Dr. William Windle first because its letterhead identified him as affiliated with the University of Michigan in Ann Arbor. I thought it might be another response to a paper of mine, "A different look at evidence from the Proterozoic Age," which had been published in the fall issue of *World Paleontology.*

Dr. William Windle's letter was nothing of the kind. He wanted to visit me. If I preferred, his funding would allow him to pay my expenses in traveling to Ann Arbor. He was engaged in a comparative study of three cases of child abuse, drawn from the DMS casebook and involving three individuals (I having been one) who had made "good recoveries," as he wrote, "from serious psychotic episodes triggered at least in part by confrontation with an abuser in a courtroom." I wondered who had given Dr. William Windle my address.

I had not heard of the DMS, but had no difficulty finding the case study pertaining to me once a librarian directed me to the book. I found the name of Dr. Frances Hartenfells in the index. Mine was not, because my name and certain irrelevant details had been changed to protect my identity. However, the basic lie had been maintained. It was their lie, the one I had been living. I checked the Behavioral Sciences Section of American Men and Women of Science. The short vita for William Windle confirmed his association with the University of Michigan. For seventy-five cents, I made a Xerox copy of the pertinent pages from the DMS. Those pages were lying on the table next to my chair, beside my reading lamp. My fingers quivering with rage, I picked them up again:

Happy Ending
(A note submitted for the DMS casebook by
Dr. Frances Hartenfells, M.D., Ph.D.)

Arnold, now nineteen, is a sophomore at college. He won
a scholarship and hopes to become a paleontologist. He lives
by himself off campus. He prepares his own meals, carries a
full load of classes and achieved academic distinction in his
freshman year. Although he has minimal social contact beyond that required by class attendance and daily necessity,
Arnold demonstrates that a remarkable recovery, within
narrow parameters, can be achieved following a severe separation anxiety with psychotic manifestation.

At age seven Arnold, a gifted child with exceptional verbal
skills, came into treatment as a result of being sexually
abused by an eighteen-year-old neighbor boy, a babysitter
for whom Arnold had developed affection.

Arnold felt extreme guilt from his participation as a victim of the abuse. Repression robbed him of his memory of
many events. Three psychologically significant events became emotionally blurred: (1) the trauma of the abuse, (2)
the threats posed by having to prepare as a witness in a
criminal jury trial and (3) his responsibility for the disagreement between his parents which led to their separation. Arnold developed extreme dependency upon his mother. He
withdrew from association with schoolmates and friends.
Remarkably, his performance in school did not deteriorate.

Ultimately, the demands placed upon Arnold became too
severe, and, while being cross-examined in front of a jury,
he suffered the first of several breakdowns. When his abuser
committed suicide at the conclusion of court proceedings,
Arnold took responsibility for the death. He suffered a further withdrawal from peer relationships—indeed, from relationship with anyone outside his immediate family, except
for a private tutor. His mother and father had reunited but
Arnold did not trust the reunion. He was unable to return to
school. His dependency upon his mother reached the point
where he shadowed her, waited at the door when she went

291

to the bathroom, sometimes slept outside her bedroom door, accompanied her on errands and became panicked when she left the house without him. On those occasions he would lock himself in his room.

His nightmares became increasingly severe and he began to hallucinate, seeing bloody monsters in his room and a menacing spider with magical properties. He complained of physical symptoms, palpitations, chest pain, choking and smothering sensation, bouts of dizziness. He was often found in bed, trembling, sweating profusely and mumbling. His fear of "doing something against the rules" became obsessive, as did his need to please his mother. His fears concretized in the form of believing himself about to be removed from his family (particularly his mother) and punished for the death of his abuser. Throughout, he clung to his intellectual achievements and, in a home tutoring program, reached outstanding levels in a variety of comparative grade-level testing exercises.

The pathology manifested itself through a loss of identity. Arnold became unable to think of himself or to express himself except in the third person, i.e., "Arnold does not want ice cream." Arnold defended himself by repeating, often verbatim, the words spoken to him in conversation.

The impossibility of treatment in his family setting was evident. However, his mother was reluctant to see Arnold removed, believing that greater damage would be inflicted by severance of the support to which he clung.

Institutionalization was mandated when Arnold suffered a complete breakdown, became nearly catatonic and unable to express himself coherently or free from gross delusion.

Removed from his home and in the course of an intense milieu therapy of eighteen months' duration, Arnold made a remarkably significant therapeutic gain.

He was able to rejoin his family. With the assistance of counseling, he returned to a new school at the sixth-grade level. While he kept mostly to himself, free from dependent

relationships, he performed well in school and has demonstrated no aggressive or self-destructive behaviors.

(Diagnosis: Acute post-traumatic stress disorder; separation anxiety disorder)

In the last twenty-four hours I had read those pages
many times. Every time it made me want to smash people.
Dr. Matt Johnson could have stopped this publication. Matt
Johnson knew the truth. He came upon the truth when I
was delirious and making absurd statements. I didn't remember some of what happened during that time but I
remembered how glad I was when Matt Johnson put everything together, even if he did find out about Mitzy Gerlach
and Heather Knowles. Matt Johnson always believed me.
Surprisingly, once I started telling him things, I wanted
him to know everything. I trusted Matt Johnson.

Matt Johnson had promised he would tell no one anything I revealed to him—not mother, Dr. Frances
Hartenfells, lawyers or anyone. "They can put me on a rack
and torture me and I won't tell," he told me. He had been
grinning but I believed him. His promise to me was probably why he had not notified the DMS publisher.

The second letter which came yesterday was from
mother. Mother wrote twice a week, so a letter from her
was no surprise. The surprise was the enclosed newspaper
picture and story announcing Mitzy Gerlach's engagement
to marry a Jason Palmer in June.

"I ran into Mitzy and her mother in the Canterbury
Mall," my mother wrote.

Mitzy will be sending you a separate invitation and said it
would mean a lot to her if you came. We ended up by going
to the Russian Tea Room where we had sandwiches and a
delightful visit. We laughed over the times you used to correct Mr. Shirley's mistakes in second grade and that silly

business that earned you the nickname "Large Charles." Mitzy will make a stunning bride and of course she radiates her excitement. She is marrying a top law student who is on the Law Review at the Ohio State Law School and graduates this June. He has accepted an offer from King and Braxton. Your father says he was the best prospect they interviewed this year. Isn't it a small world?

I found myself staring at the picture of mother mounted in a glass stand-up frame on the top of a low bookcase which was below my window. I had pictures of father and Vivian there too. I swept those pictures off the shelf. I got out of the chair and stomped them to bits on the floor. Carefully I cleaned up the loose glass and put the pieces in the wastebasket under the sink of my kitchenette. At the same time I threw away the two-pound canister of salted cashews—the latest care package which had arrived a week before the letters. I would tell mother to send no more of those. Since the start of my freshman year I had received something each month; assorted nuts, apples wrapped in red tissue paper and fitted into slots in a box, fancy cheeses from France, chocolates and caramels, grapefruits, oranges, gourmet cookies, a fruitcake, smoked salmon, smoked sardines and some I could have forgotten. On those holidays when I couldn't get out of going home, and in half her letters, mother reminded me that I was not eating enough. I might have been skinny but I felt healthy and would no longer eat her food just to be polite.

Suddenly I laughed out loud. This was the first temper tantrum I had experienced in years. My hands were shaking and I had squashed the canister of salted cashews before throwing it away. But no one would ask questions or scold me in a weekly review.

I returned to my reading chair. It was now dark outside

but the wind still pounded the window and students were still making their way to and from the library.

I sat in my reading chair and came to decisions. I would not respond to the inquiry from Dr. William Windle. But there were three actions I would take. It was time for people to know the truth. As Matt Johnson had envisioned, the time had come when I felt like telling what really happened. Other people, as well as me, could start living with the truth. If other people got hurt, it was their own fault.

I would go to Mitzy Gerlach's wedding. I wasn't sure she'd be so delighted to have me there if she knew what I was going to do. When I got to Columbus, I would look up Howard's parents and explain to them that Howard had not done what he had been accused of doing. Thirdly, I would expose Dr. Frances Hartenfells for her fraudulent case study in a scientific publication; maybe have her censured for revealing the confidences of a patient. I was pretty sure she was the one who had directed Dr. William Windle to me.

Since I had gotten away to college, I dreaded vacations. I had managed to secure employment as a research assistant to a professor who was a prolific publisher of treatises and papers. That kept me in Brunswick during the summers. I'd made excuses to miss the last two Thanksgiving vacations. Only Christmas was unavoidable. But going home for Mitzy Gerlach's wedding seemed a necessity to me.

I put the cartridge for a video game into my TV attachment. I felt good about having made decisions, entitled to waste a little time.

26

MOTHER AND FATHER met me at the airport. On the flight from Boston to Columbus, I had sat next to an elderly, inquisitive lady who reminded me of Mamsy who had died of cancer two years ago. To protect myself, I pulled down my tray, took a text from my carry-on, opened it and made marginal notations. Unfortunately the presence of the annoying woman kept me from reclining my seat and using the flight to review plans. I couldn't take the clipping with Mitzy Gerlach's picture out of my billfold to study her face.

In the four months since receiving those two letters, my

purpose had not weakened. I had, however, decided to deal
with Howard's parents and Dr. Frances Hartenfells before
the wedding. The wedding was not until Saturday, which
gave me six days. I wanted Howard's parents and Dr. Frances Hartenfells out of the way so that I could leave Columbus the day after the wedding.

On the drive from the airport to Country Club Way, I sat
in the passenger seat—mother was in back—and conversed
at some length about my school work, frequently turning
to include mother in the conversation. I described a second
paper I hoped to publish and the summer internship I had
secured at the Museum of Natural History. I would fly back
to Bowdoin the day after the wedding and go to Washington one week later. Mother and father seemed pleased to
find me so talkative. It exhausted me.

"Charles you look so much better," said mother as we got
out of the BMW—father was still driving those—to go in
the house.

I learned that Vivian would not be home for the wedding
because just two days previously she had been accepted as
a back-chair violin by the St. Louis Symphony. She had to
join the orchestra immediately as they were doing a Summer Festival tour in Europe.

I did not have a suit for the wedding, but mother eagerly
promised to accompany me on a shopping trip. She wanted
me to have other things, a second suit, slacks and a sport
coat, shirts, ties, at least one pair of new shoes. She felt my
wardrobe would be inadequate for my internship in Washington.

After supper in the garden room, I pleaded fatigue and
retired to my room, which had not changed since I left for
college. I looked up the telephone number for Dr. and Mrs.
Dwight Landis. They had moved to Muirfield Village. I
thought it best to call before paying a visit. They would

likely be home on Sunday night and I reminded myself
that no task becomes easier by putting it off.

Dr. Dwight Landis answered on the first ring. He must
have been sitting beside the telephone. I identified myself
as Charles King who used to live next door.

"Is this part of your therapy?" Dr. Dwight Landis asked.
"Something a psychiatrist or counselor suggested?"

"No." I rejected making an explanation, telling him I
hadn't seen Matt Johnson for three years, that it was my
idea to call even if Matt Johnson had wanted me to do
something back then.

"Have you any idea of the extent to which Mrs. Landis
has suffered?" he asked.

"Yes."

"I doubt that you do," he said. I heard him take a deep
breath. "I want you to listen carefully," he said.

"Yes."

"We do not want to see you. Your call and your desire to
see Mrs. Landis indicates a cruelty that I can scarcely conceive."

"No, I didn't mean to—"

"Please!" he interrupted me. "You listen! I will hear your
response after I finish."

"All right."

"Mrs. Landis has not only required counseling, but she
has been affected physically. She is crippled by arthritis.
The onset is traceable directly to the trial. I don't plan to go
into details and I don't want to hear your reaction to our
problems. I only want you to understand why I will not
. . . why I will take any step to prevent you from adding to
her misery."

I resisted the urge to speak. Until he finished, he would
not hear me.

"I came to terms with my son and his problem some time
ago," he said. "In fact, before the trial. But Mrs. Landis did

not. She will never accept that she could have raised a son with such deep-seated problems. She cannot excuse herself. But through the years, she has made an adaptation of sorts. Then you, for some therapeutic need, call, opening the wounds, heedless to what destruction you cause.

"I will not have it!" Dr. Landis's voice had risen to a shrill shout. He was so angry he was not coherent. But what he was saying shocked me. He was convinced that Howard had been guilty of abusing me. He believed Howard had been a deviate, a pederast. He refused to consider any other possibility. "You obtained your pound of flesh," he said. "Wasn't that enough?"

"But I want you to know," I couldn't keep from interrupting, "Howard didn't do what I said in court."

"Haven't you been listening?" he asked. His voice was low and cold. It frightened me, even over the telephone. "If all else fails," he said, "I will take this into my own hands. I will not allow you to add to Mrs. Landis's suffering."

"But I—"

"There are ways of stopping people like you," he said.

The phone was dead. He had hung up before I could respond.

I lay on my bed thinking about the strange conversation. It had left me shaky, frightened. As I lay there, my fright gave way to despair. I could not undo what I had done to Howard. Even if I'd tried to tell people Howard didn't hurt me, I had pointed to him in the courtroom. I could have saved him if I hadn't been protecting myself. That truth would never let go of me.

In the next days, I wasn't able to maintain the friendly, conversational atmosphere with mother and father. The day I spent shopping with mother was excruciating. So were meals in the garden room. I could not look at mother's frosted gray head or listen to her voice without the urge to pick up something and smash that head to jelly.

Sometimes when she was relating the details of Mitzy Gerlach's wedding, I wondered if she could see the way my eye involuntarily twitched, my hand started to clench into a fist or my foot would jerk in a kind of spasm.

"Charles, do you think it was wise to have taken this job in Washington without making living arrangements in advance?" When shopping, in the car, in the garden room, even when I came down to watch television with them in the leisure room, mother assaulted me with that kind of question. I was not so angry with father, but he and I had nothing to talk about.

I stayed in my room as much as possible and endured mother's repetitious expressions of delight in having my company for dinner in the garden room. I tried to close my ears to her extravagant claims of how much it meant to "catch up with" my life. I came close to calling Matt Johnson. I didn't want to. That would be a defeat. I wanted to carry this off without help.

Often, in the privacy of my room, I looked at the picture of Mitzy Gerlach. It was only black and white, on newspaper pulp, but I felt I was getting to know her again. I knew her shoulder-length, almost-black hair would be full bodied, silky. She had the same widow's peak as when she was a little girl. I saw her skin as smooth, dark olive. The slim line of her neck and jaw had grown elegant and I could almost see her wriggle her nose. She was more beautiful than the prettiest girls at Bowdoin, girls I wouldn't know how to talk to if I wanted. I didn't care about girls, but Mitzy Gerlach's picture fascinated me and I was constantly taking it out of my billfold to examine. It had been unfolded and folded so many times that white lines formed a cross which intersected just below the tip of her nose. Even so, the picture seemed alive, as if her lips were about to open, say something to me.

My old Macintosh was still in my room. I assembled the

information I had collected and typed out letters: to the American Psychiatric Association, the Columbus Academy of Medicine, the Ohio Medical Board, the hospital administrator at Childrens' Hospital and to the College of Medicine at Ohio State—all with copies to Dr. Frances Hartenfells. I kept extra copies of each letter. At the public library I had found the stories concerning my trial and paid for copies to be made from the microfilm. The old clippings and copies of the letters to the medical associations would go to the newspaper and TV stations. I wanted to be away from Columbus when what I had written became public. As I put the material together, I saw that my part in the lie was worse than anyone's.

The days did not pass quickly. I missed terribly the pleasures of my apartment in Brunswick, the satisfaction of research, study and preparation of papers. I was counting the hours until Mitzy Gerlach's wedding, until I could unburden myself of the secret I had carried for thirteen years.

It was a beautiful day for the wedding, sunny and mild but not humid. Tremont Presbyterian smelled fresh with floral greenery—bursts of color around the altar and white bouquets attached to the ends of each pew. It seemed a softer, brighter place, though still dominated by the stone walls and towering gothic arches. Down the center aisle, a spotless white runner had been placed over the crimson carpet. As friends of the bride, we were escorted to the left by a young man in a tuxedo. "Nice to see you, Charles," he said to me. I didn't recognize him, but mother said he was Mitzy Gerlach's brother, Karl Gerlach, the one I used to stay away from.

We were early. Mother chatted with wedding guests in the pew behind us and then with people in the pew in front of us. I sat on the aisle, with mother between me and father. We were seated halfway to the altar. I felt myself getting nervous. I tried to concentrate on the organ selections. Father waved a hand in greeting to someone on the groom's side.

I turned with everyone when the music swelled. The girls in the procession looked as if they'd stepped out of a fashion magazine, all beautiful and slim, striding down the aisle while smiling and nodding to one side then the other. Heather Knowles was the maid of honor. She was the tallest of the attendants and her long blonde hair fell nearly to her waist. She looked at me and smiled but I didn't think she recognized me until she saw mother and looked back at me with a real smile.

Then came the wedding march and Mitzy. Mitzy was more than stunning. She looked right into my eyes and touched my shoulder as she passed. I heard mother whisper to father, "Did you ever see a prettier bride?"

Jason Palmer and his ushers were spread in a line at the front, waiting for Mitzy. Jason Palmer looked like a fashion model too, with thick, wavy black hair and glittering teeth. He had a widow's peak like Mitzy's.

Mitzy's father gave her to Jason Palmer. For four months, since I'd received those letters, my plan had been to stand when the minister asked for their vows. I was going to announce to everyone that Mitzy had forced me to take off my clothes in her basement, that she had stuck a wooden spoon handle up my rear end, brought about the trial which caused Howard to kill himself and me to have a mental breakdown. The idea had been absurd. As soon as we arrived at church that afternoon, I'd begun to see that my plan was impossible, completely unrealistic. It was also unfair. I didn't hate Mitzy. I didn't want to spoil Mitzy's perfect wedding. It had been mother I wanted to embarrass by making a scene that she would never live down, a scene that would follow her to church, the country club, on her charitable projects and even to the Canterbury Mall. But not until Mitzy started down the aisle had I fully realized that I didn't blame Mitzy and that my only goal had been to punish mother.

All the same, I wanted to tell Mitzy that what we'd done in her basement had made the trial happen. I needed to do that before my letters became public. I would see her at the reception.

During the recessional I noticed mother sponging tears off her face with her handkerchief. Mother leaned into father and hugged him.

We lingered in front of the church, waiting to throw rice when Mitzy and Jason Palmer came out. Inside, they were taking pictures of the wedding party. Friends of mother kept coming up to me, saying how nice it was to see me and asking about school. Everyone was laughing and having a good time. Lawyers from father's law firm and father exchanged stupid jokes about Jason Palmer. I suggested to father that I go for the car, pick him and mother up in front of the church. I really didn't want to go to the reception but that would be my only chance to see Mitzy. She and Jason Palmer would be going somewhere on their honeymoon. I wanted out of Columbus and I didn't want to return.

Mother was standing at the curb with father. I could press the accelerator, swerve the car and wipe them out. My hands gripped the wheel so tight my knuckles turned white. I didn't do it. In my mind I did. I did everything but turn the car and make my foot move to the accelerator instead of the brake. The rage I felt was because I couldn't do it.

"Wasn't it a perfectly gorgeous wedding," said mother, sliding into the front seat and closing her door. "It was so special for me because when Mitzy walked down the aisle, I could see her as a little tot, not more than six years old, your little playmate." Mother was dabbing her eyes again. "Time goes by so quickly," she said.

Someone had come up to father just as he was about to get in the car. We had to wait.

"Someday you'll be having a wedding of your own," said mother. "I hope it will be as lovely as this one."

Father was taking forever, laughing with the man who had approached him, probably over nothing more than how Jason Palmer wouldn't be worth much to the law firm after he got back from a honeymoon with Mitzy.

"I've hesitated to pry," said mother, "but is there anyone you're interested in?"

I glared at her.

"Any special friend back in New England?" Mother smiled, ignoring my glare.

Father got into the back seat. I pushed the accelerator to the floor of the BMW, rubber squealing as we shot away from the curb and church.

The reception was at Mitzy's house. It still looked like a stone castle though not quite so magnificent. A huge, towering green-and-white tent had been set up to cover the swimming pool—which was filled with floating lilies—and the entire grassy area of the backyard. The floral decorations were extravagant. Circular tables, enough to accommodate the two hundred guests, were comfortably spaced under the tent and a string quartet was playing in the peninsula which protruded into the crescent-shaped swimming pool. I heard a girl say the dance band would set up there later. A portable floor had been laid beside the pool. We found our table and I saw that we would be joined by three other lawyers from father's firm along with their wives.

There was no receiving line, but shortly after the wedding party arrived I saw Heather Knowles come around the pool on the side away from the portable dance floor. She looked in my direction and headed for our table. I was sipping my diet root beer and had eaten the shrimp I got from the hors d'oeuvre table. My plate sat in front of me with twenty toothpicks lying in shrimp sauce. Mother and father were off mingling, and the two couples who had taken their seats at our table had given up trying to draw me into conversation.

"Charles, how neat to see you again," said Heather. "I gave Mitzy the devil for not telling me you would be coming." Heather leaned down to kiss me and I let her. "How *have* you been?" she asked.

"Just fine," I said.

"Mitzy sent me to get you," said Heather. "She wants you to meet Jason and share a bottle of bubbly with us before dinner is served."

"Okay," I said and followed her. She hadn't gone more than three steps when she swiveled, swinging half of her long hair across her shoulder. "I'm dying to catch up on all you've been doing," she said, "but it seemed better to wait so you won't have to go through everything twice."

I followed Heather with my eyes down, noticing her legs. She was much different of course, but it took me back to that Saturday morning in the rumpus room. I could smell the room and I could smell Heather. I could remember the creaks and groans of the house and Heather's damp, smudged legs as she pulled her panties back up.

Mitzy saw me coming and ran to me. She had taken off her shoes and was holding her wedding dress in her hands. She threw herself into me and wrapped her arms around me. "Large Charles, I'm so glad you're here," she said. She held the sides of my face and kissed me on my mouth. She wasn't as tall as I'd imagined from her picture—not nearly as tall as Heather—but in her stocking feet she was taller than me.

She grabbed my hand and dragged me to Jason Palmer, who was standing at the rim of the pool in his tuxedo shirt and cummerbund with his coat off and his hands in his pockets. He was surrounded by young men who looked like they either were or were about to be lawyers at King and Braxton.

"Jason, I want you to meet the first love of my life," said Mitzy.

I looked to see if she was making fun of me but couldn't tell.

"Uh-oh," said Jason Palmer, arching a bushy eyebrow and sliding his eyes to his friends on his right, then to those on his left. "I better not let you out of my sight." He flashed me a huge smile and extended his hand, crunching mine in a powerful grip. Up this close, I could study Jason Palmer's bone structure. I saw that his thick hairstyle masked a forehead and cranium that looked less evolved.

"Charles is an honor student at Bowdoin," said Mitzy. "He's already published one important paper in a scientific journal and he's been selected as a summer intern at the Museum of Natural History."

"That's great," said Jason Palmer.

"Terrific," said one of Jason Palmer's friends. The others nodded and smiled.

Heather Knowles ran her hair through her hand and let it fall behind her shoulder. Jason Palmer's friends watched Heather. They approved of Heather.

"Mitzy," I said, "I hoped we could talk for a minute."

Mitzy scrunched up her nose and glanced at Jason Palmer. "Just you and me talk?" she asked. "Right now?"

I nodded.

"Well, sure, I guess." Mitzy looked around, seeming to canvass the tables and all the people she would have to pay her respects to.

Mrs. Gerlach came out of the house, hurrying. "Mitzy," she called out, coming around the end of the pool. "Mitzy, your uncle Rudy is calling long distance from Zurich. He wants to congratulate you."

Mitzy pulled up her wedding dress and ran into the house. I drifted back toward our table. Mother and father had taken their seats. I looked back to where Mitzy had been. Heather Knowles was talking to one of the ushers. Jason Palmer had moved off to shake hands with the guests at the table nearest to the string quartet. I turned toward our table again.

I saw that mother had taken father's hand and was holding it in hers, above the table. I remembered her hugging father during the recessional and that she'd put her arm around his waist when we came in the tent. She'd told father she couldn't go to a wedding without reliving her own.

Mother kissed father on the side of his face. After twenty-seven years, I thought it was, they looked like they couldn't restrain themselves from touching and kissing each other. The couple across the table from them was looking at them and smiling. Though mother and father had been polite, they had demonstrated no such affection during the six days since I'd come home from Bowdoin.

I kept moving toward their table, but slowly, waiting for people who were talking in clusters between the tables to either finish conversations or notice that I was waiting to get through. Occasionally I looked back to see if Mitzy had returned from the house or if anyone in that group had noticed my absence. I did not want to be anywhere except back in my apartment at Bowdoin.

Mitzy came out of the house and saw me turning to look that way. She waved me to come around the pool to where she was standing, on the stoop of the door to their kitchen; the door through which she'd taken Moose out to pee while Heather was waiting downstairs.

I skirted a table and walked, not fast, to join her. I was thinking about the morning I rode the elevator to the ninth floor in the Hall of Justice, standing between Mr. Clay Gorman and Sgt. Fred Lutz, looking at the shiny handle of Sgt. Fred Lutz's automatic, remembering how frightened I had been walking down that rear corridor, how Judge John Van Horn surprised me by springing out of his chambers in his black robe. There had been no escape.

But now there was. I didn't have to tell Mitzy anything. I had written my letters. I had spelled everything out. I wished there were a way to correct the lie without embarrassing Mitzy and Heather. There wasn't. Maybe I wouldn't send copies of everything to the newspaper and TV stations. But it might all come out anyhow when they investigated Dr. Hartenfells, or if Howard's parents changed their minds and decided to sue someone. Mother, father, Mitzy and the court people—if any of those still cared—could deal with the truth after I had gone back to Maine and on to Washington. My interest was not in those people but in my studies, in making a contribution to science. Some day they might know me for what I had accomplished rather than as the unfortunate little boy who got abused and put through a difficult trial resulting in psychological problems.

When I got to Mitzy I told her this wasn't a good time to talk, not in the midst of her wedding celebration. She looked at me for what seemed like several minutes but probably was only two or three seconds. I had aroused her curiosity.

Jason Palmer called to her from across the pool. "All right," she yelled back.

She looked at me. "Large Charles—I hope you don't mind me calling you that—" Her eyes questioned mine and I nodded my approval. "It's how I remember you and it reminds me of how much I love you."

She didn't mean love, but I nodded again.

"I can't tell you how glad I am you came," she said. "I

really mean that," she said when I didn't answer. She was studying me with those burning black eyes. I thought she was telling me the truth.

She kissed me a third time and skipped off, around the lily-filled pool, to Jason Palmer. I watched her until she got to him and as he gave her a squeeze across her shoulders when she sidled next to him and joined a conversation with an older couple I didn't recognize.

I stood at the edge of the tent, looking across the pool at people seated around the tables and standing between the tables, holding their drinks and hors d'oeuvres plates. I was back in the courtroom facing the jury. The recess was over and I had to go back to the witness stand because I'd promised mother and father I'd try to complete my testimony. Mr. Clay Gorman was seated at counsel table and Mr. Bart Mansfield was approaching me to resume his questions. Mr. Bart Mansfield was smiling.

I blinked and shook my head. I didn't know how long I had stood there, across the pool from the wedding party. It had gotten dark; the tableware, linen, crystal and even the grass shimmered under lights mounted high on the tent posts. The waiters, all wearing tuxedos, were about to serve the soup and everyone had found their seats. At our table father was sitting beside mother. On the other side of mother was the empty chair for me.